D0309492

DISCARD
U

STEAM UP!
A RAILWAYMAN REMEMBERS

*By the same author*

Liverpool & Manchester Railway 1830–1980

# Steam Up!
## A Railwayman Remembers

by
*Frank Ferneyhough*

Foreword by
*Captain Peter Manisty*, MBE, RN(Retd.)

ROBERT HALE · LONDON

© *Frank Ferneyhough 1983*
*First published in Great Britain 1983*

ISBN 0 7090 0704 3


Robert Hale Limited
Clerkenwell House
Clerkenwell Green
London EC1R 0HT

KIRKCALDY DISTRICT LIBRARIES

391477

385. 361 /FER

CE

Photoset by Rowland Phototypesetting Ltd
Printed in Great Britain by
St Edmundsbury Press, Bury St Edmunds, Suffolk
Bound by Hunter & Foulis Ltd

# Contents

# List of Illustrations

## CREDITS

Permission to reproduce illustrations has been granted by the following: British Rail, 3, 4, 7, 11, 13–15, 17–19, 21–7, 31; Central Press Photos Ltd, 28; S. le Cheminant, 30; Tony Gregory, 9; J. R. P. Hunt, 29; Ioma Enterprises, 20; Keystone Press Agency, 12; Topical Press Agency, 10. A few illustrations of unknown source are believed to be free of copyright, but the author, c/o the publishers, would be pleased to correspond with any claimant.

# Acknowledgements

With sincere gratitude, the author acknowledges the generous advice and help he has received from friends, former colleagues, railway societies and other relevant organizations. He names particularly Eric Beavor, former locomotive shedmaster; John Dixon, railway enthusiast with an extensive library; Michael Satow, who built full-scale working reproductions of Stephenson's masterpieces, 'Locomotion' and 'Rocket', for the railway celebrations of 1975 and 1980; and George Hinchcliffe, managing director, Steamtown Railway Museum, Carnforth. Specific assistance came from former colleagues Alex Murray, Desmond Dardis, Tony Eveleigh, Ken Tucker and Frances Heckler. Thanks are due also to those countless railwaymen down the line who made life in steam railways so varied, adventurous – and happy. And finally to his wife, Joan, who shared the research, typing and proof-reading.

# Foreword

by Captain Peter Manisty, MBE, RN(Retd.)
Chairman, Association of Railway Preservation Societies

I never cease to wonder at the world-wide interest in steam railways; and since British Rail finally phased out steam in 1968, nostalgia strengthens apace, especially for the period between the two world wars when our 'local station' meant something rather special. After a lifetime's experience as a working railwayman in various roles around Britain, in country and town, Frank Ferneyhough recreates the atmosphere of those half-forgotten days. He recalls incidents of excitement and drama, and the fun and laughter ordinary railwaymen found in their daily round. He describes famous locomotives, and the thrilling runs of much-loved titled trains. Frank told me amusing stories about life on the line when we first met in the early 1960s; he was then writing speech notes for Dr Beeching, and I was giving public relations railway talks on the Beeching Plan with a brief reference to the railway societies; Beeching had been a visitor to the Bluebell Railway in 1962.

Frank Ferneyhough's story is entertaining and fast-moving – and at the same time it offers an insight into working methods and safety techniques that keep all our railways safe. This book, packed with human interest, gives the general public, and railwaymen too, a better understanding of the intimacies of running a railway, demolishing not a few myths. It also pays handsome tribute to the railway preservation societies which are keeping alive the old traditions.

# 1

# A Rough Night Out

Blissful thoughts of creeping into a warm and welcoming bed alongside Joan had sustained me in those last few freezing minutes of cycling along the darkened streets to the house, through biting frosty air at half past three in the morning. When you have been out on an emergency call, and you are frozen to the marrow, you feel you will never be warm again; and few prospects are quite so alluring as nestling closely to a bed-warm woman. Your woman.

For me, in my late twenties, luxuries such as central heating were still a distant dream. Yet such comfort would be a boon to a young relief stationmaster when he is 'on call' to attend any mishap that might occur at night on his particular piece of railway.

I had stumbled out of bed and downstairs at two in the morning, that ghostly hour when spirits are low, to answer that raucous, relentless telephone. A disembodied voice had told me that two wagons of a goods train were derailed and blocking the railway lines. At such times, the man in charge must turn out, whatever the hour, to get the trains on the move again. Returning home in my single days, I would lie awake, tired and cold and restless, aching for that elusive sleep and worrying about the line and whether I had carried out the operating rules correctly. When things go wrong, there is the inevitable inquest to follow in the cold light of day, and the cool assessment of someone higher up who could maybe help your promotion or stymie your career. Now that we were married, these nocturnal disturbances, mercifully not too frequent, had been easier to bear. But Joan? Now half awake, she turned. Gently, I placed my arm around her, and soon the vexations of the enigmatic operating inspector, Mr Goss, and the worries of the railway drifted into oblivion.

In our courting days, I had warned her about this 'on call' business. My job as a relief stationmaster often meant being 'on call' one week in two, continuously night and day for seven days, mid-week to mid-week, including the weekend, summer and winter, for any stretch of line that happened just then to be under my supervision, either sleepy branch or busy main line. Such duties earned extra pay. And even more important, they brought valuable experience.

On this occasion, the telephone had shattered my dream and turned it into a nightmare at two in the morning. Joan would not have the thing in the bedroom. Understandably. It rested on the hall table, and we always left the bedroom door ajar. But even then it seemed a most uncivilized way to be wakened. It jangled the nerves and took you minutes to recover.

How well I remember working with a big, confident and handsome booking clerk at Oxford who was given his first station – the bottom rung of the ladder. It stood on a delightful branch line, with a station house and a pretty station garden, at a low rent, for him and his new wife. But, he told me, those passing freight trains that rumbled along in the night awakened him, and he often lay there shivering and apprehensive in case one became derailed. I know the feeling. Within six months he was forced to give up the job of stationmaster and returned as a booking clerk at Oxford, where later he told me of his unhappy experience.

Now, downstairs in the hall, still bleary with unfinished sleep, I groped for the telephone handset and heard the voice of the night-shift train controller at Kirkby-in-Ashfield control office, cool as you like.

"Couple of wagons on old England at Mansfield Junction. They're on the empties for the colliery."

"Okay. I'll be at the station in under ten minutes. Will there be a lift to the junction?"

"Sure. A loco waiting for you. We've got to get these empties moving. Otherwise we'll stop production at the colliery on early shift. And they'll all go mad up there!"

"We might want a steam crane."

"Up to you, Stationmaster. The twenty-tonner's in steam if needed."

Keeping my pyjamas on for extra warmth, I dressed, mounted my bike and pedalled away in the dark, my breath like steam in the frosty air. I had donned my gold-braided peak cap so that the chaps would know who I was.

At the station platform stood an 0-6-0 tank engine. Its fire lit up the clouds of steam and smoke eerily, forming a ghostly silhouette of the driver.

He called, "Come on up, sir."

Following the customary courtesy, the driver stuffed a piece of cloth in my hand as he helped me to climb to the footplate. This cloth had a double role: to keep my hands clean and to protect them against any hot metal I might inadvertently touch. The young fireman finished topping up and banged shut the firebox doors. Gently the driver eased the regulator, and we began to chuff steadily along towards the Junction about a mile away. On either side of the line were rows of terrace houses, the occasional one showing a light upstairs. In these small hours the noise of our engine seemed positively indecent.

My job now was to assess the derailment, call for any assistance I judged might be required – a steam crane, for instance – keep the control office informed of progress and get the lines cleared for normal operations as soon as possible.

On the way I asked the driver, "A bad derailment?"

"Just two wagons. Track's damaged a bit, and a signal wire broke."

"They've called out a P-way man, and a signals bloke?"

"Control said yes. Oh, and the traffic inspector, he be on the way."

"That's fine."

Let's hope it won't be that smoothy smart alec, Inspector Goss. Knows his stuff all right. And he's had much experience, especially compared with me. But somehow he always tries to take the mickey out of me.

While passengers and day-shift miners are sleeping comfortably in their warm beds, a handful of railwaymen like me, who have spent years learning our craft and are used to mishaps in the small hours, will be clearing up the mess ready for their daily work. Indeed, anywhere on the railway system, for a derailed wagon or a major disaster, railwaymen with all the necessary skills and equipment to cope are available 'on call', continuously day and night throughout the year. And they can call, in next to no time, doctors, hospitals, ambulance, police, fire brigades. Every station, every depot, large or small, has up-to-the-minute information posted up ready for immediate use, in a highly efficient system that has taken well over a century to mature. And one of my jobs at any station was to check that all the information was kept up-to-date.

We reached the site. I climbed down from the engine and peered at the two wagons in the beam of my battery flashlight (my own, not the company's). They were looking most unhappy, each with two wheels off the rails. Up came the permanent-way man, the oily odour from his handlamp hanging in the still night air, and his breath blowing out like steam.

He told me, "Only a few chairs and keys buckled, sir. Half an hour'll put it right. I've seen Fred on signals. He's doing that wire. No problem there, he tells me."

"That's great."

To be honest, I'd had little experience of derailed wagons, and the anxious neophyte in me felt some sinking of my vitals. Maybe I could pick the brains of these chaps before that Inspector Goss arrives.

Exhibited in my office at the station, with all the emergency information, was a list of telephone numbers and the engine depots where ranges of lifting equipment were located, from timbers and jacks and packing to cranes large enough to hoist a giant locomotive.

I sounded the permanent-way man. "What d'you think, the small Kirkby crane?"

"Dunno. Reckon we could manage with timbers and packing. Up to you, gaffer. If the driver's any good, timbers'd do it. Plenty here at the junction."

Using my torch, I picked my way gingerly to the engine at the front of the train of empty wagons. The guard had gone to the signalbox to report his position and should be back soon. I called to the driver, and he jumped down to the track

"How long are you going to be on this bloody job?" he lambasted me. "We've been here nigh on an hour. And you're still frigging about doing bugger-all!"

"Eh, come off it, driver. I've only just got here."

He shone his oil-lit handlamp on my face. "Look, gaffer. I'm already on overtime. And it's Saturday morning. And it's my missus' birthday and we're going away for the weekend, see? So get bloody weaving!"

I could feel the adrenalin surging dangerously. No good fighting though. Must keep cool. Tommy Cliffe, a relief station-master who encouraged me in my teens to learn the rules, always said, "If you're in charge, keep cool. Keep your dignity and don't argue the toss." I knew it was fatally easy to make a mistake if you are upset and working with moving vehicles in pitch black. Any error and we are all in the soup.

"Look, driver. We both want to clear this job up and get home. Right? Let's get the chaps together and shove some timbers under the wheels and jack up a bit, and try a steady bit of shunting."

His reaction shattered me. "Are you raving mad? That'd take two hours! Where the bloody hell did you learn your railways, in a bloody college? Timbers is no good. We wants a crane. I seen one at Kirkby. Phone Control. Tell 'em to pull their friggin' fingers out!"

No good being aggressive with a man in such an ugly mood. We've got a job to do. Maybe he's right about a crane. Nothing for it but to play along with him. "Right. I'll go to the box and fix it."

It was about three hundred yards to the signalbox. There the signalman switched me through to the Control Office, and I ordered the crane. Despite returning carefully along the track with my torch, I skidded on an icy patch and tripped base over apex and struck my head slightly against the rail. Somewhat dazed, I just had to sit there on the ballast in the freezing cold for a minute or two to recover. I was barely half-way back when I could see two or three handlamps swinging and could hear men shouting and the sound of the engine shunting back and forth. Something was happening and I didn't know what.

Reaching the site again, I found a wagon examiner there and the engine pulling the two derailed wagons at a gentle speed over some strategically placed timbers. Inspector Goss himself was shouting the orders: "Steady, steady. Go on a bit. That's it!" And the wagons were duly on the rails once more.

From the Stygian depths a smug voice smote my ears. "Good morning, Mr Stationmaster, if it's not too late!"

"Oh, good morning, Mr Goss. I'd just been to the box to order the crane."

"I guessed as much. And I cancelled it. There's a phone in the sidings here."

"I didn't know."

There was an edge to his voice when he said, "It's very costly to use a steam crane when a few simple timbers and a little nous will do the trick, old boy!"

He slapped me on the back, and I felt my cheeks reddening.

"Much obliged," I said. "You did a good job."

In the faint firelight from the engine, I could see his round, clean-shaven face smiling through clenched teeth. Never have I seen anyone who could smile so smugly. In his mid-forties and holding a somewhat senior position to me, he always wore his black bowler at a rakish angle and had a sharp tongue for anyone who crossed him.

Lowering his voice, he said smoothly and pompously, "Please rest assured, Mr Stationmaster, I shall omit your serious error of judgement from my confidential report to the district officer."

Cheeky blighter! "Don't do so on my account, Inspector. Say just what you think you must."

"Well, I'll be . . ."

But before he could say more, I turned smartly and made off along the track towards the station. Curse the fellow! He had that tank engine at his disposal and could easily have ordered the driver to give me a lift. It would have saved me a rather treacherous walk of a mile along the track on so dark and frosty a night. But no offer came. And I certainly wasn't going to ask him.

What a stupid bunch of fellows we were, all chewing each other up because we were out in the freezing cold when we could have been warm in bed. On my way home the only thought that consoled me was that of crawling into bed alongside Joan.

And that poor idiot, Goss, wasn't even married!

# 2
# Baptized in Fire and Water

However did I get caught up in this mad, mad world of trains? How does anybody? Most enthusiasts, one supposes, can trace that magic moment when a lifelong fascination for steam railways suddenly blazed into their consciousness. It may have happened during regular travel to school or work, a trip to the seaside, a school outing or Sunday School treat, a ride along a sleepy and meandering branch line to visit the grandparents. Or it could have been an excursion with a railway society, or a visit to a main line to watch a mighty Atlantic or Pacific with billowing plume of rolling steam roaring past, its great long train thundering behind it.

For others, the hobby may have crept up on them, stealthily, inexorably, permanently. For some, it was their career. For me, my baptism in fire and water was sudden and shattering. I was nine years old, and it happened at Stoke-on-Trent station on the North Staffordshire Railway after the First World War.

At close quarters the engine appeared as a giant dragon breathing hot steam which at any second might burst into flames; it seemed to crouch over the metals in sheer concentrated animal strength; mysterious noises throbbed from its inner depths, speaking of latent power, furious power that would soon be hurtling its train at breath-taking speeds to London town.

Gripping the strong hand of my father, a gardener, I edged cautiously forward to be nearer this frightening monster. Through the open firebox doors I could see red-hot coals and could feel the heat from them on my face. The fireman, sweating at the brow, shovelled black coal into that great roaring mouth which gobbled up the black and turned it instantly into glowing red. I expect he was getting steam up ready to depart south with the long and loaded train. I had never been to London and was not to make my first journey there for another eight years. So

17

London itself was not a real place at all, just a mass of jumbled picture-book images in my mind – of Buckingham Palace and the Changing of the Guard, the Tower of London and Tower Bridge, red horse-drawn omnibuses and black barges on the River Thames.

My father grinned down at me. "D'you like it, lad?"

"It's big!"

For weeks I had pestered him to take me to Stoke station to see a big express train, and a friend of his, the station inspector, had arranged it. We were now in the mighty presence of the morning express to London. As I looked at the huge engine, the inspector, smart in his navy blue uniform, made a tempting offer.

"What about it, lad, up in the cab?"

"Oo, yes, please!"

He spoke to the driver, a sallow-faced man with a handlebar moustache, wearing blue overalls and a cap with a shiny peak. They both helped me up. The fireman had stopped his shovelling and had closed the firebox doors. On the footplate the driver warned, "Hang on to this rail, sonny, and you'll be all right. Everything else is hot. So don't touch."

"Yes, sir."

He told me about things. "This big handle, it's the regulator. Makes the engine go. And this little wheel is the brake, vacuum brake."

I noticed a glass tube high up. "What's that for?"

"Shows how much water's in the boiler. Most important gauge of the lot. Understand?"

"I think so. I've got a railway picture-book at home."

Suddenly a most terrible roaring noise hit my ears and scared me to death. It made me jump and I put my hand by accident on a pipe that was burning hot. I remember screaming, more in fear than in pain, and the driver held me reassuringly. The men were grinning as the driver handed me down to the inspector. He stood me gently on the platform, and my father took my hand and dabbed my eyes with a khaki handkerchief. So loud was the roaring and hissing that you could not possibly hear anyone speak. I looked up at the engine. Steam was spurting fiercely up to the smoke-stained glass roof of the station, creating a strong odour of hot steam and oil. Just as suddenly, the noise stopped.

"Nothing to worry about, lad," assured the inspector. "Just blowing off, that's all. You get used to it."

'Blowing off', I was to learn later, was one of several devices in the form of safety valves to release excess pressure of steam. In pioneering times many boilers had exploded with dire consequences before safety systems had been perfected.

It seemed that neither the driver nor the inspector knew I had burnt my fingers. But my father did. And he wrapped his khaki handkerchief round my hand. Unfortunately there were hardly any marks for all my pain and suffering. Snatching my hand off that burning hot pipe had been the fastest thing I had ever done. And I began to laugh in relief. Grinning from his cab, the driver teased, "He'll never make a driver!"

Added the inspector, "But he might make a good station porter!"

Then he walked along the station platform attending to the train, in its livery of darkish red, the same as the engine.

It was exciting to see late-comers scramble aboard the train, and watch the guard wave his green flag and blow his whistle. Tremendous power-ridden chuffing shook the station, and billowing clouds of steam and smoke marked the starting of the train. Pistons hissed back and forth. Great oily rods rotated the huge driving-wheels. Steadily the train gathered speed. The last carriage, which carried a white-painted tail-lamp, rumbled out of the platform into the morning sunlight, and the train swiftly disappeared into the mysterious distance, leaving the station strangely quiet and deserted.

Wandering along the platform, I spotted a model of an old locomotive standing in a glass case. It was called 'Rocket'. Put a penny in the slot, the notice directed, and see the wheels go round. A penny, my weekly pocket money, was all I had, and into the slot it rattled. Wheels began to spin in a most realistic way, and the pistons went up and down. 'Rocket'! What a wonderful name. I must remember that. I knew that fireworks rockets whizzed up into the sky with great speed. And I wondered what speed the real 'Rocket' locomotive reached in the olden days. It must have been a hundred miles an hour! My nine-year-old mind was full of wonder as we took a local train home to Bucknall, nearly three miles away.

From early childhood I had been taken with the family on an occasional Sunday by train from Bucknall station to Stockton Brook, just four miles distant, to visit our grandparents. Horse-hair upholstery on the carriage seats scratched the back of our bare legs and made them itch. The train of two or three carriages simply rattled along at the most fantastic speed, at least twenty or even thirty miles an hour – diddly-dee diddly-dum diddly-dee diddly-dum – shooting under bridges and flying high on the top of embankments. Most puzzling, the scenery seemed to be travelling backwards, while the train seemed still. Lineside tele-graph poles ran a losing race with the train; the telegraph wires dipped and rose from pole to pole in an even rhythm, like some gigantic magic trick. I asked my father why the wires kept waving up and down. He said, "I wouldn't bother your young head about things like that," which left me even more mystified. One day I would find out.

I tried to count the bridges as they came and went with a whoosh. Steam and smoke wafted through the open carriage windows. Occasionally a speck of ash would blow into your eye, and for a moment you would be the subject of brief parental anxiety.

Throughout the journey the regular, rhythmic beat of wheels on rail joints and the chuff-chuffing of the engine made an agreeable and reassuring sound.

Only fifty yards from the terrace house where I lived on the edge of the country – two up and three down, gas lighting, one water tap, zinc bath for Friday nights at the fireside, outside flush toilet, tiny back yard, tinier front garden – ran the railway, parallel with our road. A branch line, winding sleepily through country villages for twelve miles between Stoke and Leek, it crossed the River Trent only yards from our back door and not many miles from its source. I must have seen and heard my very first trains from my pram.

Virtually from birth, in all my innocence and ignorance, I was hooked and caught, bound hand and foot, gagged and brain-washed by the vivid sights and sounds of steam railways. They ingratiated themselves into my senses and invaded my very bloodstream along with mother's milk. Against such infiltration, what chance was there for a chaste and unprotected child!

To and from the infants' school, four times a day, we passed under a stone and iron bridge, and if we boys and girls could see a train approaching, we ran excitedly, to be beneath and wait to be terrified by that great thundering noise as the train rumbled over the top. And to laugh with relief when we found ourselves still safe and sound.

On moving to the 'big school' at the age of seven, the lane we used crossed the railway. A big boy named Billy Bowen, who was a bully and a show-off, one day climbed to the parapet as a dozen admiring boys and girls gathered round. A train approached and he tried to drop an empty salmon tin down the chimney. But a powerful chuff hurled it back and blacked his eye. When grown-ups asked him about it, he just said, "Fighting!" Billy could walk along the top of the wooden palings that fenced the railway, arms outstretched to balance, like a tightrope walker: something I would not attempt. He even walked along one of the rails on the track. But this stopped after a policeman called on his father.

Now and then we would put a halfpenny on top of a rail. When flattened by a passing train, to our eyes it looked just like a penny. I took mine round to Clough's corner shop and said, "Penny bar of chocolate, please." Mr Clough reached for the chocolate as he took my coin. Then he bellowed, "Eh, off you go, you young imp! Kids have been trying this for these twenty years!"

Back at the railway bridge, Alf Madeley had his halfpenny ready. When I told him my story, he changed his mind. So we sat on the stone parapet and watched a long train of coal wagons uncoil itself from the sidings and rumble underneath, hauled by a North Staffordshire Railway 0-6-0 tank engine. The rumbling faded into the distance, and the train tucked itself away in the secret folds of the distant low hills. Sometimes we saw short coal trains pulled by a tiny black engine with four coupled wheels. It was such a filthy old thing that we kids called it 'Dirty Dolly'. We could see on the open, unprotected footplate that even the driver and fireman had black faces, like miners returning from work in the pit.

In our street little girls played traditional skipping-rope games, in one of them calling out simple rhymes which included the words 'North Staffordshire Railway Company', which, when you come to think, has a splendidly poetic feeling about it.

Several of the menfolk in our terrace worked on the line, and of course the NSR was the only railway in our part of the world that was worth talking about. After all, its main and branch lines totalled over two hundred miles of route. Occasionally we heard talk of foreigners such as the Midland or the Nor' West and even one they called the Great Western. But they were only names to Potteries folk, and none of them stirred the blood like the old 'Knotty', known as such proudly among local railwaymen because the famous Staffordshire Knot was the railway's very own emblem.

Unbeknown to me in my youthful innocence, things were afoot in the world of railways in the early 1920s, and in 1923 our beloved railway, along with 119 others, large and small, was submerged in a smother of amalgamations. Four main-line groups were formed. They were named London Midland & Scottish, London & North Eastern, Great Western, Southern.

Formed in 1845 during the Railway Mania three years before George Stephenson died, the North Staffordshire Railway had fought for, and enjoyed, its vigorous independence for seventy-eight glorious years. Now it was just one of thirty-three former railway companies making up the LMS, one of the four gigantic groups. But for years the little girls on the sunny streets continued to play their skipping-rope games to the words chanted in childish rhythm, "North Staffordshire Railway, I call number one," the cue for the next girl to jump in.

Generations of Staffordshire men, sons following fathers, nephews following uncles, had served with pride and loyalty this stalwart railway that linked the pit shafts and blast furnaces, waste heaps and bottle-shaped kilns of the ugly industrial parts of the Potteries with the beautiful surroundings of hills and valleys, steep and gentle, many of them thickly wooded, and connected with the network of the nation's railway systems. For a long time the line would still be called affectionately 'the Knotty', or 'the North Stafford', and sons would still follow fathers in a calling that offered such a wealth of human interest. People all round Britain, one supposes, felt a warm affection for their own little railways that were similarly being swallowed up by one of the four big ones.

The LMS was barely four years old, and I was approaching sixteen when my father one day said, "My boy, I must try and get you a job on the North Stafford."

# 3

# The Mysteries of Running a Station

A job on the North Stafford! The very thought made my blood tingle. Perhaps I would be a porter at Bucknall station and wear a smart uniform and polish my silver buttons to sparkle like diamonds and shine my shoes as we did on Sundays for Sunday School. And load parcels and mails and milk churns which make such a lovely noise from a truck into the guard's van and close the doors behind passengers boarding the train. Maybe I would have a whistle, tell passengers the times of trains and where to change (how would I know?), collect the tickets, go into the signalbox itself. I had seen the porters, the clerks and the stationmaster at Bucknall do all these things.

Then my father told me, "You can't get on the North Stafford without a relation on the line. So Mr Stonier's going to be your uncle."

Mr Ewart Stonier was the inspector at Stoke who had shown me that locomotive six years earlier; he and my father, when single, had been in lodgings together. But this adopted uncle business worried me. It did not seem quite right. However, I met the inspector on Stoke station, and he took me for an interview with the great Mr L. P. Briggs, the stationmaster, who seemed terribly tall. He had just returned to his office from seeing the Manchester train away and looked most impressive in his tail-coat and tall silk hat, the first I had ever seen, except in books. His pale face was adorned by a luxuriant black moustache.

Nervously I answered his searching questions and proffered a sample of my handwriting, which my teachers had usually said was appalling. However, he raised his dark brows at my Pitman's shorthand speed of forty words a minute (learnt at school in an experiment), and his serious face threatened to crack into a smile when I said I had won a prize at school for an essay entitled 'The Effect of Temperance on Character'.

I noticed that the Staffordshire Knot was woven into the dark

red carpet on the floor, and the letters 'NSR' engraved on a large
bevelled mirror on the wall. Upholstery of the chairs was in a dark
material similar to that in some of the trains. On another wall
were two vividly coloured posters of NSR trains steaming along
through beautiful countryside, while along the corridor could be
heard the sound and bustle of the busy station.

Mr Briggs left us for a minute or two, and Inspector Stonier
murmured encouraging things and reminded me to call him
'Uncle'. Apart from my former headmaster, the doctor and our
vicar, Mr Briggs was the most important person I had ever met. I
savoured the atmosphere of his dusty office, which, I thought,
smelt exactly as a stationmaster's should – like the station
itself.

When he returned, he said briskly, "Yes, Inspector, I'm willing
to recommend him to Derby headquarters as a junior clerk. Then
he's on his own."

Junior clerk! Secretly I had been hoping for that. A few days
later a letter arrived from LMS headquarters at Derby (no HQ at
Stoke now), and a free railway ticket was enclosed. I was to take a
written examination. At home I spent time studying my modest
collection of railway maps and an old North Staffs timetable.

From Stoke the journey to Derby was thirty-six miles. I allowed
time to see the engine, a 2-4-0 passenger tender type in a splendid
dark red livery. We went through stations whose names I had
heard and which had a romantic ring about them – Blythe Bridge
with its level crossing; Uttoxeter, odd with its triangular platform
arrangements, leading to a branch line along the pretty Churnet
Valley to Leek and Macclesfield connecting to Manchester, and
another short branch to Ashbourne; then Sudbury and Tutbury,
and Egginton Junction with a line to the old Great Northern.
Beyond Tutbury was a junction for Burton, with connections for
Birmingham, Gloucester and South Wales, and Bristol for the
West Country. We clattered over the bridge that crossed the River
Dove and finally a span across the River Derwent, then into the
high-roofed station at Derby. Our Knotty 2-4-0 did well, arriving
two minutes early.

In the awesome head offices at Derby, built in the last century
for the Midland Railway, with other lads I was ushered into a
room and instructed about the examination. It was mainly con-

cerned with writing, arithmetic and reading, which, thankfully, I found quite easy.

Officials were pleasant enough but everything was deadly serious and you did not speak unless you were spoken to. Before catching the afternoon train home, I watched several express trains arrive and depart, the massive engines filling the station with thunder and steam. It was all very exciting. Some day I would learn all about these engines. One of them, an official told me, was a Midland compound 4-4-0 with three cylinders and enormous driving-wheels for speed and painted in that lovely Midland red. He said it was about twenty years old, a great age to my sixteen years.

Within a month I was offered a post as a junior clerk at Hanley passenger station. A job on the railway and a dream come true! What more could a lad wish for? I was to be a clerk and not a porter. But I knew I would work alongside porters and ticket-collectors, guards and drivers, and even signalmen. Best of all, there would be the sight and sound of trains in and out of the station from early morning to late at night.

Whenever I was near the railway, I think it was the clanging of wagon buffers combined with the squeal of wheels on rails that thrilled me most: sounds I had listened to all my life, sounds I heard in bed as I was drifting off to sleep. They were sounds with a million associations and belonged as much to the bright and sunny days of summer as to the crisp frost and snow of winter. For me, the railway was full of secret enjoyments that were difficult to share.

Half an hour's walk from home and five minutes from the town centre, Hanley station stood on a loop line between Etruria and Kidsgrove to the north and two miles from Stoke station to the south. A friend and I had often gone to Hanley to watch the trains. Because the station and platforms were in a deep cutting on a sharp curve and with heavy gradients, the thunderous noise and vigorous vibrations from a heavy goods train rattled the windows of the booking and parcels offices at street level above, until you felt sure the building would come crashing down. Working there would be like being paid for your hobby.

Starting salary would be £45 a year. It worked out at 17s 3d a week (86p) for a week of forty-eight hours, payable fortnightly.

On my first day I met Mr Payne, the stationmaster, in his private office. A big man, he had short-cropped grey hair and a military-style moustache. His uniform jacket in dark navy-blue serge was double-breasted with two rows of shiny brass buttons. His gold-braided peaked cap carried the words 'Station Master' in a gold-coloured thread. His deep, dark-brown voice seemed to rumble right down into his shoes. To me he was the acme of railway authority and style.

"Ah, Ferneyhough," he said, "I saw your uncle at Stoke the other day."

"Who, sir? Oh, er, yes. My Uncle Ewart." The thought of a counterfeit uncle made me go hot.

"A lot to learn here, lad. We send parcels and merchandise all over Britain. And large loads come in daily on the trains for delivery round the town. Our two horse-vans do the collections and deliveries. There's a man and a boy on each. Every commodity you can think of. In the parcels office, some of the transactions are cash, and others – mainly regulars – are monthly credit. So there's plenty of paperwork and book-keeping to do."

"I see, sir." Having done none of these things, it was all a bit vague and frightening. Since leaving school at fourteen, I had worked at a butcher's shop in Hanley. As the eldest of four children, the money was needed at home.

"Later you'll do booking-office work, issuing all kinds of tickets and keeping the books." He fiddled with a wide gold wedding-ring on his finger. "The passenger business isn't what it was. First the trams, and now all these buses. Oh, we have two theatres in the town. And we get new companies in and out each week. That means issuing their travel tickets and despatching big loads of their props and scenery. Plenty going on there. You'll learn a bit at a time with the other clerks."

"I'll do my best, sir."

"Good lad. In time you can have a go at compiling wages bills and paying the men each week and making up the cash for the daily banking."

A goods train was reverberating through the station platforms down below. You could tell it was a goods by the rhythm of the wheels over the rail joints, different from a passenger train with bogies. The thrusting engine rattled the windows, and I could feel the very floor under my feet vibrating. What a thrilling thought – I'm now working on the railway.

Mr Payne said, "You'll start in the parcels office. Let's go there now."

Friendly clerks and porters helped me to learn the work. Customers brought in packages, to be weighed, charged and have numbered red railway stamps affixed, showing 'Hanley' and the value. Book records included 'cash' or 'credit', and at the end of the day figures were totalled and cash balanced. Porters loaded the parcels onto two-wheeled hand trucks and wheeled them down a covered timber slope – there were no lifts – to the platforms for conveyance in the guards' vans of trains.

Several times daily the two horse-vans arrived. They had delivered 'received' packages around the town, mainly to commercial firms and factories, and had collected those for despatch by train. The vans were hauled by two of the most clumsy-looking but lovable shire horses you ever saw – dapple grey, adorned with massive manes, long, full tails occasionally plaited with straw, and floppy fetlocks that splayed out as the animals walked. One answered to 'Captain' and the other to 'Blossom'. Sometimes one of the horses would stand outside the parcels office, with a nosebag of oats, contentedly chewing away. As he neared the bottom of the bag, he would toss his head for final mouthfuls, spilling some on the ground. Then he would be joined for the meal by cheeky, chirpy, quarrelsome sparrows who would peck up the grain furtively, keeping a beady eye on those massive, iron-shod hooves.

Several horse-drawn drays – flat vehicles on four wheels – were attached to the goods station across the road. As they ambled leisurely along the busy streets with their various loads of merchandise that was carried on the railway by goods trains, they were a familiar sight. Though motor vehicles were now growing in numbers – for bakers and coal merchants, milk deliveries and timber merchants, fruit and vegetables – horses were very much a part of the daily life of the town, and better-off people still rode around in a gig or trap, a pony cart or a barouche, all still very fashionable in the late 1920s.

As the months went by, my work became easier. I committed my fair share of bloomers – a wrong charge, a parcel sent to the wrong destination, or mistakes in the book-keeping. Errors were always worrying, but in between the work we made our own fun.

A parson asked parcels porter Jack Merrill if he could see the chief clerk, Mr Grocott, who was in the rear office behind a glass partition. To my eyes Mr Grocott, the most gentle person, was a caricature of a man from an earlier age. Pince-nez spectacles perched on the bridge of his nose had a fine gold chain connected to a hook round his ear. Inside or outside, he always wore the curliest of bowler hats at the back of his head. Sprays of grey whiskers sprouted out of his ears and nostrils. His grey, straggly moustache was stained with blue ink marks from his habit of putting his dip-pen to his mouth.

Taking the parson towards Mr Grocott's office door, Jack said, "In there, sir. You'll have to shout. He's very deaf."

Through the glass partition we watched discreetly the two men and listened through the slightly open door. In the loudest voice, as though from the pulpit, the parson boomed, "I'm sending a trunk of valuable books to my son at Cambridge. Can it be insured?"

Mr Grocott looked pained and jerked away as though he had been struck. He said quietly, "You don't have to shout, sir. I'm not deaf!"

When the parson came out of the private office, he glanced round crossly for the culprit. But Jack had vanished.

In handling the numerous packages in the office, work in which the clerks shared, we often threw them to each other to save time, for example, from loaded truck to weighing scales. Sometimes, with much puffing, Jack would struggle with a large parcel and pitch it over to me. I would splay my feet and brace myself for the heavy catch, only to find that it was feather light, and it would bounce from my arms up in the air. Jack always found this very amusing, especially when I was on the receiving end. One afternoon he threw a quite small parcel as though a few ounces. Actually it was so heavy that I lost my balance and fell. Jack grinned mischievously but behind his back the stationmaster suddenly appeared. He glared at us, each in turn, and rumbled heavily from the bottom of his boots. "If I catch you at that again, it'll be the sack for both of you. We've enough claims without the staff throwing the goods about!" We were instantly subdued and never did such a thing again – not for weeks.

Taking packages from the parcels office down to the station platforms could cause problems. It took two or three men to wheel a loaded hand-truck down the slope; there was one slope to each of the two platforms, both connected at the top by a covered overbridge; bridge and slopes were also used by passengers.

That afternoon it was a particularly heavy load for two of us. Half way down, the pace began to increase and we gripped the handles for dear life. In a panic Jack shouted, "Hold on tight!" But once the momentum had begun, we rapidly lost control, and the barrow ran smack into the wall at the bottom. What a mess! Fresh cream from four large cans spattered big blobs of white onto the walls and floor. Some streaked down my face and trickled into my mouth. As the train ran in, passengers looked out and grinned. Noticing so much white, one comic called, "Merry Christmas!" We cleaned up as best we could, despatched the undamaged packages by the next train, and in the office Jack compiled a detailed report headed, "Goods damaged in Transit".

Mr Grocott read it, then said, "Jack, lad, it'll have to go to the stationmaster."

"I know. But it's the first time it's happened to me in ten years."

In these early months at Hanley, I worked from 12 noon to 8 p.m. Mondays to Fridays and 7.30 to 3.30 on Saturdays. A permanent late shift was not too marvellous, for I could not meet my friends very often, and no Saturday afternoons to watch football. That's railways. They never stop running. And I made the best use of those spare hours, mainly in study.

In October, after I had worked there for four months, Mr Payne sent for me. A call from the boss always brought butterflies but was usually worry for nothing. This time it was different.

"Sad news, I'm afraid, lad," he said in his private office. "Derby HQ say I have to give you two weeks' notice of dismissal."

Standing there in front of his desk, I was stunned. The sack! My poor dad would be worried because of the money.

Mr Payne added, "Sorry about this, young Frank. But your appointment letter did specify a junior post for the summer months only."

I could only answer, "Yes, sir."

He gave me the handwritten letter confirming what he had said. Then I asked, "Have I done anything wrong, Mr Payne?"

"Oh, no. You've done very well, and I'm pleased with your progress. So's Mr Grocott. I'm writing to Derby. Let's hope they'll take you back soon. Don't be too despondent, my boy."

That fortnight under notice to quit dragged heavily. It was not easy to carry on working with the station chaps and be cheerful and look happy. After leaving, I signed on for the 'dole'. We'll skip those unhappy weeks, for eventually I was given a job at Crewe, fifteen miles from Stoke, to work on locomotive accounts in the offices of the famous Crewe Works. It seemed the accounts were in arrears, and junior and senior clerks from miles around (some juniors had been sacked like me) swooped on Crewe like a swarm of locusts. They travelled daily from places as far away as Manchester, Warrington, Rhyl, Chester, Lichfield and Stafford.

In a large L&NWR office of early Victorian vintage, some forty of us perched on tall stools at sloping desks and used for our work dip-pens with steel nibs and pots of ink sunk in the stained desks. The chief clerk handed us large piles of small forms which we sorted according to engine numbers and workshops, then totalled the hours worked and the costings for transfer to another, bigger form. Main activities in the Works consisted of building new engines and repairing and maintaining those taken temporarily out of service. Our paperwork was for repair and maintenance jobs and included work on fireboxes and boilers, pistons and cylinders, wheels and frames, for a great variety of engines. Slowly it came through to me that this work was part of a system for calculating the amount spent, and how it was spent, on every individual engine going through the workshops. This gave me a glimmer of a mysterious technique they called statistics.

At lunchtime we took our sandwiches into an enormous canteen provided for hordes of workmen. We paid a penny for a large mug of strong and bitter tea which the men seemed to enjoy but which tasted like poison to us. It was noisy with talk and laughter and the clatter of crockery, and we chatted with the chaps about their work. It was hard to realize that these men, in rough clothes or overalls, were building real live steam-engines soon to be pulling mighty trains on the main lines of the LMS, and it was exciting just being with them in what I knew would be a spell of only a few months, never to be repeated.

A special workmen's train was run for the men from Stoke. They had been made redundant by the closure of the locomotive-building works of the North Stafford after the amalgamation of 1923 and for various reasons did not want to move their homes to Crewe.

To save a long trek from the office to Crewe station, Philip Hawkes and I often travelled home on the works train. It meant walking through the Works for a quarter of a mile, stepping over railway lines in the dark winter evenings and keeping a wary eye open for moving wagons that were being shunted around the place. Had our bosses known, we would have been in dead trouble, and I realized later that what we were doing was suicidal.

On the train the men played cards. Some smoked thick twist tobacco, strong and pungent. A few chewed the stuff and spat on the floor or through the window. Soon the compartment was heavy with the effluvium of tobacco and stale sweat. Because we were young clerks dressed in suits, we suffered legpull and ribaldry and were usually not sorry to reach Stoke.

On the way through the Works to the train, we had to pass several workshops; we would stand there and, with Longfellow, "look in at the open door". For the first time we saw dazzling molten liquid running like water and sparks flying up like vivid red fountains, and massive blocks of white-hot metal being stamped by an enormous steam hammer that shook the floor beneath your feet like an earthquake. We could see the men with sweat on their lined faces that glowed in the fierce heat which we could feel even by the doorway. All this crude metal being shaped up to make railway engines.

In the foundry we watched men pouring molten metal from crucibles with long handles into moulds of sand that had been shaped by wooden patterns in the pattern shop. We peeped into the boiler-making shop. But the angry rat-a-tat of the rivet guns that bored deep into our ears was more than we could stand. Once, for a few minutes, we saw inside the huge erecting shop, with overhead travelling cranes and lifting-hoists high in the roof. Components had been assembled onto the main frames, and a real locomotive was taking shape before our very eyes.

Going for the Works train one dark evening, Philip and I could hear wagons moving. Buffers clanged and wheels were squealing on the rails as we waited for a clearance. Then, quite suddenly, Philip ran across the several lines. In the gloom I heard him shout something. So when it seemed safe, I scurried over, horrified to find him lying still on the ground. But he grinned up at me.

"Phil! Are you all right?"

I helped him up and could feel that he was trembling.

"I reckon so. I managed to jump clear. But a wagon bumped into me and I stumbled. Just a bit shaken, that's all."

I was shaking too. And my mouth was dry.

"Let's go to the station," I suggested, "and give the Works train a miss, eh?"

"We'll do that. I'll never go on that bloody train again. Besides, I can't stand their tobacco."

We never mentioned this near-miss to our colleagues in the office, nor even to each other. It was a terrifying lesson for two lads of sixteen, newcomers to the railway, about the crass stupidity of taking chances on the lines.

Crewe was a true railway town created entirely by railways, whose shareholders built for their workers schools and churches, clinics and libraries, sports grounds and social clubs; and Crewe for us in the late 1920s was a superb station for watching the trains go by. Lines fanned out to Chester and North Wales, Liverpool and Manchester, Stoke and London, Derby and Nottingham, Shrewsbury and on to Hereford and South Wales. Particularly exciting were trains bound for Glasgow and Perth, Aberdeen and Inverness, names which, for me, were still only dots on a railway map, fascinating places one day to explore – by train.

In a railway magazine I read about a famous train with its own name that travelled via Crewe. Its title, 'Royal Scot', had been confirmed officially, complete with tartan nameboards on the carriage sides, in summer 1927. It had been hauled by a 'Claughton' 4-6-0 and piloted by a 'George the Fifth' class 4-4-0, to give non-stop runs, except for change of engines at Carnforth, to both Glasgow and Edinburgh. In its early days I was lucky enough to be on Crewe station one day when it went through.

Though my spell in the offices of Crewe Works was for only a few months in the winter of 1927–8, it had been a stimulating experience. There I became familiar with the names of numerous locomotive parts listed in the paperwork we handled, from piston rods to number nine headed screws, and smokebox doors to engine whistle cords, and had a glimpse of locomotives actually being made.

# 4

# The Monocled Man and other Theatre Characters

From Crewe, back I went to Hanley. It was great to see the chaps again, and their welcome was flattering. Though I did some work in the parcels office as before, I began to learn the procedures in the booking office which Mr Payne, the stationmaster, had outlined to me earlier. There was a lot of detail and I found it a bit of a strain at first. On most days passengers for the trains were not very numerous.

Light relief came from booking the two theatrical parties each week, plus their props and scenery, for the companies on tour visiting our two local theatres. At the Grand Theatre it was usually a music-hall style of variety entertainment; the Theatre Royal generally presented a play or featured a musical programme by the D'Oyly Carte or another opera company.

In the booking office one morning the windows were rattling as a particularly heavy coal train thundered through, and above the general noise came a loud knocking at the door.

I called, "Come in!"

The door was flung open in a most dramatic fashion and in strode a gangling man of around fifty. He wore a suit in a check so loud that it shouted at you, a wide-brimmed Mexican-style white hat and a huge yellow-spotted red bow tie. He waved a big cigar and in one eye wore a monocle which was attached to a black silk cord clipped to his lapel. His pale face was deeply lined and mischievous, like that of Arthur English in later times, and the bags under his eyes were big enough to deposit in the station left-luggage office.

His very presence frightened me a bit, but I guessed he must be connected with one of the two theatres. I greeted him cautiously. "Morning, sir. Can I do something for you?"

With a flourish, he removed his hat and laid it on the booking office counter, revealing a mop of wavy, silver-grey hair.

"Yes, indeed, laddie. You can, so you can." You would think he was addressing a crowded audience in a smoky theatre, and his voice sounded as though he laced his whisky with rusty nails. "Our distinguished company's playing in the Gaiety in Manchester next week, laddie. So I'll need thirty-two theatrical tickets, at reduced fare, mark you, to travel on Sunday morning. Six of them to be first class for our six most dazzling stars."

I wrote down the details and noted from him the amount of scenery and props they would be sending, for which the station foreman would need to order a special van from Stoke control office.

"Very good, sir. I'll see the chief clerk, and we'll have the tickets ready for you tomorrow, Tuesday." Parties of theatrical performers were allowed specially reduced fares.

"Right, laddie. As Shakespeare has it, 'I will return to thee on the morrow at the appointed and fateful hour, then abscond, never to cast mine old eyes on thy ugly young mug ere again.' And that, my deah fellah, if thou knowest thy bard, is from Act II scene 1 of *As You Like It*, or 'Why bother with it', I'm not quite sure."

It was all rather embarrassing, and I felt uncontrollable giggles come on. "You're making me laugh, sir!"

He suddenly flung both arms up and gazed aloft, as though pleading to the heavens. "Laugh? Ye gods and teeny little fishes! My dear sonny, I'm a tragedian not a comedian. You're looking at a true Thespian in the Garrick tradition who has played before the Duke of York and other public houses!"

His booming tones suddenly changed to the intimately conversational. "Here. Two tickets for the show tomorrow night. Take your girl."

"Oh, that's good of you, sir. Thanks!"

"Good of me? No, laddeo. It's bad of me. Bookings on Wednesday are bad, not good. Good-day to you, me bhoy!"

He moved briskly to the counter, grabbed his ridiculous hat, replaced his dangling monocle into his right eye and swept out of the office, noisily banging the door behind him. Whew, and whew! His departure left a cloud of cigar smoke and a big gap of emptiness and silence. Never before had I met such a larger-than-life character with such an overwhelming presence, and I stood there a moment or two trying to collect my scattered wits.

I had been going out with Millie for only a few weeks. At nearly eighteen she was about my own age, and we were still very shy of each other. Yes, she would like to come to the theatre with me. All I knew about the show was that it would be a musical-hall programme with about a dozen different acts – singers, dancers, acrobats, a magician, comedians, sketches and the like.

Our seats were in the upper circle (which I could not afford), just below the 'gods' as the balcony was called. It was all very rowdy and exciting, with lots of noise and colour and movement. We enjoyed the programme, including the lively music from the orchestra deep in the pit below the stage. Then the two com-edians bounced onto the stage, garbed in check suits, large flat grey caps and bright red socks. It was not so much the crazy new songs they sang, such as, 'I've never seen a straight banana', and 'Horsy, cock your tail up, keep the sun out of my eyes.' It was the jokes they told. To us, then, they were so smutty and crude that we two innocents sat there in stunned and silent embarrassment, while the rest of the audience, especially the women, were screaming with laughter and dabbing the tears from their eyes. In your teens, you are so idealistic, so sensitive. A few weeks later Millie and I parted company.

About that time there were five cinemas in Hanley, and some cinema- and theatre-goers travelled by train. But more and more were being lost to the marvellous new motor buses coming on the roads. Many railway passengers had already been lost to the electric trams with overhead wires that whined and screeched up the steep road by our station. But in 1928 the trams in the Potteries were withdrawn, ending yet another era.

We should have earned a lot of passenger business from the cinemas, a form of entertainment that already threatened the 'live' theatres, but it was only marginal. Talking pictures had now arrived and cinema-goers would soon be changing their affec-tions from screen sweethearts Mary Pickford and Douglas Fair-banks, comedians Charlie Chaplin and Buster Keaton and romantic Rudolph Valentino to Al Jolson and Clark Gable. It was a slow process, but our loop line was losing to the buses, and the theatres were losing to the cinemas.

Some months after my débâcle with Millie, I was working in the parcels office on late shift finishing at eight o'clock. On the Monday, in walked a youngish man in a grey sweater, slacks and a brown bowler hat: not the quintessence of sartorial elegance but certainly compelling to the eye. And I was not surprised to find he was a theatrical. He held a rather rough-looking one-wheeled cycle.

"Hallo, me ole dahlin'. In the left-luggage office till next Saturday OK?" Now that American talking pictures were popular, 'OK' seemed to be on everybody's lips.

"Right, sir. Here's your ticket. Threepence, please."

He handed me a threepenny bit. "Keep the change, me ole son. And don't you get ridin' me ole bike when I've gorn!"

After he had left, I said to my colleague, Jack Podmore, a year my junior, "I'm going to ride that blighter when things get quieter tonight. Even if it kills me."

Jack grinned. "It probably will. Rather you than me."

So I examined the vehicle, if that is the correct term. It consisted of an ordinary cycle wheel, pedals and a saddle. It was a dowdy old thing and had a circular panel attached to the spokes carrying the words, 'The Three Pirates'.

That evening we balanced our books and cashed up in good time. Then Jack and I cleared a space in the left-luggage office, and warily I tried to mount the unicycle. Whoosh! – the wheel shot forward, hurling me backwards, and I fell smack on my backside. Jack laughed. I tried again. This time the wheel shot backwards from under me and threw me forward, flat on my face. Jack rocked with laughter. I was not amused.

Then he suggested, "We ought to have an ambulance standing by!"

After fifteen minutes of experimenting and sprawling, I was flushed and breathless, and my cheap Burton's suit was covered in dust. However, five evenings and fifty bruises later I had mastered it enough to ride it six or seven yards across the left-luggage floor. Next day the owner collected it, putting further temptation out of my way. Just as well, really.

The next week, lured by advertisements for the Three Pirates and trick cycling, Jack and I visited the Grand Theatre. We wanted to see our old unicycle in action. Our sixpenny seats were high in the balcony. After the interval three acrobatic comedians in sailors' suits cavorted around the stage far below us, one of them finally riding just once on the old unicycle from one side of the stage to the other. And that was all!

"Well," said Jack, after the applause had faded, "What a disappointment. *You* could have done better than *him*!"

But the final act was indeed trick cycling *par excellence*, a dazzling and skilful display on all kinds of machines, from a tiny one ridden by a chimpanzee to a single-wheel model with the seat perched on an enormously long steel rod, a lengthy chain from the crank driving the wheel. To a background of dramatic, pulsating music, the cycles sparkled in the spotlights, ridden fast and furiously by sylph-like girls and Adonis-shaped men in multi-coloured tights: a truly exciting finish to our evening.

As we moved down the many staircases with numerous people chatting excitedly, Jack remarked, "Folks wouldn't believe you if you said it was fun working in a railway left-luggage office!"

In the parcels office we handled quite a few consignments of livestock for conveyance by passenger train, usually in the guard's van. Dogs, cats, goats, cockerels, day-old chicks by the dozen cheeping boxful, pigeons, ferrets, rabbits, cage birds, crabs, lobsters and even squiggling, writhing maggots for anglers. Some birds and animals were extremely valuable and highly insured for despatch by the Fur and Feather Society members to their exhibitions and shows.

It was impossible to handle such a quantity and variety of livestock as we did without a *faux pas* or two. Jack Merrill, the parcels porter, brought a goat on a lead and tied him to a table leg in the office. "There's trouble here," he said. "This fellow's got no come-from or go-to. He's chewed his label."

Loss of a label was a common-enough occurrence, despite instructions to senders and rail staff to make sure strong labels were used and affixed away from the animals' voracious jaws. I wrote telegrams of enquiry for Congleton, Macclesfield and Manchester because the animal had arrived on a train on that line. The telegrams would be transmitted on the telegraph instrument in the booking office of the railway's own telegraph wires.

For statistical purposes a dog on a lead was a dog on a lead. But a dog in a box was a 'parcel'. A box holding a little terrier arrived on a train, one morning, and as soon as Jack Podmore had entered it on a delivery sheet, the door opened and the little dog escaped. Jack chased him up the street and shouted, "Stop that dog, it's a parcel!" He managed to catch the little fellow and secured him in his box, duly converting the dog to a parcel once more. Which shows just how devastating to the English language steam-railway statistics can be.

One Saturday morning several crates of cockerels arrived from Lichfield. They were clucking away and pecking up what food was left. As a country lad I had learned several animal noises, but my *pièce de résistance* was to crow like a cock. In the country I could count on a challenging riposte from the farmyard cock who feared for his feathered harem. I had never done it at the station but, when I saw the crates, I could no longer resist greeting them in their own native tongue. Besides, I had an audience of several clerks and porters. Then out it came, the most realistic crow I had ever crowed. Within seconds one or two of the birds responded, then another and another. A few customers had gathered at the counter, and their faces creased into grins. Just then the station-master, Mr Payne, appeared. I was not sure whether he was angry or amused, but he shouted above the din, "What's going on here? It sounds like a bloody farmyard!"

We handled more pigeons than cockerels. Potters and miners in the Potteries were great pigeon-fanciers and built pigeon lofts at the back of their terrace houses. Baskets of birds were sent by train to a distant station where the station staff would release them to fly home, write on the label the time of release and return the empty basket by the next train to the sending station. Special flat baskets were used with a handle on the top or, for larger baskets, a handle at each end – easy for two people to carry.

Charlie Robison, a swarthy, rugged miner with a gravelly voice, was one of our regular customers. He sent his birds by train two or three times a week. His was a large basket to hold about two dozen birds, and his teenage son helped him to carry it. At home they had built a large pigeon loft, and you could hear the birds cooing away and flapping their wings a mile off. A cheerful and happy chap, Charlie entered pigeon races and won cups which, he told me proudly, he displayed in the front-room window on a special table by the aspidistra where passers-by could admire them. He sent his baskets on railway journeys for many miles from the Potteries and in all directions.

At Hanley station we also received baskets of homing pigeons occasionally, from places as far distant as Congleton, Market Drayton and even Nuneaton, for release. Jack Merrill released pigeons arriving by train, and several times he allowed me to release them. Most exciting. As you opened the basket door, a mad panic of fluttering beat around your face. And off they flew in a flock, rose high, circled the station buildings a few times, then suddenly made off in a specific direction – home. How homing pigeons find their way back for hundreds of miles is one of those delightful mysteries of nature which one might prefer to remain an enigma.

One bright morning in walked Charlie and his son carrying their basket. "My prize birds, them," he said. "I want 'em to go to Lichfield."

"That's a long way, Charlie," I told him. "But we've got a good connection forward from Stoke off our next local. Guard'll see to it."

I made the entry in the books, took his money and stamped the address label, and a porter took it with other merchandise down to the station platform. Charlie and his lad departed.

Within twenty minutes Charlie was back. No smile. No cheery chatter. Face as black as thunder.

"Eh up," he bawled angrily across the parcels counter. "Them birds got back home afore us did. They're prize-winners, but they're not that fast!"

I could surmise what had happened. And it had. Our new junior porter, seeing a basket of pigeons on the platform and no train in, thought they had just arrived on a previous train and released them. All that could be done was to apologize to Charlie Robison and promise him a refund; alternatively he could have free despatch for the next lot, an option he accepted. The young junior porter was upset when he realized his mistake. The stationmaster ticked him off and told him to be more careful in future.

When I first went for training in the booking office, I saw something I had never seen before, a telegraph instrument. It stood on the counter, a small polished wood contraption. In its centre was a single vertical needle which, on pressing the left tapper, would strike a metal pin on the left; and the right tapper would make it strike the right pin. Small metal soundboxes behind each pin created a musical ping at each strike, the right one being higher in pitch than the left. The two tappers could be operated by either two hands or one.

A dot was represented by the higher pitch, and a dash by the lower one. Dots and dashes formed the signals for letters and words based on the Morse code. I was to learn later that the celebrated American Samuel Morse (1791–1872) invented the code in 1837, an alphabetical code in dots and dashes. By the mid-nineteenth century the Morse code and electric telegraphy were coming into wide use on the railways, mainly for train signalling and for internal communications; the telephone then was still locked in an arcane future.

And here was our very own ancient instrument, which I had not yet appreciated was part of a nationwide network. From lineside batteries the electric current was transmitted to the station instruments by those overhead wires seen from a carriage on almost any railway journey.

You can imagine my astonishment when I saw Albert Smith, one of the booking clerks, operating the instrument without looking at it and chatting at the same time. Such a performance, I assumed, could be executed only by a genius. Albert was a friendly, encouraging chap of about thirty. He carried a brown leather Gladstone bag for his sandwiches and personal things, wore a smart dark grey suit, a curly-brimmed bowler hat and highly polished black shoes. In winter, to keep his feet warm, he wore light grey spats, fashionable among clerks who took a pride in their appearance and with 'posh' people such as doctors and solicitors, headmasters and parsons.

I soon discovered why Albert could chat while working the telegraph instrument: he was merely calling Stoke by the repetition of the call-code letters 'ST' – dot dot dot pause dash.

I asked him, "Is it hard to learn?"

"Not really. Nothing to it."

"Could *I* learn it?"

"Sure. *Any* idiot could!"

"And those who aren't idiots?"

"Easier still," he grinned.

When we were not too busy with passengers, he handed me a booklet to study, containing the Morse code and instructions.

"Take it home and bring it back after the weekend."

At home in Bucknall I could not leave it alone and found myself tapping out words in Morse with my feet, fingers, tongue or voice or just in my mind, or scribbling it out fast on scrap paper, until dots and dashes were deeply engraved on my heart. Monday morning did not come fast enough for me to get my itchy fingers on those tappers. Within a few weeks I could send telegram messages, consisting usually of ten to twenty words, at a fair speed; it took longer to learn to read incoming messages.

Forwarded and received messages, all for internal use, we wrote out by hand on small printed forms headed 'Telegram'. They concerned all kinds of railway activity too urgent for writing letters (we had no typewriting machine at the station). Many were enquiries for parcels and luggage, quotations for special fares, rates for van loads of theatrical scenery, twenty cattle by goods train for the goods department across the road, vans for circus animals for a local fair, or fifty milk churns for a dairy show. On Saturday afternoons when we were tied to the office, we found the telegraph instrument useful for sending and receiving cricket or football scores with our friends along the line, all very irregular.

Albert was pleased with my progress. One thing I found at Hanley station was that all the senior clerks, the chief clerk and the stationmaster did all they could to teach me the work and were patient when I erred. I sensed a real family feeling, and there was always plenty of legpull and banter.

Albert was not the only one to polish his shoes. Most people did, including the two junior porters. Staff who wore uniform usually kept their clothes brushed, wore presentable collars and ties and kept themselves clean and tidy. Mr Payne, the station-master, set a good example. The man at the top makes all the difference. You felt that every man working at the station was proud of his calling, and in the community generally a man on the railway was a fellow to be respected, if not envied, especially as he had a job for life! Each man (except the clerks) wore his uniform cap; it had a shiny peak and the shiny letters 'LMS' clipped to the front. But then hats were worn by almost every-body: old and young, rich and poor, boys and girls, men and women, as can be confirmed by outdoor photographs of the period. People who did not wear a hat in the street, even in flaming June, were considered a little odd. Unquestionably, the ubiquitous hat was *de rigueur*.

Once a fortnight Mr Henry Huthwaite came to the booking-office window for his pension. He was so old he made me feel I had still got a million years to live. On a cold morning, if I was not too busy, I would invite him into the office to warm himself by the old iron stove with its stovepipe pushing up through the ceiling. I had already gleaned from him something of his story. As a clerk he had worked in Liverpool for the Lancashire & Yorkshire Railway but had recently moved from Lancashire to live with his married daughter whose children had grown up. His new home was not far from the station. I loved to hear him talk about the old days of the railways and could have listened to him all day. That frosty Friday morning he sat in the chair by the open stove, gazing into the bright red coals.

"Mr Huthwaite, when did you retire?"

"It were 1904, lad. I'd done nigh on forty-seven year on the railroad afore they pensioned me off."

He removed his mittens, opened his thick brown overcoat and took off his old brown trilby hat. A whisper of silvery-grey hair barely covered his head, and the lines on his pale, clean-shaven face were deeply etched. A few hairs sprouted out of his ears and nostrils. He leaned on his gnarled walking-stick, and his rather high-pitched voice carried a strong and unmistakable Lanca-shire accent.

"You were born in Queen Victoria's time, then?"

"Yes, and what a gradely lady she were. My old dad, you know, was an engine driver on the Liverpool and Manchester."

I couldn't help smiling at the thought of his 'old dad'. "When was *he* born, then?"

"He were forty when I were born. That makes it 1804."

"Golly! That was before Napoleon was bashed at Waterloo!"

"Eh?"

"There weren't any railways then, were there?"

"No. You're reet, lad. No railroads. George Stephenson built 'em. My old dad seed him once on Liverpool station. He got on the old man's train going to Leeds."

"Did you ever see him, Mr Huthwaite, this Stephenson?"

"Nay. He died when I were about three years of age, my old dad told me."

"I think it's marvellous!"

"What is, lad?"

"All these stories. Real history. And you were there!"

"You like history, son?"

"Oh, yes. Especially railway history. My favourite subject. You make me feel very close to history, Mr Huthwaite. I can hardly believe you were born while this Stephenson fellow was still alive!"

The old man looked thoughtful as he warmed his hands at the stove. He seemed to be rifling through the faded pages of his distant memories.

"Tell thee what. I got an old railroad book from Victoria's days. By a bloke name o' Smiles. Daft name if you ask me. A friend gave it me years ago. All about Stephenson and his new railroads. Would you like it?"

"Oh, yes, sir. Very much. I really would."

"Reet, then. You do me a note and I'll put it in me pension envelope. Just your name and Mr Smiles. I'll forget otherwise. I can't call to mind what happened yesterday. Though I can remember every detail of when I were young like thee."

I helped him on his way to the street and wished him good-day. But never again was I to see the old gentleman. Within two weeks we had a letter from HQ ending his pension because of his death. It brought a lump to my throat. I had just begun to enjoy the dear old fellow.

You can imagine my surprise and delight when, some months afterwards, an elderly lady – she must have been over sixty – came to the booking-office window. She confirmed my name, then handed me the note I had scribbled for Mr Huthwaite. I guessed the lady was his daughter.

"He talked a lot about you," she told me. "And I found your note among his things only this morning." Then she handed me a large envelope. "It's the book. He wanted you to have it. I hope it brings you much pleasure. That book was very precious to him."

I thanked her warmly and detected a tear as she smiled gently, "Good-day to you, lad."

My recent promotion from junior clerk to senior at the age of eighteen had taken my salary from £55 a year to £80. To qualify, I had attended Derby HQ with other LMS youngsters for an efficiency examination of written papers. Included was a test in Pitman's shorthand at sixty words a minute or more. All young clerks on the LMS were required to learn shorthand. A colleague from Stafford who hated the stuff was given two extra chances, still failed and was reduced to station porter. He later left the railway and got a better job.

In an experimental class at school from twelve to fourteen, I had learnt shorthand, which fascinated me, and I reached forty words a minute. At seventeen, private lessons took my speed to a hundred, and typewriting to sixty.

Such were the employment conditions that I knew that by annual increments of £10 my wages would rise to £200 a year when I was thirty – good money for a man of that age at a period before inflation had been invented and when prices remained much the same for year after year after year. My conditions included eight free tickets a year, plus unlimited railway travel anywhere in Britain at a quarter of the full public fare.

At nineteen I was transferred to Derby HQ as a 'youth showing promise'. There I found many other young fellows who, presumably, also showed promise!

One thing I looked forward to was to see some really large engines and main-line expresses, for Derby was a vast and notable railway centre. There were also extensive works for building locomotives, carriages and wagons, originally set up by the old Midland Railway. I could think of no better better place to work.

# 5

# Fairy Stories from Fare-Dodgers

On my first day at Derby I joined the eight clerks of various ages and grades under a chief clerk, in the motive-power operating office. Head of the department was Colonel Harold Rudgard, who later made a distinguished career in steam motive-power developments.

Most of the work concerned keeping track of locomotives, whether in service or in either local locomotive sheds or the Locomotive Works at Derby for maintenance or repairs. Another function was to keep locomotives moving in the direction of the 'home' depots and for locomotives owned by the other railway companies to get back to their own territories. My job was to keep the files, sort out various forms and pass them to the right clerks for action. Drivers, firemen and other motive-power shed staff who made errors and committed irregularities in the operating rules were disciplined by this department, sometimes by the colonel himself.

After a few weeks' training, I compiled several weekly reports about locomotives that were being specially monitored because their performance was faulty. Details came in, by internal telegram or letter, from various motive-power depots describing exactly what train work had been performed during the previous week and, if any were on the sheds or in Derby Works for attention, just what was needed and an estimate of the time required. A locomotive 'out of traffic' was not earning any revenue, and such periods naturally had to be kept to a minimum.

On my list for special monitoring were the Sir Gilbert Claughton types, and there was a continuous interest in the office week after week to see how individual locomotives in this class were progressing.

Because I could 'touch-type', I typed the reports myself on an Underwood typewriter; this was quicker than writing them out by hand, sending them to the typing bureau along the corridor, then checking the details. It was common practice, however, for the clerks to send their work, written in shorthand, to the bureau. How the typists managed to decipher the shorthand from many people, some of whom must have learnt it in the 1890s, I shall never know. But the system seemed to work. Male clerks needing to visit the typing bureau knocked on the door and were attended by the supervisor; they were certainly not allowed inside. One newcomer innocently strode right through the door. Twenty typewriters suddenly hushed and twenty girls just giggled. But the middle-aged supervisor, battle-axe fashion, glared so furiously that the poor fellow nearly threw a nervous breakdown.

I learnt one morning in the office that a 'Claughton' was on the London train that was due shortly. With difficulty I persuaded Bill Fenton from the staff department to come and see it, for it was now lunchtime. And there it was, a superb piece of machinery, a 4-6-0, a picture of power and elegance heading one of Derby's most important expresses. Several interested people gathered round as the guard's whistle sounded, and those great driving-wheels, 6 feet 9 inches in diameter, began to move.

'Claughton' cylinders were 16 inches by 26 and boiler pressure 175 pounds; tractive effort was well over 23,000 pounds. The design of this class was the brainchild of Charles Bowen-Cooke, who had been the chief mechanical engineer of the L&NW Railway from 1909 until his death in 1920, aged seventy-two; but the engines were known as 'Claughtons' in honour of Sir Gilbert Claughton, chairman of the L&NW Railway 1911–21. No. 2222, built in 1913, was the first of 130 of the class. Claughton, it was said, was a much-loved man in all ranks of the railway service. A snippet I also recall was that his father was at one time Bishop of St Albans, an attractive and historic city in which I was destined one day to settle down for good.

Meanwhile, Bill and I were watching the 'Claughton'-hauled London train fade far in the distance, and Bill was growing impatient.

"Can't understand what you see in these locomotives. Big lumps of dirty old iron, with chimneys stinking of sulphur. And when they blow off steam, they burst your eardrums! They're just useful, I suppose, for pulling your train from A to B."

"Hard to explain, Bill. It's something you feel inside." We filled in the rest of the lunch hour drinking tea in the refreshment rooms on platform one. "Books about the great engineers of the railways are more exciting than a Sexton Blake or an Edgar Wallace."

"What a load of old rubbish! I'd rather see some motor-racing any day!"

Then off we went our separate ways.

Another famous locomotive that came my way at Derby was a Midland compound No. 1000. It had been built in Derby by S. W. Johnson in 1902, a 4-4-0 with three cylinders – two outside at 21 by 26 inches, and the other inside 19 by 26. Boiler pressure was 200 pounds and drivers massive at 7 feet. It was originally numbered 2631 but was changed to 1000 in 1914 when rebuilt by Sir Henry Fowler (1870–1938).

Fowler was chief mechanical engineer of the Midland Railway 1909–22 and of the LMS until 1930, when he was sixty. Just before he retired in 1930, the year I had been transferred from Hanley to Derby, I saw him cross the long footbridge spanning Derby station right into the Locomotive Works, the offices topped by a squat clocktower. Well built and balding, he wore a full moustache and a pair of those clip-on pince-nez spectacles with gold rims which have long fallen out of fashion.

Because Fowler was at Derby and I had actually seen him in the flesh, this encouraged me to find out more about him. A great series of engines he designed was the 4-6-0 'Royal Scot' class 6P (Passenger), of which the first, No. 6100, had been launched in 1927. This class had three cylinders and six-feet nine-inch drivers. Fowler had twenty built at Derby and commissioned the North British Locomotive Company of Glasgow to build fifty others. While working in the motive-power office, I learned that all seventy were about completed, this in little more than three years. A new locomotive type or class usually goes through rigorous prototype trials, but these were not necessary with the 'Royal Scots', a tremendous tribute to the competence of Fowler and his team. Ordinary test performances were staged on the Euston-Carlisle run, the locomotives then doing their best work on the Anglo-Scottish services on the LMS West Coast route between London (Euston) and Glasgow.

They were not the only successes of this highly gifted engineer.

He had introduced locomotive superheating on the old Midland Railway; he designed the heavy 2-8-0 freight engines for the Somerset & Dorset Joint Line, the seventy-two mile route linking Bath and Bournemouth, later worked jointly by the LMS and the SR. He also produced in 1919 the large 'Decapod' 0-10-0 bank engine to assist trains up the heavily graded Lickey Incline – 1 in 37·5 for over 2 miles – near Bromsgrove on the Birmingham and Gloucester line in Worcestershire. It is one of the severest inclines on main lines in Britain. On a visit to the district, I watched the bank engine move behind a heavy freight train with about sixty loaded wagons, then push off with thunderous noise and a spectacular exhibition of steam and smoke thrusting into the sky. As usual the banker went uncoupled and left the train at the top of the gradient. Then it coasted down again, ready for the next customer.

Tom Kitley, the chap I worked for in the office, replaced his telephone after a call one morning, then grinned at me. In his late twenties, Tom had the most amazing knowledge of railway locomotives, those of the other main lines as well as the LMS.

"Frankie, me boy, if you pop out to the platforms in about three minutes, you'll see a marvellous engine on the Glasgow express."

"Which engine?"

"Go and see!"

If Tom said so, I knew it would be good.

Tingling with anticipation, along the corridors I strode, then through the door from the private offices onto the public platforms. A train was just steaming in, and all the noisy activity that greets the arrival of a crack express was in full spate. And there she was, Midland 1000 herself. Smart and shiny in the vivid LMS livery of maroon red, with bright lining. Aged sweet twenty-eight and barely out of the bloom of youth. In those halcyon days, who would have thought she would still be steaming in the 1980s to thrill new generations of railway enthusiasts! What a beautiful locomotive! What a joy to the eye! If my colleague Bill Fenton had been with me, even he might have appreciated her elegant lines, her sizzling steam giving more than a hint of the latent power that would haul the express confidently up those challenging inclines on the undulating route to Glasgow.

Since my transfer to Derby, several others, including Jack Podmore, had arrived from the North Staffordshire. A friendly gang, we travelled together regularly from Stoke. That dark Tuesday morning, any minute now the eight o'clock train to Derby would be steaming in from Crewe. The previous day I had been absent.

Always a leg-puller, Jack said. "I'll bet you this train will be gas-lit."

"Eh? I don't believe you." I had never seen any such in my young life. Carriages would look funny by gas light.

"Bet you a bob," Jack challenged.

A shilling was the cost of my lunch of meat, two veg and sweet in a cosy restaurant on those days I could afford it. So I halved the bet to sixpence. "Make it a tanner and you're on."

I was quite sure he was wrong. Indeed, it would be a shame to take his money. All the carriages I had ever seen had electric lighting. And I recalled reading in a railway magazine that the North Staffordshire Railway had changed over from oil lighting direct to electric about 1900. I kept this from Jack and felt certain of winning. But I noticed that he looked cocky and grinned knowingly at the other fellows. On our daily journeys scoring points off each other was always good fun.

In came the train, and we scrambled aboard. Immediately I looked up at the ceiling, and the lights were blazing down at me – gas! Complete with incandescent mantles. The lads laughed at my discomfiture.

As we sat down, Jack demanded loudly, "Sixpence, if you please!"

"Tell me, Jack, why were you so sure?"

"A bit of low cunning, old chap. They were gas yesterday. And when I chatted with the guard, he said this stock would be on all week. But they're not old Knotty carriages. They're on loan from somewhere."

"I'll get you for this!"

That lunchtime I went to a back-street café in Derby for a bun and a cup of tea for sixpence. To my surprise Jack Podmore was there.

"I'm broke as well," he grinned.

We talked about gas-lit carriages, and Jack said he had read about fearful train fires where two such trains had collided. And after a blazing inferno in 1915 in Britain's worst-ever train disaster, the Government's inspecting officer recommended the abolition of gas lighting on trains. Sixteen years later there were obviously still some around.

After many months in motive-power operations I was transferred to the chief operating manager's staff office. Podmore was already there. So were some seventy other clerks, including a dozen girls, dealing with wages bills. We perched on tall stools, worked at sloping desks and used steel-nibbed dip-pens. Ink was contained in a small earthenware pot sunk into a hole in the desk. Much-needed blotting-paper was in plentiful supply.

The girls operated hand-worked comptometers, each with well over a hundred keys, adding, subtracting, multiplying, dividing and calculating percentages, concerning thousands of stations on the LMS. The machines were new to me, and the shapely lady operators were adroit as well as distracting.

Clerks' ages ranged from about twenty to sixty, retiring age. Most dressed well, wearing clean and tidy linen and polished shoes. They filed and scrubbed their fingernails, greased and parted their hair, a fastidious few wearing a sparkling white handkerchief tucked just inside their jacket sleeves. Some older men wore white, stiffly starched collars about two inches deep and seemed fearful of turning their heads round too vigorously lest they chopped off their ears. Higher grades carried expensive leather cases and furled umbrellas and in winter wore grey spats over their shoes. These colleagues were friendly and helpful and noticeably courteous. Many had relations on the railway, some going back several generations, and when they talked about them, you could see it was with real pride.

All this gave the department a family atmosphere. Yet discipline was firm. Within the pyramid of the structural management, we all knew our proper places and paid the appropriate respects. Punctuality was taken for granted. No one smoked in the office (few ladies smoked), and no man wore his hat. Except Mr Turnbull.

Douglas Turnbull held high office in operating HQ and was a nephew of the late Sir Robert Turnbull who had been big in the L&NW Railway. Mr Turnbull would walk the length of our large office to see the chief and keep his rakish trilby hat on and puff smokily on his curly pipe, quite unperturbed by the many disapproving glances which I guess he secretly enjoyed.

A handful of the hundreds of clerks were young men of style and confidence, their leadership-potential already apparent, men whom you knew instinctively would rise to high positions in the world of working railways, and later I was to see my judgement justified. Already I had identified myself as not being one of these. Having ended my formal education at a village elementary school at the age of fourteen, I was deeply conscious of being ill-equipped for the competition. But it spurred me on to acquire as much knowledge as I could, especially about railways.

As for working methods, the former Midland Railway people in our office, for example, thought their old railway far superior to the London & North Western or the Lancashire & Yorkshire or the Glasgow & South Western, and the North Staffordshire they dismissed peremptorily as a 'little colliery line'. Good-natured legpull and banter were plentiful among such a human miscellany. And their old company loyalties were touching.

Quite a few were snuff-takers. You would see a beautiful tortoiseshell or mother-of-pearl snuff-box removed from a waistcoat pocket, opened, finger and thumb take a tiny pinch and apply it delicately to the nostrils. The more sophisticated tipped a tiny portion on the back of the hand and sniffed it from there. A senior named Edgar Hooley, a tubby fellow with short white hair, a high white collar to match and a suit in brown, perhaps to camouflage the snuff dust on his waistcoat, kept a large pile on his desk. But though he took snuff all day, he never sneezed.

He offered me his box. "Try a sniff. It'll clear your tubes."

Nothing like trying everything once. "How much?"

"Oh, just a tiny pinch."

The pinch must have been too big, for I sneezed so many times that many grinning heads turned to see who the victim was. It was not a habit I took up. I was told after that Mr Hooley was always seeking new dupes.

Regulars, it seemed, did not sneeze. They had their own built-in immunity. Then, quite suddenly, a large accounts book slipped off a rack above Mr Hooley's desk. It fell to the desk with a bang. His heap of snuff flew up in the air in all directions. Within seconds all of us, including me, were sneezing our heads off until the tears rolled down our flushed cheeks. Though subdued, the laughter caught the ears of the head clerk in his glass-fronted office. And to show his displeasure, he walked, tall and straight, quietly from his large desk, all the time looking straight ahead, then passed silently back again. There is a piece of subtle discipline for you!

If fellow snuff-takers came from different railways, it did not discourage the old loyalties and the consequent amiable arguments. Former Midlanders were proud that, of all the talented engineers among the old railway companies, it had been a former Midland man, Sir Henry Fowler, who, in his capacity of chief mechanical engineer, had taken over the design and building of locomotives, carriages and wagons for all the LMS. Midland men gloried in their 4-4-0 three-cylinder compounds with seven-foot drivers that would romp gaily through the Derbyshire hills around Matlock and Buxton with the greatest of ease and match any Nor' Western power on the Anglo-Scottish runs via Crewe. Not only were the compounds still running well, they were serving as a model for new LMS building programmes.

Nor' Western chaps reminded us that their railway had long been known as the 'Premier Line' and boasted of the performance of their engines on the heavy Scottish gradients and over formidable Beattock and Shap. They claimed too that HQ should be in London and not in the 'wilds of Derby', run by bumpkins with straw in their hair. Only a real Cockney could regard Derby as in the wilds of anywhere!

Other contenders for past glories came from the Furness Railway, the Caledonian, the Shropshire Union and the Yorkshire Dales. Running through the banter was an obvious pride and affection for anything to do with railways, and though the North Staffordshire, on which I had been nurtured, was only a comparatively small line, I was glad to work with this marvellously mixed group of men and to enjoy their romantic railway tales of bygone days.

With Derby being the central headquarters of the LMS and the home of such extensive workshops, nearly all the town worked on the railway. Every morning, just before nine, a fleet of Midland Red buses arrived at Derby station from the surrounding suburbs and disgorged its human cargo. Before one o'clock they would be back again to deliver the hordes home for lunch, bring them back at two with stomachs full, then home again after five. And when men in overalls massed through the works gates and out again, it resembled a cup final day at Wembley.

Some clerks, however, who had been transferred to Derby preferred, for family and other reasons, not to move their homes. Two of them, aged around forty with young children, travelled from Crewe to their work at Derby six days a week, fifty miles each way, six hundred miles a week, fifty weeks a year, for at least ten years. They had clocked up about three hundred thousand miles, poor devils! Twelve hours a day away from home to work a seven-hour day, and on Saturdays seven hours with travel to work only three.

Sometimes Jack Podmore and I travelled with them. On the journey they read, gazed out at the passing scenery and dozed. Mr Crane was short and thick-set with a round, pink, clean-shaven face and curly fair hair. When you got into his compartment, he did not bat an eyelid or show the slightest reaction. To me, little over half his age, he was an enigma. We youngsters took great care not to upset him. I often wanted to, just for the hell of it. He and his friend always travelled in a non-smoking compartment, and if anyone lit up in his presence, he would tap them on the knee, point to the label on the window, lean forward and say quietly through gritted teeth, "It's a non-smoker!"

One bitterly cold morning in January, Jack and I boarded the train at Stoke and found ourselves in a non-corridor compartment with Mr Crane and his friend. Mr Crane always sat with his back to the engine, so that, if the window were down, he would not feel the draught. Two strangers followed us aboard, clerk types around thirty. The ginger-headed one held a newly lighted cigarette in his hand. As the guard waved his green flag, and the locomotive made the usual businesslike starting noises, Mr Crane was buried deep in his daily newspaper. Soon cigarette smoke must have penetrated his sensitive nostrils, for he lowered his newspaper and cocked a cold eye on the culprit sitting in the corner seat opposite him. Ah, now for some fun, I thought. Jack and I, pretending to read our books, watched unobtrusively.

Mr Deadpan Crane tapped the fellow on the knee, pointed to the label on the window, leaned forward menacingly and said quietly through gritted teeth, "It's a non-smoker!"

Ginger grinned. "Oh, I shouldn't let that bother you."

Mr Crane's round pink face reddened very slightly. Otherwise there was no sign of disturbance to his nervous system. He lifted the leather strap and sharply let the window down to the bottom, then returned to his newspaper.

A cold and biting whoosh of January air blew smack onto the smoker with such force that he bawled angrily, "Eh, what the hell!" Snatching at the strap, he slammed the window up again.

Mr Crane waited two seconds, then, grabbing the strap, he lowered the window again. You could see now that Mr Ginger Smoker was livid. This time he stood up, cigarette still in mouth, and heaved at the strap, snatching the window up with such violence that the glass broke and smashed onto the floor. In the excitement the cigarette dropped from his mouth, and he accidentally trod on it.

Mr Crane did not flicker an eyelid but sat there pretending to read his paper. Suddenly tension was eased as Mr Smoker and his companion burst out laughing. We all joined in – except Mr Crane. Mr Smoker managed to kick most of the broken glass under the seat. The train slowed and then stopped at Blythe Bridge, six miles from Stoke, and Mr Smoker alighted. Standing right by the open door was the stationmaster, who, I thought, surprised him with a tactical ploy: "Well, now, sir. How did you manage to break it?"

Before he had time to deny it, the fellow said, "It was an accident."

"Right. You'd better let me have your name and address, and your ticket number."

The door was closed and the train moved off. With this great yawning gap, it was bitterly cold, despite the steam heating. I looked across at Mr Crane. He was still reading his newspaper, or pretending to. On his round pink face was just the slightest hint of a smile.

In Derby, railway lectures were given on railway premises by railway experts about this and that. Jack Podmore showed me a notice on the staff board. "Just up your street," he enthused.

"MIC tomorrow evening. Six o'clock. Then home on a later train."

"Who's this MIC fellow?"

"Not a fellow. Mutual Improvement Classes. For locomen."

That clinched it. "I'll be there."

Fortified by a station buffet snack, off we went to the meeting room in a nearby office. About twenty people were there, some in overalls or uniforms. We learnt that they were mainly drivers and firemen, fitters and engine cleaners. In front of a blackboard on an easel, the lecturer was preparing. Of medium height and build, with dark hair and trim moustache, Mr Elkins looked smart in his navy-blue uniform suit, white stiff collar and grey tie. A man to stand no nonsense. Introducing himself, he explained he had been a top-link driver based at Crewe, taking crack expresses down to London and up to Glasgow on the LMS west-coast main line. This made him an instant hero for Jack and me. He was now a locomotive inspector.

While some of the men cut up their thick twist tobacco with a penknife, rolled it lovingly in their palms, loaded their pipes and charged the air with its pungent aroma, and others rolled cigarettes, the lecturer was saying, "We're going to talk about boiler tubes, their furring up, how to avoid it, how they are treated either in the loco sheds or in the workshops for mainten-ance." His chalked drawings on the blackboard were simple and clear and told us much about what goes on under the engine cladding. He explained the LMS plans for more water-softening plants for main loco depots. During question time the lecturer enlivened his answers with anecdotes of his life as an express driver. Telling us he was born in 1885, he gloried in claiming that both his father and his grandfather had been engine drivers.

Jack and I attended several lectures. Never before had I realized what complicated pieces of machinery steam-engines were, and how, even with engines of exactly the same class and specifica-tions, each needed careful coaxing by a skilful driver, for every engine was different in some foible or idiosyncrasy and could be different today from what it was yesterday. Engines, said Inspec-tor Elkins, were like women. Though basically the same, each was a one-off, and woe betide the man who ignored this! "I know," he said. "I've had experience with hundreds of 'em." A driver in front of me raised laughter by asking, "Which, engines or women?"

Reminiscing, the inspector said his grandfather had worked on the London Brighton & South Coast Railway where the chief engineer was William Stroudley, a man who had come from the Highland Railway which stretched to Thurso and to Wick in the northernmost corner of Scotland. A robust individualist, Stroudley treated his enginemen as individuals. Each driver had his own engine with his name in the driving-cab and took a pride in its appearance and performance. Stroudley obviously understood how temperamental engines could be and the need for them to be looked after by one man. He had introduced a sparkling green livery that drivers needed little encouragement to clean and polish.

One evening water troughs were described, that brilliantly conceived contrivance for locomotives to scoop water into their tanks while travelling at high speed. I whispered to Jack, "Ask him why water troughs have to be laid on dead-level track." Jack replied by kicking my ankle.

In our office a minor panic had arisen in the late afternoon. It concerned Birmingham New Street station. Mr Caplon, a senior clerk who handled problems in the West Midlands area, was speaking on the telephone. "Hallo, Birmingham. Yes, I'll find you someone for tomorrow morning certain for the 8 a.m. shift. We'll move a youth from Dudley. He's done similar work before, so don't worry."

The vacancy at New Street was for a station messenger, the regular junior porter having reported sick. His main duties were to deliver internal railway telegrams and other messages concerning minute-to-minute operations to various parts of the station and environs; these included the telegraph office, booking offices, parcels office, station foreman's room and station inspector's room. Then there were the enquiry office, stationmaster's office, passenger shunters' cabin, passenger guards' cabin, porters' mess room and several signalboxes.

Messages were multifarious. Horse-box containing racehorse expected from Newmarket in half an hour to connect with a train to Worcester, for which a shunter would be ready to disconnect the horse-box from one train and have it ready for the next; the station foreman and signalmen at two signalboxes would need to know, and a message would be sent to Worcester as the train left New Street. A train from the south is reported half an hour late leaving Rugby and, as the guard of that train is scheduled to work another starting from Birmingham for Wolverhampton, he will arrive too late and another guard must be allocated to it quickly. A parcels van contains many baskets of racing pigeons for release at Oakengates on the Shrewsbury line and is to be attached to a stopping train from New Street. A signalman reports a door not properly fastened on a train due in a few minutes. Four old empty coaches are coming from Crewe to be stabled in the carriage sidings ready for next week's excursion to Blackpool. Extra loads of newspapers and magazines are expected on the night newspaper train, and two extra parcels porters must be added to the unloading team. Twenty Japanese travelling in the rear of the train from London will need to change quickly to catch their connection to Lichfield. A special train of vanloads of various animals will arrive at seven o'clock the next morning from Bristol for a local circus. Thirty air cadets with two officers will arrive from Cheltenham at seven in the evening and will be met by a motor coach on the station forecourt etc, etc, etc.

The poor lad was at everybody's beck and call. But you can see that a bright young porter working as the station messenger could learn much about the working of the railways. You can see also that the lad was absolutely indispensable to the efficient working of a very busy provincial city station in the heart of the industrial Midlands.

But at New Street there was one man, and one man only, who could be absent for a day or two and everything would function quite normally. The stationmaster.

A broadly similar pattern of daily operations at New Street could be found at most large provincial stations on the railways, and my experience in the HQ staff office, where all kinds of personnel matters were dealt with, proved fascinating.

At Derby other changes came for me. I was to work in the accident office, manned by about a dozen people. Each morning stacks of reports came in from all parts of the LMS system of every kind of accident you can think of. Daily, people jumped on or off moving trains or left open doors swinging, with dire consequences. Level crossings (most of which have long since been closed) accounted for many mishaps, serious and otherwise. Rarely was there a passenger train accident, but that called for a full investigation by the government's inspecting officer of railways. Accident prevention occupied much of management's time. Apart from the human suffering, the railways could not take out general insurance against train accidents, for the simple reason that the premiums would be formidable.

Also an eye-opener was my short period in the passenger travel irregularities office. A dozen or more clerks were engaged handling refunds of fares for lost tickets, tickets not used or whatever cock-and-bull story the more unscrupulous could cook up.

Every kind of ticket fraud you can think of came up in the paperwork on my desk. Here is one I liked: a passenger from Watford to Liverpool, by some ruse, retained his ticket at Liverpool. Weeks later he bought a ticket from Watford to Kings Langley, which he did not use. With a razor blade he then sliced both tickets and glued the top of the costly long-distance ticket to the bottom of the cheap Kings Langley ticket which had the new date stamped on it – a new date on an old ticket. But if I give any more examples, you might one day find it too tempting.

In these headquarters offices yet another move came for me, this time to the signalling section with about twenty people. As in other offices, they came from various pre-grouping railways, complete with ethnic accents and fierce loyalties, plus their own brands of humour.

Meantime, I had left my Potteries home where I was the oldest of four children (my mother had died when I was twelve, but we had a good father) and found lodgings in Derby. By the time I had settled into a new social life, with dances, parties, roller-skating, swimming, weekend walks in the lovely Derbyshire Dales, playing my violin in an amateur orchestra, and railway lectures, strong personalities of pro-Midland and pro-London & North Western had been battling it out behind closed door, and our office was transferred, bag and baggage, to Euston in London. Typical of railway life, there was a rule for it, Rule 1; it began: "All employees must reside at whatever places may be appointed

. . ." In practice, management showed fair consideration, especially for those with families or domestic or financial problems, and assisted in house hunting.

I found homely lodgings in Harrow.

# 6

# A Railway Bumpkin in the Great Metropolis

London at last! Our office was on the sixth floor of a brand-new nine-storey building called Euston House, only a train's length from Euston station. On arrival we made our own fun sorting out our papers and desks and pens and ink and emptying the enormous hampers of files brought from Derby. This was in 1934, just after the new office block had been opened officially to a fanfare by Edward, Prince of Wales, whose passionate affair, and later marriage, with an American divorcee named Mrs Wallis Simpson lost him the crown; gained him the title 'Duke of Windsor' and supplied Press and populace with months of speculative and sensational gossip.

At twenty-three, my salary was £130 a year, plus a special London allowance of £10 a year. The lot would not buy much champagne, but it might run to an occasional visit to a London theatre – up in the 'gods'.

Work in our section consisted of everything to do with signals and signalling. One simple project might be to move a signalpost a few yards to improve its sighting and visibility for drivers; or a really complex one could be a resignalling of a long section of line with new electric colour-light signals and electrically operated signalboxes costing millions and taking years to complete. All the operating rules and regulations were brought up to date, amendments being required by changing equipment and conditions, and recommendations by government inspectors of railways following an accident. Our senior men also compiled the special operating instructions that were needed in most signalboxes to meet local conditions not covered by the standard rules and regulations. Our work covered the whole of the LMS system and was a key responsibility, under the chief operating manager, at the very centre of safe and efficient operation of the railway. Always the prime philosophy was safety.

Apart from large and costly installations, much routine work brought improvements to mechanical and electrical interlocking between signals and points, locking-bars and electric circuiting; these and other techniques and equipment were bringing higher standards of safety, reducing the dangers of that fickle element, human error. Contacts were maintained with our opposite numbers in the other three main-line railways through the Railway Clearing House, to seek as much standardization as possible.

Other projects included closing signalboxes and amalgamating the work of two or more in economy measures. Changes in any of the signals and related equipment were notified to all the operating staff on the line in weekly and fortnightly printed notices. That was one of my tasks, and I had to check and check again to avoid error. You can imagine a driver on an express who had not been informed of a signal being moved from one side of the line to the other, saying to his fireman, "Eh, who's pinched our bloody signal!"

Being the youngest, mine was a minor role: keeping the files, chasing up replies to urgent letters, answering telephones and trying to see what the hell it was all about!

Fortunately the chief clerk was a great guy in all senses. In his forties, Jim Pearson ('Mr' to me) was hugely bulky. He had the largest head I had ever seen. In his absence, to amuse colleagues I would put on his bowler hat; it fell right over to my chin. His round, florid face was clean-shaven, and he wore the quietest of plain grey suits. Yet in the summer, on a scorching hot day, he removed his jacket to display a pair of screaming scarlet braces, and when he sat down and pulled his trousers up at the knee in the usual manner, I saw that his sock suspenders were a screaming match. Freud would have had something to say.

But he took me in hand, trained me and gave me increasing responsibility. One such was to assemble all the letters that came in from various LMS centres certifying that all the signalmen had been examined in their knowledge of the operating rules and regulations and found satisfactory. Signalmen in every signalbox on the system had to be examined locally by an inspector every two years, and from the certificates I received, I drafted one certifying letter which went to the Minister of Transport, confirming in effect that all our signalmen were properly qualified. Similar arrangements were made for other operating staff including passenger guards and goods guards, drivers and firemen, and even stationmasters. Fog-signalmen, who were drawn mainly from permanent-way gangs, were also thoroughly examined; it was their job to stand by signals during fog or falling snow and signal with handlamps or flags to show yellow, red or green to drivers of approaching trains. The wider use of electrically lighted signals replacing the ancient oil models eventually made fogmen redundant.

Mr Pearson had a knack of explaining things simply. He was a Lancashire & Yorkshire Railway man and glad to say so often in his strong Lancashire accent. If he got going, the Midland and Nor' West men did not have a chance, never mind the fellow from the Furness. When the others accused me of being a North Stafford man, I twitted, "It was four years after the amalgamation that I joined the LMS. So I'm the only LMS man here!"

Keeping track of the important files was a problem. They were often taken away by some of our senior men on their travels round the provinces or to meetings in London. Jock Tavish sometimes ragged me about a missing file. A slim and ginger Scot, he had joined the Highland Railway at Aberdeen; promotion took him to the Caledonian Railway at Edinburgh, followed by a post at Glasgow on the Glasgow & South Western Railway.

"Frrank!" he called from his desk. "In a week we start that new signalling scheme on the Leicester line. And I've to write several wee letterrs. But all the details are on the file. For the thirrd time, where is that wee file, laddie?"

"Forr the thirrd time," I imitated, "that file is not on the file, Jock. It's oot!"

"Who's it oot to?"

"I dinna ken. But I'll hae anotherr look."

"You'rre holding up a £2 million scheme. There'll be operating chaos, and passengerrs will go starrk staring mad if it's delayed. Just waiting for yourr bits o' paperr!"

Shortly after, he went out, and I found the file under a pile in his bottom drawer and placed it on his chair. And I put the file cover sheet in his bottom drawer as evidence.

His face lit up on his return. "Laddie, you're a genius. Who lost it?"

"You'll never believe me, Jock. Open your botten drawer."

He did. "Ah, I knew you'd find it if you really tried!"

Jock knew a lot about locomotive and carriage design in Scotland, and we enjoyed some great talks together. But I sought a companion of around my own age and found one in Freddie Cook, recently transferred from Derby, and we renewed our friendship.

Some evenings and weekends we spent visiting London's main stations. The frontage of Euston station was magnificently impressive. Its famous Doric arch, designed by Philip Hardwick, had been built in 1837 for the opening of the London & Birmingham Railway. Its spectacular pillared arch, "higher than any other building in London", said a contemporary writer, formed an eloquent epigraph of the railway's Victorian power and prestige, a symbolic monument, a sort of grand gesture by a comparatively small railway with big ambitions. A luxury hotel was added. At the birth of railway travel, it was really the first long-distance route out of London; George Stephenson had selected the route, and his son, Robert, had built the line. The magnificent Great Hall, the boardroom and surrounding HQ offices were built by Hardwick's son within the station precincts in 1846–9, and in 1852 a huge statue of George Stephenson was erected. Elaborate and elegant, the Great Hall was fashioned like the main hall of a splendid English palace. Its divided, balustraded staircase led to a balcony running high along the walls.

With some trepidation lest some pompous high-up should complain, Freddie and I one morning walked round the Hall, which was public, up the impressive staircase, then round the balcony. (Minions such as us should use the back staircase.) Coming down the stairs, we noticed how worn they were. What mighty feet had trod there! We stood in front of the massive Stephenson in marble, and I said to Freddie, "I wonder what he's thinking?"

"Ah, I know exactly. 'What the hell do you two young squirts know about railroads!'"

It was our lucky day, for I spotted two impressive gentlemen mounting the Great Hall staircase.

"Look, C. R. Byrom," I said. "The chief operating manager himself. Who's that with him?"

"Gosh, Sir Josiah Stamp!"

Stamp had been appointed in 1926, the year of the General Strike which had closed the railways, to the top job on the LMS – chairman and president of the executive. Formerly a director of the ICI, he had a high salary which had provoked lively newspaper controversy. He replied that if his salary were to be divided among all the shareholders, it would be worth only a ham sandwich each: a nice line in polemics in which he was notably adroit.

Freddie and I watched some splendid locomotives leave Euston with their express trains. On the few occasions when we saw titled trains, we followed their progress with the help of timetables.

Still feeling that Euston was 'our station', we later visited other London main-line stations. At Paddington, a station built by Brunel in 1854 and still in full use, among the many locomotives we were most excited by the 'Kings' and 'Castles', 'Halls' and 'Manors'. At Waterloo the 'Schools' class were on the up and up. They had been launched by Maunsell in 1930, and by 1935 forty had been built. Reputedly they were among the best 4-4-0 types ever constructed up to that time. Fitted with three cylinders, 6-feet 7-inch drivers and boiler pressure of 220 pounds, they caught our attention occasionally on a Bournemouth or a Portsmouth train. Other stations we particularly enjoyed for their variety of locomotives and rolling stock were King's Cross, Liverpool Street and Victoria. To our eyes, everything there looked strange and 'foreign'.

But we were not in London just to go train-spotting: there was work to do. One feature that came through to me strongly in the signalling section was the absolute enormity of the ceaseless travail to keep the railway system safe. Other departments were in the safety business too, of course; our section had no direct responsibility, for example, for erecting signals, laying or inspecting the track and the physical safety of structures, nor, indeed, for the mechanical safety of locomotives, carriages and wagons. Naturally, we felt that signalling was the most important of the lot!

One thing that bothered me was that my knowledge of railway operating was mainly theoretical. That is why I applied for permission to visit the main-line signalbox at Harrow which controlled four main lines between Euston and the north. I had to convince Mr Pearson, the chief clerk, that evening visits to the box would further my railway knowledge and my ambition to be a stationmaster one day. I knew also that I would see some fine expresses roaring through the station.

Armed with an official signalbox permit, I walked from my lodgings after tea. There stood the signalbox between the fast and slow lines at the north end of the station. Up the box steps I climbed, entered the door marked 'Private' and showed the signalman my permit. To mind came the words of Rule 72: "Signalboxes must be kept strictly private, and signalmen must not allow any unauthorised person to enter."

"Yes," said the signalman. "The stationmaster had a letter. He said you would be coming. It's quiet a minute, so I'll show you round."

Windows were so numerous that the box resembled a large greenhouse, and the potted bright red geraniums on the floor added to the illusion. Slight fumes rose from the iron stovepot, whose chimney vanished through the ceiling. It was the biggest signalbox I had ever been in, and the entire set-up was over-whelming to the senses. Why wasn't I playing tennis with Reg Blain who shared my lodgings, or taking a nice girl to the pictures?

However, the signalman was quite pleasant and as relaxed as if watching a game of bowls in the park instead of dealing with express and local trains steaming by at frequent intervals on four lines of track. Adjacent were two other tracks, electrified, con-necting with the Underground system and controlled from a small signalbox on Harrow station.

In the main-line box I was sufficiently familiar with the system to know that, of the numerous levers in the signal frame, red levers operated 'stop' signals, yellow ones 'warning' or 'distant' signals, and black ones were for operating the switch-points. In my mind I began to work out which block telegraph instruments referred to which lines and trains.

On a long board above the lever frame was a diagram of all the lines and sidings controlled by the signalbox. Tiny lights came on and off as trains moved along the tracks from signal to signal: a marvellous visual indication of the train positions, day or night. Known as an 'illuminated diagram', it was wired up to the rails, the rails themselves carrying a low voltage of electricity. As wheels ran over rails that were 'track-circuited' (wheels and axles are welded solid and carry the electricity), they operated the tiny lights. It was the kind of installation we dealt with in the signalling office.

Within an hour or so, comments by the signalman ("Call me George"), coupled with my own observations, began to reveal a general pattern. It was dark by the time I departed, after nine o'clock, with aching eyes and tired brain. George called out cheerily, "See you tomorrow night." His was a lonely job.

But I saw George that very night. In my dreams. He was pulling levers furiously, banging away on the telegraph instruments, shouting angrily into telephones, waving his fist fiercely at passing trains which shot by red signals at terrifying speeds in great clouds of steam. In a panic, I was trying vainly to help, but I infuriated George even more by trampling over his precious geraniums. Maybe I should not have stayed in the signalbox so long that first time.

At breakfast next morning Reg, of the accountants department at Euston, eyed me quizzically. "Well, can you work it now?"

"Work what?"

"Harrow signalbox."

"No. And I never will. How one man can hold all that detail in his head and not go stark staring bonkers, I'll never know!"

"Tennis tonight, then?"

"Well, er . . ."

That evening in the box was not quite so awe-inspiring. I found I was able to follow George's moves for one or two trains right through his sections. One startling thought that came to me was that he could be involved in signalling up to a maximum of eight trains at the same moment. On the fast line he could have a train coming from Hatch End in his rear and another on the same line ahead of him going towards Wembley. He could have the same on the up slow line, and similarly two trains on the down fast line and two on the down slow. Or, in an occasional gap, he could even have none at all. During the evening, quite often he would be coping with three or four trains at once, the peak periods being commuter times in the morning and early evening rush hours, when he signalled train after train after train.

Timings of all the movements he made in pulling signal levers and operating the instruments he entered in ink in his train register book. Sometimes a driver, fireman or goods guard would come in to make a telephone call to the Train Control Office at Euston or to report about their trains; each was required to sign his name on the next vacant line in the train register book and to record the time of signing. There was an official rule in the rule book to say so. Such records were essential for any future investigation that might be needed in case of irregularity or mishap. By reference to train register books along the line, the detailed timings of the passage of a particular train can be traced, months or even years afterwards.

George was often on the phone to London Control or the boxes on either side of Harrow. Every job has its jargon. So did this one. Snatches of one-sided conversation reached my ears: "He's at my up home board" (train standing at the up home signal); "I've got him pegged" (signalled); "I'm not giving him the back one because he's got to stop at the home peg until twenty-five's cleared" ('back one' is the distant signal being approached by a passenger train, and 'twenty-five' is a freight train, known by its number in the internal freight train timetable); "The Brains say we've got to give a good run for the down express" ('Brains' meaning the Control Office); "Tell Harry two score cabbage on this down local" (cabbage plants from the station foreman at Harrow for his old uncle, signalman at Headstone Lane).

Three evenings that week I spent in the box, staying on the last evening till ten o'clock to meet Ted on the night shift who would be 'noons' the following week. I found he was a little younger and faster than George but just as cool. On his shift he allowed me to make a few entries in the train register book and occasionally to send bell codes on the telegraph instruments and to pull a signal lever.

In that second week, instead of going over the footbridge above the two electrified lines, I crossed them on foot. It was something I would have to get used to some time, so why not now! That first time, I felt my blood fairly freeze with terror. Stepping gingerly over each rail, live or dead, I knew that the live fellow, hiding innocently his six hundred volts, was ready to shrivel up my being if I did not pay him the proper respect. But after a few weeks I thought nothing of it, except to concentrate like hell. Indeed, nothing concentrates the mind so wonderfully as the danger of imminent death. When, later in my career, I had to walk across electrified lines, I was to be grateful for this initiation at Harrow.

I resumed my visits to the box when George was on the afternoon shift again. Under his close direction he allowed me to signal one or two freight trains and local passenger trains when things were fairly quiet. I operated instruments and pulled levers. His confidence in me was appreciated, for we both tacitly understood that it was really 'against the rules'; yet this is how most people learnt the ropes. If my masters in the signalling office knew, there wouldn't half be a row!

George said, "Fast freight coming up on the slow soon. Have a go." One beat on the appropriate instrument sounded. "That's him."

It was Hatch End box. I acknowledged his 'call attention' by repeating it. Next came the 'Is line clear?' bell code for the freight. After acknowledging it by repetition, I turned the block instrument from 'normal' (or 'blocked') to 'line clear' on the dial. That gave the signalman at Hatch End permission to place his signals for the up slow line to the 'clear' position.

Hovering, George said, "That's fine."

A few minutes later two beats on the bell from Hatch End signified that the train was entering the section, and I turned my instrument to the 'train on line' position. Then I repeated this process to Wembley box.

My next move should have been to place my signals – distant, home and starter – to the 'clear' position. George had been watching me closely but was called to a telephone, and this distracted both of us. At this moment I was feeling tense from the involvement. Returning to my side, George's expert eye swept over block instruments, illuminated diagram and signal levers. Immediately he rushed to the lever frame and slammed two signal levers over smartly. What had I done? Looking out of the windows, I saw that the freight train was in view but had obviously slowed down, and the driver was glaring angrily from his cab. George hurried to the door, stood on the top of the steps and, as the locomotive went by, moved hands together and apart at waist level. But the driver was not to be assuaged; he turned his head away and shook his fist.

George returned, grinning. I realized that I had failed to pull the signals clear for the freight train. "I let you down, George. Sorry!"

"Not to worry. Nothing terrible. That phone interrupted me. I expect that driver was upset because we slowed him down, and his train's already half an hour late, and his dinner's stewing in the oven!"

"What was the hand signal you gave him?"

"Within these four glass walls, and not a word to Euston, it meant 'signal wire broke'."

"Was it?"

"Oh, no. Just trying to kid the driver. Anyway, I got the home and starter boards off, just to keep him moving. It's nowt serious!"

I flopped into George's wooden chair with an old red cushion on it. He signalled an up express and a down local. An uneasy feeling gnawed at me. I did not want to get the fellow into any trouble.

He sensed my mood.

"Don't worry, lad. We all go through it. Don't let it beat you. Up local's due soon. Things are quiet awhile. You take it right through."

"I'm not sure . . ."

He spoke sharply. "Come on, lad. It's now or never!"

Happily, every detail went right, a real confidence boost. I stayed until ten, the end of the shift, and enjoyed every minute. After George had handed over to the night man, I said, "It's a pint on me tonight, George."

"Okay. Pegs are all clear!"

In the 'Railway Arms' across the road, George talked about his early youth as a porter at Euston station before the First World War. Private carriages drawn by fine horses would rumble into the station forecourt, and the porters took turns in carrying the baggage for the gentleman in a tall silk hat and a lady in long flowing skirts. For him, this seemed pure nostalgia. "People weren't in such a hurry," he said. "They had time to talk to you."

In due time I sent a note to thank him. Those few weeks had narrowed the gap between theory and practice, and I had gained a new respect for railway signalmen.

Back now to Euston in the mid-thirties. As in Derby, the subject of accents and dialects came up often. Austin Knowles, a true Lancashire man around thirty, amused us by trying to southernize his speech. He never quite knew whether to say 'barth' or 'bath', 'farst' or 'fast'. But it became really incongruous when he said words such as 'parssenger', 'harppy' for 'happy', 'dard' for 'dad', 'narture' for 'nature', 'marp' for 'map'. All this lot, interwoven with his pure Bolton sounds, was always good for a larf. In keeping with the beautiful English language, not a thread of logic nor a hint of consistency could he discover. But Austin was no fool; he just enjoyed making nonsense of English phonetics.

My remaining time in the signalling section was most instructive. I had made new friends, enjoyed sight-seeing in London, visited theatres, cinemas and exhibitions, gone to dances and parties, played tennis, walked in the Chilterns at the weekends, attended railway lectures and shorthand speed lessons, joined the LMS staff orchestra as a violinist and played at public concerts. Then, at twenty-four, I was a reluctant transferee to Bletchley, a busy railway centre set in the wilds of bucolic Buckinghamshire. It was summer 1935.

Ah well, there's bound to be some fun somewhere.

# 7
# Now for Some Real Railway Work

What a contrast from my job at Euston! Bletchley, a sleepy town of ten thousand souls, boasted quite a large station. Eight platforms. Barely forty-seven miles from Euston. Branch lines ran eastwards to Oxford – thirty-two miles, to Banbury via Buckingham and Brackley – thirty-one miles, and westwards to Cambridge – forty-six miles.

My job was in the district control depot office, along with a senior clerk and a typist. Of the several offices on platform eight, next door was the train control office, the operating nerve centre of the district covering the main line from Tring to south of Rugby, to Northampton and part of the Peterborough route, the line towards Market Harborough, and several branch lines – to Oxford, Cambridge, Aylesbury, Dunstable, Newport Pagnell, Wellingborough, Towcester.

Marshalling yards and engine sheds at Bletchley and North-ampton, and sidings at most of the stations, added variety to the operations in this predominately country territory. Through the district passed every kind of train, including crack expresses of the LMS that thundered through Bletchley station and shook the very ground under you. Clearly Bletchley was the right milieu for me, a microcosm of the entire network.

My work entailed visits several times a week to the marshalling yard and signalboxes. Along the track and in the busy sidings among moving engines and wagons, you really had to concen-trate on what you were doing. One morning I was about to pass a large engine standing on the Bedford branch when I suddenly stopped, just in time to miss a shower of red-hot ash being thrown from the driving-cab by the fireman. I could have been severely burned. I shouted, "Oi!" and the fireman leaned out grinning. "Sorry, mate! OK. I've finished now." He had been clearing his fire out and should have looked out on the track first. An early and frightening lesson in a new environment.

One task of mine was to compile statistics about locomotive productivity in the yards. Engines worked there day and night throughout the year. Some were used for shunting wagons into train formation for onward transit and sorting out those wagons which had arrived from many other places and were bound for another stage on their journeys. Others were train engines, arriving or departing and doing some shunting work. The 'shunting time' and 'standing time' of all these engines were recorded in the train register books, and later analysis of the details I extracted revealed any waste and led to improvements.

As I set off along the platform with record books under my arm, my ears were soon greeted by that indescribably lovely sound of several engines busy in the yard, steam rising high in a summer sky, engines blowing off steam or sounding their whistles. Guards and shunters were shouting their orders to drivers and signalmen and signalling with their whistles or flailing their arms like race-course tic-tac men, in that mysterious sign language so familiar to the work-a-day railwayman.

Every few minutes main-line expresses, fast goods trains and local passenger trains would whiff their magic smell across your nostrils, making noise enough to thrill you to the marrow. Sometimes you would see fine old engines that had first seen the light of fire early in the century, such as the 'Jumbo' 2-4-0 passenger engines, the big 4-4-0s and 2-4-2 tank engines, all still earning an honest living.

Walking in the sidings in sunshine or rain, stepping over rails and keeping a wary eye open for moving vehicles, I thought – ah, this is the life. Right among the action. In the signalboxes (there were five) and shunters' cabins, accepting a hot and friendly cup of tea, taking the good-natured chaff which the chaps in uniform reserved for the clerks, you had to be quick-witted to hold your own, yet perceptive enough to avoid the sarcasm or smart-alec stuff that spoils good friendships. Many of these fellows I came to know quite well, and I heard about their families and personal problems, hopes and disappointments. They were the salt of the earth. For the most part, they did their job well.

In a branch-line signalbox, I occasionally signalled a train, unofficially but under the guidance of the signalman.

Ted Mosey, a signalman in Bletchley No. 5 box, and I were

good friends. Clean-shaven, he had a shock of black curly hair. Of medium height and slight build, he usually worked at high speed in his shirt, uniform trousers and once-white pumps with rubber soles and canvas uppers. With many shunting movements to work, it was a busy box. He tore round the place like a boxer in training, pulling levers, working the telegraph instruments, shouting on the telephone, bawling instructions to shunters and drivers through his open window, swearing, joking and laughing all the time. His flushed face always seemed wet with sweat.

"Have a go at the local," he told me.

Exactly as I had learned at Harrow, I went through all the motions for the incoming passenger train from Cambridge. Soon I heard in the distance the engine whistle, then into view round the bend came the train. To describe the thrill of that moment would be embarrassing if not ridiculous! But, joy of joys, up in front of the six carriages was a Stanier 2-6-4 class 4 tank, with two outside cylinders, the familiar taper boiler and oval buffers. Across the large side tanks were emblazoned in yellow letters on a black background 'LMS', 'my' company.

Stanier had been a hero of mine for a decade. Born in 1878, he was to live until the great age of eighty-two to enjoy his memories after a distinguished career. Though from the Great Western, he joined the LMS in 1932 as the chief mechanical engineer, later to be briefed by Sir Josiah Stamp to 'scrap' and 'build'.

These thoughts were interrupted as, with mischief in his eyes, Ted Mosey called, "Hey, pull off the down branch home."

Going to the signal lever, I placed one foot on the signal frame and pulled hard. It would not shift. In the distance the engine whistled.

Ted bawled, "Hey, pull the bloody thing off. Train'll be here in a jiffy!"

I simply could not shift the thing, not even enough to waggle the red signal arm which I could see through the window a hundred yards away.

"You clerks with your pansy biceps. Outa my way!"

As I watched, I noticed that he stood very close to the lever, then threw the whole weight of his body to pull it right over. It looked so easy.

"Just knack," chuckled Ted. He was enjoying himself.

Two minutes later he shouted, "Hey, pull number seven points lever."

Meanwhile, as he kept busy, I tried number seven. It would not budge. Not even half an inch. I stood close by the lever, then threw my body back, like Ted. Still it would not shift, and I began to sweat. Then I heard Ted laughing his head off. He shouted to a shunter through the box window.

"Come up here, Bill. We've got a Control man here, trying to shift number seven. Somebody oughta tell him. It's been out of order these ten year!"

I leaned on the lever, sweating and panting. Ted slapped me on the shoulder and handed me an enamel mug of tea.

"Drink up, lad."

He meant well. And I had to drink that thick brown over-brewed poison that had stood for hours on the stove, if it killed me. I'll miss him next week. He'll be on nights.

Another interesting task that took me out on the track at Bletchley was that of investigating lengthy train delays. Though the signalman would have reported each delay to the control office, more detail was needed by the district control officer. The work took me into our three large main-line boxes, high above the track, giving a bird's eye view of passing expresses. One box overlooked the engine sheds and locomotive coaling plant, always a hive of activity – fire-lighting, cleaning out ashpans over the pits, running repairs and final preparations for an engine to go out for its scheduled train.

Express delays of over five minutes I had to explain in writing. Causes were as multifarious as changes in the weather. Here are some. A goods train has been allowed to precede a passenger train without adequate headway (if the signalman is not sure, he should consult the control office, but either could misjudge); a faulty signal or failure of block telegraph instruments; lineside telegraph wires blown down; a landslide; a cow on the line; passenger communication cord pulled; carriage door swinging open; faults on locomotives such as poor-quality coal, damaged vacuum brake or steam-heating pipes; signalman answering an insistent call of nature. There are hundreds more.

Friends often complained to me that their train had stopped in the middle of nowhere for no apparent reason. I agreed that we on the railway were not as good as we should be in giving information to passengers. Rest assured that, when things went wrong, it may have seemed that the last person we thought of telling was the passenger, but always our overriding first thought was for the passenger's safety. I would explain: "You're sitting in your train which has stopped in a quiet country place. All you can hear are the birds and the bees and whispers of steam from your engine. But look up at the telegraph wires. They are humming with coded signal messages and buzzing with talk between anxious signalmen and worried train controllers. They all want your train on the move as soon as possible."

At Bletchley, I was surprised at the large number of staff employed and the variety of their skills. In addition to the usual people, there were carriage and wagon examiners ('wheel-tappers'), permanent-way gangs, signals and telegraphs maintenance men, masons, painters and a few more.

Among the operating grades, the rules were often discussed. The rule book, a red pocket-sized volume, consisted of well over two hundred pages and was a subject of controversy. Chatting in the office, goods guard Harry Jones commented, "Them rules is made to protect the management and to lay the blame on the men!"

He winked at Ron Aitken, a senior train controller. Ron replied, "Some people argue that, if you ignore them, you can cause an accident. Others say that, if you work strictly to the letter, you'll stop all the trains."

"Which is right, Ron?" I asked.

"Neither. But somewhere in between. Commonsense is the key. Take rule 61. It says that points not frequently used must be occasionally worked by the signalman to assure himself that they are in order. What do 'occasionally' and 'frequently' mean? It's a matter of commonsense. But the rule is needed, otherwise a points lever rarely used could get stuck for want of use."

Harry asked him, "What about train working?"

"The same. Commonsense. If you're the guard in charge of a passenger train, you have to satisfy yourself that the doors are properly closed and fastened."

"Right."

"So if it's a commuter train and late-comers keep coming, some time you've got to wave your green flag!"

"Sure. But the rules is in terrible language. Hard to understand. If them had been in ordinary words, I reckon I'd been a guard ten year afore I were!"

And so it went on.

In addition to the standard rule book, there were separate books about the working of the block telegraph system and about various methods of working single lines of railway. Add to this lot a few local instructions specific to the place, and you can see there is a lot to absorb.

Normally the rules say who is to do what and when and how. Let us say someone has pulled the communication cord on a passenger train 'miles from anywhere'. It was the duty of the guard to attend to the passenger concerned (he could tell which carriage by a peg on the top edge of a carriage which will have been turned, and which compartment by the chain hanging down); and the fireman had to walk back showing a red flag (red lamp at night) and with explosive detonators to place on the rails for a distance of up to three-quarters of a mile, to warn any following train. If there were two guards on the train, the rule said that the rear guard should go back to 'protect' the train, and the front guard attend the passenger. If, for any reason, there is no guard, the driver has to attend the passenger. In your mind's eye you can see a burly, bewhiskered driver with hands grimy from his honest toils climbing into the compartment of a damsel in distress and reassuring her, "Don't be afraid, ma'am. I've only come to do my duty. It's all in Rule 181!" On occasion, a cord has been pulled because a pregnant lady has started to give birth before the appointed time. The mind boggles . . . (Pulling the cord makes only a partial braking, otherwise the train might stop just short of a station, entering a tunnel or half-way across the Forth Bridge.)

The rules said what but not why. If reasons were included, the book would be ten times as thick. But because they had to be couched in quasi-legal terms, a close and protracted study of them was pure and unadulterated masochism.

My own system of study was first to write the rules in my own words, followed by what I thought to be the reasons and logic behind them. Then they began to make solid sense. Lectures I had attended in Stoke, Derby and London were good basic theory. Now that I was working on the railway proper, the pieces were coming together. A thorough knowledge of all the rules and regulations would be essential for promotion on the operating side.

Anyone hoping to become a stationmaster, however small the station, needed a thorough knowledge of booking and parcels office clerical, administrative and accounting work of a passenger station, plus a similar knowledge for a goods station; the main reason for knowing both was that many of the smaller stations dealt with traffic for both passenger and goods train services. He would need also to know the procedures for banking the takings and paying out wages and how to balance the monthly accounts. He must be able to deal with a Sunday School outing to London or a first-class passenger for Dublin, and a wagon of pigs to King's Lynn or a vanload of gas cookers for Manchester.

On top of this lot there are the rules. He would be required to know all the operating rules and regulations, including those for drivers and fireman, guards and shunters, traffic inspectors, station supervisors, permanent-way men, delivery-van drivers – in fact, everybody concerned with the operating of the railway. Main lines, branch lines, marshalling yards, carriage sidings, private sidings – the lot. He had to know what action each man would take in any accident or emergency, failure of engines, rolling stock, signals or any equipment on the track – in blazing sun or raging storm, in moonlight or the blackest night, whether or not he had a headache, a heartache or a raging hangover! In later years, changes would come in the techniques, though not in the basic principles.

Yet in the 1930s there was always a small queue of men of latent ability ready, in their sweet ignorance, to pitch their wits against these odds – for the glory of being the master of a little station.

Railway managements always encouraged employees, of whatever age or grade, to take courses of study in their spare time in all these subjects and many others. Lectures were free; so was travel when needed. Lecturers were mainly stationmasters, operating inspectors, goods agents and other specialists. Terminal

The author, Frank Ferneyhough, in 1947.

Hanley station, Stoke-on-Trent, closed by Dr Beeching in 1964 after just a hundred years of use. This is where the author started his railway career as a booking clerk in 1927.

This photo of a Great Western parcels delivery van reminds the author of his own days in the parcels office.

Above: Frank Ferneyhough has good reason to remember working with milk churns (see Chapter 3). Below: Many of the older type of signal cabins, like this one, will continue in use on the less busy lines.

The Great Clip-
board Fiasco —
see Chapter 12.

The quiet dig-
nity of Euston's
former Great
Hall.

Frank Ferneyhough when he was appointed to write speech notes for Dr Beeching, the British Railways Board Chairman.

Frank Ferneyhough with Ann Ritchie, chairman of Bassett-Lowke, Northampton, in the Bassett-Lowke marquee at the Rainhill Trials on 26th May 1980 — the trials were staged by British Rail to celebrate 150 years of railways.

Sir Nigel Gresley, the loco designer, photographed at Waterloo station in 1938, *en route* for South Africa.

Sir William Arthur Stanier (1878–1966), chief mechanical engineer of the LM&SR 1932–44, formerly of the Great Western. He became famous for his 'Black Fives' and 'Duchess' class locomotives.

An appropriate honour for Robert Riddles (loco boss in the newly nationalized BR) in 1981.

Harry Turrell MBE, the last stationmaster at Euston, who retired in 1965. The post was re-organized and designated 'station manager', and later 'area manager'.

The grandiose frontage of St Pancras station and its hotel, terminus of the old Midland Railway, contrasts with the simplicity of Culham station, Oxfordshire, built in 1844.

examinations were held under strict academic invigilation, and graded certificates of proficiency issued to successful students. Details went on staff record cards. Top winners received their certificates from top people at Euston HQ and were fêted. In my years at Bletchley I attended lectures at Bletchley, Northampton and Rugby and gained good qualifying certifications in all the subjects.

When I first moved to Bletchley in summer 1935, I was shocked to see a great hulking dapple-grey shire horse with massive mane, long tail and floppy fetlocks ambling happily along the main line in the station. Peggy Carrington, the blonde teenage shorthand-typist, was amused at my demeanour.

"Never seen a shunt horse before?" she smiled.

"Not in the middle of an express route, no!"

From where we stood on platform eight, I then spotted the shunt-horse driver just behind. Harry Barnes and Bob, I learnt, had just shunted a loaded horse-box from the rear of a down express across to the Oxford train for the journey to Winslow. That was typical of their work.

In Buckinghamshire hunting, gymkhanas, jumping and other equine pursuits were highly popular among the local gentry, and the comings and goings of horse-boxes, loaded or empty, to and from all parts of Britain, gave Harry and his shire plenty of work around the station. They handled other vehicles, too, including varied merchandise and occasionally circus animals. Notice of expected arrivals was received by telephone or internal telegram, so that everybody and everything was in the right place at the required time.

On those occasions when a van off the rear of an express had to be left by itself on the running line until the shunt horse could move it, the station inspector, who supervised such movements, pressed a plunger on the platform marked 'VOL', which gave, in the nearby signalbox, the indication 'Vehicle on line' by the block telegraph instruments as a reminder to the signalman of the vehicle's presence.

Horses for station shunting (there were lots at Newmarket) were specially trained and did no other work. They became impervious to the roar of a passing express, the piercing screech of a locomotive whistle and the deafening buzz of safety valves 'blowing off steam'. They ignored the clanging of buffers on a loose-coupled goods train and obeyed the instructions of only one man – the handler.

When walking from my lodgings to work, I often saw Bob, duly harnessed and reined, clip-clop from his stable across the station approach road, nose open the wicket gate that led to the track, then wait for his master's call. I have walked many miles over railway track of all kinds with numerous hazards, but it amazed me how Bob stepped over or round the rails, sleepers, lengths of point rodding and signal wires without catching his great feet on them. Just horse-sense, I suppose.

Some Sundays I spent in the marshalling yard or riding on a branch line in my own time, to get the feel of the railway. This time it was a ride in the brakevan with a train of empty wagons bound from Bletchley sidings to Millbrook, ten miles along the Bedford branch. They were wanted in a brick company's sidings ready for loading bricks for London the next day. Billie Beere, the elderly goods guard, was in charge. A gentle and agreeable soul, he was of medium build, with a round, pale face with smiling blue eyes.

Getting ready in Bletchley yard, wagons needed coupling together. Billie handed me a coupling pole with its specially shaped metal hook at the sharp end.

"Have a go," he invited.

I did. But I could not even lift the iron links.

Billie laughed. "Watch this."

He hooked his pole in a link, swung it back, then flung it deftly onto the hook of the adjacent wagon. It looked so easy. Eventually, with a struggle, I managed it. Skill counted far more than brute strength. Cast in heavy iron, the couplings made the most beautiful clanging noises, music in my ears, sounds that had been with me from childhood.

Soon we were chugging away, through the crisp autumn air. Up in front was a rather old 'Jumbo'-type 2-4-0 passenger engine, with the driving-cab open at the rear to the sky. Just imagine running tender-first on a wet night with the rain driving right in at you over the tender! – a journey to avoid. Our thirty wagons, all loose-coupled, had the usual hand brakes but not automatic vacuum brakes. Wagons clanged together according to the pull of the engine or the effect of the gradient, rising or falling. Much skill by the driver – no snatching – and the guard – with his brakes van – was needed for a smooth journey. When travelling in the guard's van, you had to hold on to the handrails, otherwise you could easily be thrown to the floor. Billie showed me how to work the wheel-operated handbrake.

Standing on the small balcony at the rear of the brakevan and watching the scenery move gently away was delightful. We passed those charming country stations Fenny Stratford and Woburn Sands, fashioned, like many wayside stations, in the style of pleasant country villas, including a house for the station-master and his family, and now gay with dahlias and Michaelmas daisies.

When we climbed down to the track from the brakevan in Millbrook sidings, Billie said, "Ride on the engine while we do the shunting. Charlie Marks is the driver. Nice feller. He won't mind."

On the footplate Charlie said, "Eh, Mister. Have a go with the shovel."

The fireman, in his mid-twenties same as me, grinned and handed me the implement. He opened the firebox doors, and I felt the enormous heat. "You have to spread it out all around that there fire. Else it clinkers up and makes a mess."

I could not throw the coal very far, and the fireman showed me again. With a vigorous swing of the body and a fling of the arms, his shovel threw the black stuff to the furthest corner of the firebox, where it turned to blazing red before it was gobbled up in the ravenous furnace.

Charlie, the driver, told us, "In the general strike of twenty-six, we had them college lads from Cambridge, you see. One feller, he bring a pair of kitchen fire tongues, you see. And he said, 'Drivah,' he said, 'do you want one lump or two?'"

During a brief break in the sidings the fireman polished his shovel with a rag until it shone like silver. Then he broke four eggs onto it and added rashers of bacon, held it in the firebox for a short time and – hey presto! – their meal was ready. Driver and fireman sat in the corner seats to enjoy a hot meal off their enamel plates. Next came the tea. On his shovel the fireman balanced two blue enamel cans, somewhat chipped, the tops forming the cups, and gave them the heat treatment, and in seconds they were nice and hot for drinking.

We returned to Bletchley E & B (engine and brakevan). Billie and I ate our lunch in the brakevan. I had ham sandwiches. He produced from his leather guard's shoulder-bag half a loaf, sliced a couple of thick rounds with crumbs rolling down his trousers to the floor, cut a hunk of cheese and a large slice of raw onion, then proceeded to tuck into the lot with relish. He heated his tea on the iron stovepot which had a chimney pipe going out through the roof; a bucket of coal stood in one corner.

Now that a dazzling saffron sunset shot with orange fire had faded behind the clouds this early autumn evening, it was nice and cosy in our van, and Billie talked about his life on the line. Riding in a rattling, oscillating goods van and sitting on a hard wooden seat, with smoke blowing in from the chugging 'Jumbo', recalls the comfort of an upholstered railway carriage. But for me it was part adventure, part learning: coupling up wagons, stoking an engine, watching for signals and seeing at close quarters a regular and routine operation out on the track – this was really railway work. Once you have ridden in a loose-coupled train of goods wagons, you appreciate the skills and teamwork of the three trainmen, in maintaining good speeds and avoiding wagons, loaded or empty, bumping together with such force as to damage the goods carried or make a wagon jump the rails.

From the control depot office one morning, in the distance we could hear a continuous engine whistle. Most unusual. It could spell trouble. As the sound came closer, several of us hurried onto the platform. We could see an express approaching from London, about half a mile down the line, and knew it was not scheduled to stop here. Obviously it was slowing down, so two of us nipped across the bridge to the platform in which it might stop. It did. Walter Nursar, the brisk station inspector, hurried to the driver. At such close quarters the whistle was deafening. A 'Royal Scot' class, it was a 4-6-0 6P, a really massive engine. Both the driver and fireman jumped onto the platform, screwing up their faces and covering their ears. The driver shouted to Mr Nursar, "Whistle's jammed. It's terrible! We'll want a fitter."

A fitter with toolbox was already approaching; he must have heard the noise from the nearby engine sheds. A few curious passengers had gathered on the platform. Many heads bobbed out of the carriage windows. Onto the footplate climbed the fitter, and in a moment the screaming whistle was suddenly silent and would remain so awhile. He had hit it hard with a hammer.

Back on the platform the fitter said, "I've buggered your whistle, driver. You'll want a replacement loco."

That put all of us on our toes. It must have been twenty minutes at least before another express engine was brought across from the sheds and the 'Royal Scot' shunted into a siding. Now recovered from the strain, the driver and fireman climbed aboard the new engine; they gave a 'pop' on the whistle; the guard waved his green flag; the train steamed away, and onlookers dispersed. Behind the scenes, train controllers would be in touch with the adjacent control at Rugby, with the divisional control at Crewe and with nearby signalboxes about the change of engines and consequent alterations in related train working.

To some people it might appear strange that a faulty whistle would halt a mighty 'Royal Scot' engine and take it out of service. But the whistle is vital in train working. Out of the 240 rules in the standard rule book dated 1933, fourteen concerned many locomotive whistle codes. A driver must sound his whistle when men are working on the line and when the train is approaching a level crossing, entering or leaving a station or a tunnel, and in a long tunnel frequently.

If an engine is assisting a freight train from the rear, the guard gives the signal to start to the rear driver; the rear driver then gives two crows – in the rhythm of cock-a-doodle-doo – which the front driver acknowledges by repeating it. Bystanders have been known to raise their eyebrows, as though the drivers were indulging in some Gilbertian whimsicality; no challenging riposte comes from farmyard cocks, though one or two might flap their wings in jealousy.

On a goods train of unbraked wagons, if the driver needed help from the guard's van brake, he would give three whistles. Incidentally, if the guard wanted the train to stop, he would put his brake on and off to attract the driver, show a red signal (flag or lamp) and, after it had stopped, walk the track to the engine. One goods guard said to me, "Some day I'll talk to my driver on a telephone."

What about a cow on the line? Rule 155 (b) reads: "The driver must, if he see cattle on the line . . . sound his whistle and exhibit a danger signal to any train he may meet . . ."

Drivers being what they are, a few 'unofficial' whistles sometimes struck the ear. A popular greeting was in the rhythm of, 'On Ilka Moor baht 'at'. It was not easy for one speeding driver to shout to his mate, "How are you, Tom?"

Bletchley driver Arthur Pooley had his own personal call when on the morning shift. As his goods train passed his home just out of town, he whistled one short and one long, which, in Morse code, is 'A'. And his young son, Andrew, was always thrilled.

Yes, that 'Royal Scot' needed its whistle.

# 8
# Learning to be a Stationmaster

Each time I cadged a ride on the footplate, in Bletchley sidings or on a branch line, I was bursting my boiler to ask, "Can I have a drive?" But the words failed me. Engine drivers can be formidable fellows. When necessary, they can cut you down to size by doing nothing – just ignoring your very existence in a deep, dark grey, stony silence. For me they were a very special breed. Not like ordinary chaps. So you could not quite put the question as you would to a friend, like, "Can I have a ride on your bike, Mike?" There was this tremendous invisible barrier. First, it was against the rules for a chap like me to drive an engine. We all knew that. It was almost like asking a policeman, "D'you mind if I commit a burglary, just a small one?"

This particular Sunday morning, I might be lucky. Inspector Johnson, my colleague and mentor, had fixed it. I was to go with him on the footplate. Popular Edgar Webb was the driver. Only the other week I had answered his phone call, and he asked a favour: would I tell his wife – they lived near my lodgings – that he had been delayed at Rugby and would be unable to take her shopping.

Starting very early, we were on a short maintenance train, off along the Oxford branch to repair some drainage culverts near Bicester. We stopped at Launton wayside station level crossing for the fireman to open the gates, and the moment seemed propitious.

"Edgar, d'you think I could start her?"

He removed his pipe, and his lined face crinkled into a grin. "Think it's easy, eh?"

"You make it look easy. I'm sure it's harder than it looks."

He glanced at his fireman, who nodded, then at Inspector Johnson, who stroked his chin. "Very irregular, y'know. Very irregular. Still, Edgar, we might as well watch him make a fool of himself!"

Edgar released the vacuum brake, saying, "She's all yours, m'lad."

I knew exactly what to do – in theory – and had watched drivers many times. My pulse quickened and I breathed deeply. First I pulled the cord to sound the whistle, then put my hand on the regulator handle. Immediately I snatched it off again. It was rather warm. The others just laughed.

Edgar growled, "Always use the cloth!"

In my tense excitement, which was hard to conceal, I had completely overlooked this simple footplate precaution.

"Now push the regulator an inch or so. And as soon as we start to move, ease it back just a fraction. Then push it forward again. Gently."

Stupid butterflies began to flutter and I breathed deeply as I placed my hand, with cloth, onto the regulator.

"Now push!" Edgar urged.

I pushed. Too hard. Six coupled driving-wheels spun round and round without moving our train an inch, and our ancient engine juddered in angry and agonized protest as though about to disintegrate, thick black smoke shooting out of the chimney. Quick as a flash, Edgar knocked the regulator back to 'closed', and the wheels came to rest. How they all laughed at my expense! I tried hard to join in. I knew exactly what I had done – opened the regulator too much and too soon.

"Try again," said Edgar. "Gentle and firm this time."

Using two hands, I did as bid. The driving-wheels turned slowly, and steadily we began to move along. I opened up a fraction more and could feel the power of the old engine surging forward, sense the thrust of the two pistons and the rhythmic beat of virile steam. The other three clapped their hands in mock applause, and I acknowledged with a mocking bow. We picked up speed, and I experienced an unforgettable exhilaration which I knew could never be repeated, a memorable 'first'.

Warning or teasing, I was not sure which, Edgar called, "Remember. You got to look for them signals as well!"

In the excitement I had quite forgotten about signals but was certain Edgar was watching. A few minutes more and our speed must have been twenty-five to thirty miles an hour. I saw some rabbits scuttle away and wanted to shout, "Eh, bunny-rabbits, look, I'm driving an engine!" A few starlings darted overhead and made for a nearby copse. I resisted the urge to call, "So you can fly. But you can't drive an engine!" Steam from the chimney floated like cotton-wool clouds above the trees on the lineside in the magic velvet of a warm and sunny morning. Green fields drifted sleepily by, the pattern broken briefly by an occasional farmstead. No harm in telling the animals and birds about my driving, but I would keep it quiet in the office.

Edgar, relaxing with his pipe, reminded me, "No need to hold the regulator all the time. It won't drop off!"

This I knew and took the hint. Yet it did not seem quite decent just to stand there on the footplate and let the thing run along all by itself.

Inspector Johnson ribbed me. "He'll make a good driver, Edgar. Look at him, driving with no hands!"

We must have covered five or six miles when the driver took over, though all he did, it seemed, was to continue sitting in his seat by the window, glance forward from time to time and keep his pipe alight.

That memorable morning I had been privileged to achieve a special railway ambition.

Some time later Inspector Johnson met his promise by giving me practical but unofficial tuition in working trains over one line while the other line was temporarily blocked – called 'single-line working'. It would be a pre-planned operation. In emergency an operating supervisor – stationmaster or inspector – has to turn out night or day and organize the arrangements on the spot. So I needed to know for the future how it worked.

That bright and sparkling Sunday morning we set off from Bletchley engine sheds about five o'clock while sensible people were enjoying their lie-in. Our short goods train rattled along the Oxford branch. And here was I, with the inspector, again on the footplate, the class 4 0-6-0 goods engine trundling along without a care in the world. It was a dream world really, and I held no authorized engine travel permit. All somewhat irregular. Such was railway life in a rural area, where every Jim and Tom knew every Dick and Harry.

Driver Albert Gadsby and his fireman, Mick, were good sports. Being somewhat crowded on a class 4 footplate meant that you had to have your cloth ready in case you touched something hot. I noticed that a blue enamel tea-can stood precariously on the engine's warm drip-plate directly above the firebox doors.

Albert sported a huge black handlebar moustache. He wore blue overalls and a greasy old cloth cap. Sitting in his corner seat, he was filling his big-bowled curly pipe casually, relaxed, as though in his favourite fireside chair at home. The footplate flaps between the tender and the engine oscillated and rattled, and whiffs from Albert's pipe infiltrated the hot steam-and-oil odours of the engine to lazy chuffs and throbs.

In the peaceful quiet of that Sunday morning, our short goods train disturbed the wild life. Rabbits, little white tails a-bobbing, scurried hoppity-hoppity, frightened, along the grassy banks by the track and vanished like lightning into the safety of their burrows. Pheasants' wings flapped noisily as they took to the air and flew away from the noise of danger. On the lineside, dew-drops cupped in foxgloves and coltsfoot sparkled like diamonds in the brilliant sunshine.

I thought of those countless sunny Sunday mornings I had squandered in bed. What a waste of young life when these hours of early morning beauty were just waiting to be enjoyed. Yet I was not on this engine primarily for bucolic or pastoral pleasures but to absorb the railway ambience. Workmen, their tools and equipment were being conveyed in maintenance wagons to repair a bridge. On the four-mile section between Marsh Gibbon and Bicester our train would work while occupying the 'down' line; the 'up' line would remain open for the few other trains, in both directions, that were expected.

To simplify an elaborate procedure, the principle was that trains could be allowed on the 'single-line section', in either direction, only if accompanied right through by a 'pilotman' (Inspector Johnson was scheduled for this) or sent through the section by the pilotman personally. This was to prevent two trains being in that single-line section at the same time with the danger of collision. When done correctly, risk was negligible. Set out in the standard rule book, the system enabled trains to keep moving should one of the two running lines be obstructed for any reason. Causes could be anything from an earth fall to a derailment. In charge of such an operation, the pilotman would be a stationmaster, inspector or other qualified operating supervisor. In an operation as today, it is easy. Details are planned in advance. But if it is an emergency in the small hours in a blinding snowstorm or drenching rain, a pilotman is shocked from his cosy bed by a loud thumping on his front door, or screaming rings on his telephone. Blearily he gathers wits and clothes and walks or cycles to the railway, ready to take charge.

To prepare me for the future was why Inspector Johnson kindly offered to train me that day to be a pilotman under his direct supervision. On my sleeve I wore the red armlet on which were the bold letters in white, 'PILOTMAN'. The rule book even specified that it should be worn strapped on the arm above the left elbow. Not for a moment did he leave my side. We both knew that, if anything went wrong, only he could take the rap. I hid my slight tension from drivers and firemen, goods guards and signalmen, I hoped, behind a veneer of studied casualness and light banter. Here, out on the line, I could learn the ropes at leisure to qualify for stationmaster; at twenty-six, time was rolling by.

Throughout the day, as we climbed up and down locomotives, up and down signalbox steps, gave hand signals, shouted orders and wrote entries of every move in the train register books, we must have looked an odd pair. Tall and slim, clean-shaven and fresh of complexion, the inspector looked smart in his navy-blue uniform and, of course, a bowler hat, a beautiful curly bowler: that unofficial symbol of supreme railway authority down the line. I, too, had taken to a bowler and wore an old dark suit. As I was several inches shorter than the inspector, we must have looked a comic pair and provoked amusing comments. Realizing that, if I were too officious, the comic effect would have been heightened, I cracked a few jokes and made the chaps laugh. In which I seemed to possess a modest proclivity.

When my friend (later my best man) Tom Beech, who shared my lodgings, had first seen me sporting my new bowler hat, I could see that his face was cracking in the struggle to be serious.

"It, er . . . suits you fine," he managed at last.

"Could I pass for a railway official?"

"Look, Frank. We're friends. Let's be candid. You look just like a bloody broken-down bookie!"

"We're friends, you said? *Were* friends!"

We laughed. And he warned, "Don't ever get like your play-mate, Inspector Johnson."

"He's a great guy. Why not?"

"He goes to bed in his bowler. Only takes it off to comb his hair."

"How d'you know?"

"Instinct."

Come to think of it, I had never seen Inspector Johnson minus bowler. Whether he was well thatched or as bald as a coot I knew not. Even on a scorching hot day in summer in his tiny office on Bletchley station, there he sat, writing, with his jacket and tie off and his shirt sleeves rolled up above the elbows, the inevitable bowler hat rested firmly and curly in its official position. But he was a good fellow and able in his job. Part of his work was to train new signalmen and examine their knowledge of the rules, to inspect level crossings, of which some twenty were on his terri-tory, and to investigate minor mishaps. He was known as a 'good railwayman' and was proud of it and liked by those above and below him.

And here he was, on that Sunday morning on the Oxford line, helping me to learn the work, knowing that if any 'high-up' heard he was allowing an unqualified man to act as pilotman, even under close supervision, he would be rebuked. And he knew I appreciated it.

In between the train working we watched the craftsmen get on with their bridge repairs. At noon we sat on a pile of old sleepers smelling slightly of creosote, to eat sandwiches, drink hot coffee from a flask and talk railways. Sunny skies had turned to rain when we boarded an engine to take the maintenance train and men home mid-afternoon. Inspector Johnson cheered me no and when he said, "You did fine. We've another job at Verney Junction. Hope you'll come with me."

During that summer we went out together on several Sunday jobs, not always with single-line working – on the Cambridge line, the Aylesbury branch from main-line Cheddington, and the Dunstable and Luton branch from Leighton Buzzard. Before each occasion, to protect Inspector Johnson, I mentioned it casually to our district officer, who usually nodded agreement. After he retired, I did the same with his successor, a much younger, ambitious man, in his private office on platform eight. He blew his top.

"You're telling me, Ferneyhough, you've been pilotman in single-line working, with passenger trains? And on the footplate without even a locomotive permit?"

"Well, yes, sir. But Inspector Johnson never left my side."

He sat at his desk, an expression of disbelief, genuine or dramatized, on his long, pink face.

"If anything had gone wrong, Inspector Johnson would have been in trouble. And if headquarters had got to know, they'd give me a roasting."

"Sorry, sir. I don't want to embarrass Mr Johnson. He's been good to me. Teaching me."

Mollified a little, he said, "Even so, I can't allow it. If you become a stationmaster, OK, that's fine. But you know as well as I that, if anything goes wrong with a passenger train, a government inspecting officer could be on our tails."

"I understand, sir. It won't happen again. Mr Johnson's been first rate, and I appreciate it very much."

"Quite. And I don't want to discourage you. But we all have to do the proper thing when we're dealing with trains. Now you can go."

Leaving his office somewhat shaken, I was not yet ready to face colleagues, so I adjourned to the refreshment rooms on platform three and took the *Daily Express* from my pocket. As I drank tea, smoked a cigarette and gazed unseeing at the news pages, one clear thought stood out: if you're in charge of railway operations anywhere, my boy, the only thing that really matters is – safety. Those trusting passengers put their faith in the train that is carrying them, in the track and signals and in the men behind the scenes, men with a sense of responsibility and a pride in their calling.

Those were the days of fabulous cinema shows featuring Greta Garbo and Myrna Loy, Spencer Tracey and Clark Gable, larger-than-life stars of make-believe, people who attracted ever-growing audiences during the film industry's booming years. And one Sunday the railway film-makers descended on Bletchley. In the twenties and thirties railway companies were making black-and-white films with a dubbed sound track; some were for public audiences to promote the passenger business, and a few were for staff training. LMS men Bill Brudenell and Charles Potter did much work on these films, an activity initiated by the London & North Western Railway as early as 1910; that was four years before Charlie Chaplin made his first film, seven years before Buster Keaton's and ahead of the fame of Douglas Fairbanks and Mary Pickford, 'the world's sweethearts'.

But nothing so glamorous for Bletchley! The railway film team were to use railway staff to make a short instructional film featuring various obstructions on the line. The Oxford branch was used. I walked along to see the fun. So did several colleagues. Few trains ran on the branch on Sundays. For the filming a special train of two coaches moved backwards and forwards to instructions by hand, whistle and shout. Cameras whirred.

Mr Gordon Rogers, our presentable assistant district officer in his forties, 'acted' as a passenger. His task was simple. On noticing that his train had stopped, he would lower the window of his first-class compartment, thrust his head out and glare fiercely up and down the line.

As filming progressed, the sun sometimes vanished behind a singularly unco-operative cloud; the cameraman was not ready; the engine driver misunderstood the director's instructions; the train was moving too fast or too slow, or Mr Rogers forgot to lower his window at the precise moment. All this occupied hours, with retake after retake after retake. What a way to spend one's only day off! They were still at it when I left.

Many months later, local staff were invited to a church hall in Bletchley to see a staff training film. We were all agog to see our little bit on the silver screen. So was Mr Rogers, seated at the back. Suddenly it was there. A train in the country. It slowed down, then stopped. The window of a first-class compartment is lowered and an angry face glares up and down the line. We found it hilarious to see our boss screened as a film star and loyally cheered him to the rafters. Mr Rogers, who sat by the vicar, stood up, twirled his moustachios, gave a dastardly leer, aping a wicked villain in Victorian melodrama, then bowed to the audience like a seasoned Thespian.

On the screen, right after the angry man scene, came another shot – a cow on the line. The audience rocked with laughter. Merriment reached a new crescendo as we watched the antics of our old friend, goods guard Bill Newton, dressed as a farmer, cloth cap askew, straw in hair, brandishing a pitchfork like a shunting pole and no doubt cursing to himself about this stupid old cow, who fancied herself as a film star. In the audience, Bill sat behind me. He said it took all afternoon for the film people to shoot the cow scene they wanted. Yet the entire scene of angry passenger and cow-on-the-line flashed on and off that screen in less than two minutes. Two days' work just for that! Goodness me, no wonder the big-time film makers spend a million pounds to produce a full feature film. Bill Newton was really put out. "D'you know," he grumbled to me, "they film folk paid that fat old farmer five quid fee for his old cow. Yet they gen me only thirty bob!"

Walking in the marshalling sidings at Bletchley one dull July morning in 1937, I was suddenly stopped in the track. An unbelievable sight, the most beautiful old locomotive I had ever seen. On the top arc of the wheelguard, her name stood out clearly – 'Cornwall'. Thank heavens she was standing still. Equally unbelievable, no one was noticing the grand old lady. My Kodak box 'Brownie' was in my office drawer, and as I turned to run back to get it, I nearly knocked over the marshalling yard inspector.

"Steve, that old loco," I said breathlessly. "How long will she be there?"

He removed his peaked cap and scratched his head. "Oh, maybe an hour. Maybe two."

"Thanks. I want to take a photo. Where's she going?"

"Willesden. There's a show or something." He grinned. "It's only junk!"

"Junk? You're joking! That's sacrilege – like saying the Mona Lisa's only paint!"

When I had collected my camera, two colleagues joined me.

But the engine was missing. My mouth must have dropped, and one colleague accused, "Eh, Ferney, is this one of your corny gags?"

The other, a controller, assured us, "It's around somewhere. We had it reported from Wolverton."

We found it shunted further up the sidings behind a raft of high box vans. Relief all round. I managed to take three snaps.

In the control office I learnt that 'Cornwall' No. 3020 was on her way, 'dead' (fire out), to Euston. She was to join other vintage rolling stock to celebrate the hundredth anniversary of the London & Birmingham Railway, which had been opened between Euston and Boxmoor in Hertfordshire on 29th July 1837. From that moment I was determined to visit that exhibition.

Meanwhile, I discovered that 'Cornwall' had been built in the Nor' West workshops at Crewe in 1847 by Francis Trevithick. A 2-2-2 with a boiler pressure of 140 pounds, the two outside cylinders were horizontal and measured 17½ inches by 24 inches. You could not possibly look at this locomotive, or even its photograph, without being struck by its amazingly large driving-wheels which, at 8 feet 6 inches diameter, are higher than your ceiling at home. Until the turn of the century she had done well hauling expresses on the Nor' West main lines and in 1902 was temporarily withdrawn from service. In 1907 she was 'elevated to the peerage', as you might say, pulling a special saloon for the use of the Company's directors. Retiring twenty years later (the year I joined the LMS), she was tucked away in a corner of the paint shop at Crewe Works, her original home.

From a grand old lady to royalty, a king. In Bletchley I saw a real king driving a locomotive. It was also the very first time I saw that magnificent streamlined train and streamlined locomotive, in a startling blue and lined in a striking white. In the driving-cab at the regulator was King Boris of Bulgaria himself.

In the control office we had seen confidential details of the special train workings days earlier and had anticipated the event in great excitement. His Majesty, coupled with that magic name of our new train 'Coronation Scot', had scattered the monotony of our daily routine. All the arrangements with headquarters had been made in cloak-and-dagger secrecy. Innocent, peace-loving citizens of Britain, brainwashed in melodramatic fiction, harboured all sorts of fancy ideas about those mysterious countries in Central Europe, all connected by the 'Orient Express', where kings were bumped off like bootleggers in wicked Chicago; however, precautions for Boris matched those for a journey by one of our own Royal Family.

Several of us left our warm offices and stood expectantly on platform eight in bleak November and watched the train arrive – the 'Coronation Scot' itself. King Boris, we learnt, was a genuine steam-locomotive driver of international repute, and he had official cèrtificates to prove it. He collected countries in which he had driven engines as a boy collects cigarette cards.

A phalanx of our top officials from London were on the platform as the train drew in. Others were on the train. Then we saw King Boris himself in a sparkling white boilersuit. A tall man, immaculate and distinguished – even in his working clothes! – he climbed down from the beautiful streamlined locomotive, a 'Pacific' 4-6-2 newly built by Stanier. He was cordially greeted in that peculiarly English manner which saves you learning the language – broad smiles, vigorous handshakes, nodding heads.

Peggy Carrington, our eighteen-year-old shorthand-typist, had brought her Woolworths autograph book. She had told the chief clerk, "I'm going to get his lordship's autograph!" And smartly she showed a clean pair of high heels before he could say "No!" Important officials, noticing this excited-looking girl with something in her hand approaching His Majesty, tried to intercept her progress. A blonde. A shapely one at that. Could she be a spy? But our Peggy was nothing if not persistent. Her eyes were afire, and she was on Cloud Nine as she confronted the King and begged his royal signature. Boris charmingly obliged and gratuitously inserted the date too. C. R. Byrom, chief operating manager of the LMS, in command of operations, chided the girl gently for such cheek. So she asked for his signature too. A note of the event appears in my 1937 diary for 5th November.

In those few years at Bletchley the real railway had come alive for me. Armed with the right paper qualifications, I sought a post as relief stationmaster as being more interesting and offering wider experience than being SM at just one place. Besides, RSMs had to deputize at stations up to two grades above their own, and occasionally three, with larger staffs and on main lines.

But there was one sizeable snag: my eyesight. One eye was much weaker than the other. I knew that, when called to Derby HQ for such a promotion, I would face a medical and eyesight examination as well as taking a lengthy verbal examination, a severe grilling, in my railway knowledge, especially in what to do at any kind of mishap or emergency. So off I went to the Bletchley optician. Yes, he said, your sight is excellent. But that very lazy eye should be made to do more work.

Generally stationmasters, traffic inspectors and other operating supervisors did not wear spectacles. Seniors told me that spectacles could bar you from these posts. The reasoning was that a man could be called out to a mishap or other emergency in heavy rain, thick fog or a snowstorm, sunny day or Stygian night – and smudged lenses could temporarily impair his vision to the point of danger and perhaps even lead to disaster.

Eventually I was invited to Derby for a rigorous test of knowledge and health. Brand new spectacles in pocket, I caught my train. I was in a mild state of tension because, if my eyesight failed the test, my years of study could be worthless. Today, I realized, was vital to my career. At the end of it all, my knowledge survived the ordeal with ease, and the doctor who tested my eyes, with and without the spectacles, proclaimed me a 'fit and proper person' to do the job.

One plain and one strong lens made up my spectacles. Originally the optician had teased, "You could have a monocle. Just think!"

"I am thinking."

"It would be unique for a stationmaster. I could supply a nice black cord for your lapel to go with it. You know, it could make your name. But you'd need a thick skin."

"My skin is thickish, I think. But not that thick!"

Now that I had been approved, I awaited an appointment. Being single, I could go anywhere. It could be Carlisle or Gloucester, Sheffield or Leicester – anywhere on the LMS.

When the letter came through from Derby HQ, it was – of all places – Bletchley.

# 9

# Gold Braid at Last

So now, a real job. In the new post of relief stationmaster, I was lucky to be based at Bletchley because already I had learnt much about my district and had made many good friends among railwaymen of all grades. Neither would I have to change my excellent lodgings with Bert and Lucy Cobb. Two other RSMs were located within the area, both senior to me, and they took the bigger stations. They offered to help when needed, a friendly gesture I found typical on the railway.

Moving up to a position of authority, even so minor, among people I knew well, might lead to legpull and familiarity: an interesting challenge. I read somewhere in the classics that "New faces have more authority than accustomed ones." Quite! And there was the insight of Shakespeare in *Measure for Measure*: "Man, proud man, drest in a little brief authority, most ignorant of what he's most assured."

Brief authority? Full uniform in dark blue serge went with the new post: a jacket, waistcoat and two pairs of trousers each year; a heavy velour overcoat in charcoal grey and a cap every two years, and less frequently a mackintosh, in dark blue. Double-breasted, the jacket had two rows of brass buttons carrying the LMS emblem. The peaked cap was gold braided, and the words 'Station Master' were picked out smartly in gold thread. Off duty, I carried the cap in a brown leather case, along with my sandwiches and rule books, and donned a soft trilby hat.

Our staff uniforms were ordered from the LMS clothing store in Manchester. Basic measurements on a printed order form ensured a reasonable fit. No Savile Row sartorial elegance here; just practical work-a-day clothes. But, oh! that jacket, straight up and down like a sack. Not being a very tall stationmaster, I would try to be a trim one. So off to my tailor I did go, to transform the sack to a tailored jacket, complete with a top outside breast pocket to take a sparkling white linen handkerchief. Black polished shoes completed the outfit. One must look the part and appear confident. About that time I had been dipping into a translation of La Rochefoucauld's *Maxims* and registered a response to one of his epigrams: "A man, in order to establish himself in the world, does everything he can to appear established there." Point taken.

On a similar theme, in later years an Oxford graduate colleague told me, "Cambridge fellows walked around as if they owned the place. But at Oxford we ambled round as though we didn't give a damn who owned the place!"

My main work was to deputize for stationmasters taking their two weeks' annual leave, spanning the period from April to October, and covering vacancies and sick leave including some clerical posts. You got through each job as best you could, and learnt all the time.

Garbed in my new uniform, one station I went to for a fortnight was Blunham between Bedford and Cambridge. A Bletchley controller had warned, "You'll find a goods porter there who's really cantankerous. Needs careful handling."

At Blunham I soon learned that Herbert was a widower, whose only son had emigrated to Canada. You could not help feeling sad about that. My first brush with him came about like this. On the platform one day I said, gently I thought, "Herbert, we ought to get that wagon load of hay sheeted and away on the afternoon goods. Think it'll be ready?"

"How the hell do I know! I'll do me best, that's all."

"We promised the farmer it would be away today. If you want a hand, I can get the platform porter on it with you."

"I don't want no help from nobody. Leastways him!"

"OK, then to ring Control and say it'll be on the goods?"

"No, sir. It won't. I always ring Control. My job to. You can't chuck your weight about-here, gold braid or no!"

This was a losing battle. I began to walk away as an engine approached hauling a train of empty wagons.

But the irritable Herbert shouted angrily, "Eh, I'm talking to you!"

A few passengers had gathered to catch our next train to Cambridge, and I was conscious of furtive glances. Then, to my amazement, Herbert suddenly grabbed my uniform cap and flung it into the passing wagons; chuntering to himself, he marched off to the goods shed. Seething, I walked along the platform, through the booking office where the clerk was issuing tickets and into my small office. There I sat awhile, to regain my lost composure. What a ridiculous situation. And no rule to cover it!

Searching the cupboards, I found the hat of the regular station-master. It was rather large but fitted somewhat better after I had lined it with two pages of the *Daily Mirror*. Squealing brakes told me that the Cambridge train was arriving, and the porter and I attended to it. When it had gone, I rang Bletchley Control: "The empties for turnips from Potton went through some minutes ago. Could you get the guard somewhere, for a message?"

"Sure, what about?"

"My cap's in a wagon near the end of the train."

"Aha, Mr Ferneyhough. Today's funny story. How'd it get there?"

I told him. He just laughed and laughed. I simply had to join in.

"Not much hope," he warned. "It could get buried under turnips. But I'll try."

When I arrived in my little office the next morning, there was my hat, a bit dusty, on the desk, sitting on the largest turnip I have ever seen. Its crudely carved eyes, nose and ghoulishly grinning mouth were looking up at me. I never knew whose handiwork it was. But for my remaining time at Blunham I was even more cautious with goods porter Herbert. In fact, I was careful with everybody. Some of the middle-aged and elderly might resent taking orders from a stationmaster of twenty-six. And I owed them the respect than their age and experience deserved. When a train came in, I shared loading and unloading of parcels and closing doors. Guards also assisted. Though it is the guard's responsibility to signal a train to start by a hand signal – flag by day and lamp by night, he must have first received a hand signal from the man in charge of the platform. Our guards were usually smart. Their uniforms were neat and tidy. They wore clean collars and shirts, polished their shoes and often wore a flower in the buttonhole of the lapel. A rose or carnation as a 'buttonhole', garnished with a sprig of gossamer fern, was popular among the menfolk at a wedding party or for church. But for many of our guards a colourful flower at the lapel was almost part of the uniform and frequently earned compliments from the passengers. They were a credit to the railway, and their appearance was a mark of the loyalty they felt for the service they provided.

One such man was Clive Morgan. Dark-haired and fresh of complexion, he was one of the few who sported a large moustache, the ends waxed to points. But he had the risky habit, favoured by some guards, of jumping into his guard's van as his train was moving from the station. Long practice had brought much skill. Rather like the fellows at fairs who jump lithely onto whirling roundabouts to collect the coppers.

Sometimes I wondered about a train going without the guard. Late on an afternoon at Woburn Sands I was seeing to the semi-fast train to Cambridge which had come through from Oxford via Bletchley. My special interest was that that week it was being hauled, maybe experimentally, by one of Stanier's popular 'Black Fives' of recent building, the 4-6-0 type with the high, squared-up firebox, tapered boiler and outside cylinders, an engine I found a joy to watch. She was now blowing off steam and rarin' to go. From mid-train I signalled to Clive Morgan, the guard. Standing on the platform a carriage ahead of his van, he signalled the driver, and the powerful engine quickly got on the move.

Idly I watched Clive, in his stance of leaning forward, green flag under his arm, ready to jump into his van, the door opening inwards. But a small boy, waving to his grandad, bumped into him, and he lost his balance and stumbled. The porter shouted to the enginemen, but neither responded. In a flash, as the guard's van passed me, I jumped in through the open door, leaned out and yelled to the porter, "Phone Control!" Looking back along the platform, I watched Clive rise to his feet and shrug. Well, I thought, he's not hurt. As the train gathered speed, I pondered the comic, juxtaposed situation. Clive on my station and I in his van.

Our next stop would be a little too soon to expect action by my controller friends at Bletchley. It would take that lot ten minutes to stop laughing at my predicament. I was rolling away rapidly towards Cambridge when I ought to be returning to Bletchley for my evening meal, not to mention my date with a girl in a foursome to see Fred Astaire and Ginger Rogers in *Top Hat* at the County Cinema.

I had no means of telling the driver he had a stranger in the guard's van. In an emergency I would have applied the vacuum brakes partially by moving the lever and watching the pressure gauge, normally seventeen to twenty-one pounds. The driver would feel the braking and see a wagging finger in his brake dial, and he would know that only a guard in trouble could wag a finger at him with impunity. But this was no real emergency. Safety was not at stake. However, a train must have a guard for many safety reasons, and he is in charge of the train. I just had to make that attempt.

Station staff on the route must have been told, via the Control; meanwhile I sorted parcels and letters, put some out at stations, took some aboard. At Bedford St Johns I rolled out a couple of empty milk churns which clanged musically on the stone platform. Now a goods guard approached me. "I've just brought a goods train from Cambridge and usually return on the cushions. But I'm your relief, sir. Control just phoned me the story."

My turn to call Control now. They would have made several changes to meet all the needs and agreed I could make my way home.

In making my written report to the district officer, I checked with Clive so that we both kept to the same story. I omitted reference to his trying to board a moving train, and felt that the shock of it would be adequate discipline for a man of his quality. I reached home just in time for my cinema date after all.

It so happened that some years later, when I worked in another district, the guard on a train from Nottingham to Worksop missed his train at Hucknall where I was the RSM. As the train moved off without him, he looked round wildly and spotted a bicycle on the platform. He grabbed it, cocked his leg over and was soon pedalling away on the road to Linby, the next station, barely a mile away. I hurried to the telephone, and the train was held there for a few minutes until a panting, sweating guard arrived to take charge again. I had already telephoned Nottingham Control.

It was a few days after that I received a telephone call from the guard. I had forgotten all about that bike. He told me, "The police have been to see me. They thought my explanation was a bit fishy. Thought I'd let you know."

"Thanks, guard. What happened?"

"It belongs to a chap in Nottingham, they told me. Said it was labelled with his name and address to go by train. They might check with you."

Sure enough, in the afternoon a plain-clothes police officer called on me at Hucknall to confirm the story.

"Officer," I said, "that's the second time I've known a guard miss his train. Most unusual. Anyway, we found the bike at Linby yesterday, properly labelled, and we put it on a train for Nottingham. The owner should get it soon. I've posted a letter of apology to him."

"He'll never get your letter."

"Oh, how come?"

"He's been pinching bikes from stations for months and labelling them to himself in various parts of the country. But we got him this time. He'd left his real address in the saddlebag."

Back now to the Bletchley district, to Verney Junction, a railway crossroads that sat, with awesome improbability, in the midst of the Buckinghamshire fields. On my first day there I made my usual daily call in the signalbox. Deep in pleasant country barely ten miles from Bletchley, trains branched on the left fork to Oxford and on the right to Buckingham, Brackley and Banbury. It was not a very busy place, and the signalman had a fine crop of tomatoes running alongside the inside window that caught the sun. I climbed up the outside steps and entered the box. An amusing sight met my eyes. In a chair sat the junior porter, and the signalman, thick-set and balding, was cutting the lad's hair. In between the snips he signalled a train. So what does a human sort of a fellow do? Maybe I should have ignored it and sidled out. But discipline is discipline. Yet, in the path of the self-righteous, I reflected, nature has its way of strewing banana skins.

"Morning, sir," said George. "You be gone and caught me proper this time!"

"We're not a barber's shop, you know, George."

"Bit quietish just now, sir. Not much traffic about. Won't be long."

In the train register book I entered the time of my visit and signed it.

"You really ought to do this job in your own time, you know, not in the Company's."

"Oh, but it grows in the Company's time, sir!" Snip snip.

"Not all of it, surely?"

"Well, I baint a-cutting it all off, be I?"

He had me there. Snip snip, snip snip.

"If the district officer should catch you, George, there could be trouble."

"Well, sir, last time he come to this box on hair-cutting day, I gives him a rabbit. Then he didn't seem to notice them scissors. And if you're round this way tomorrow, I'll be have another rabbit, I shouldn't wonder."

"George, you're an absolute scallywag!"

He had just finished. The junior porter swept up the hair and went back to the station without uttering a word. George signalled the local goods train for Banbury, then turned to me.

"I spose you be a townie, sir. Not used to our country ways. There baint no barber shop these miles around, see? At Verney, it's always been the bobby's perks, the two of us, to earn hisself a copper or two. Goes back to Queen Victoria's days!"

"George, you old rogue, you can tell a good tale. I'll call for that rabbit in the morning. My landlady would be pleased. How much will it be?"

"Oh, for you, sir? Nothing. It don't cost me nothing. I got some good snares. And I might have a mushroom or two for you tomorrow."

As I walked through the door, he called, "And if you don't mind me saying so, sir, your 'air be getting a bit on the long side!"

This incident I related to a clerk at Northampton while doing a stint there. It reminded him of his uncle, a signalman at Spratton, six miles down the Market Harborough line.

"He was there for years. They called him the village barber. He did the haircutting on Saturday afternoons, in his signalbox, when there were no officials around with bowler hats."

"What did the stationmaster say to this?"

"No problem there. He cut his as well. And his two small boys."

Ah, country life down the line. Travelling in the guard's van on the Oxford branch, when the train stopped at Bicester the station porter gave the guard a large bundle of beansticks.

"Tom," he called. "Can you throw these out at Claydon? I promised old Harry. He's just getting his beans in."

It was much the same on the other branch lines. Sometimes a score of cabbage plants, a bushel of apples, a chip of strawberries. Not quite according to the book of rules. But what could a transient, here-today-gone-tomorrow young RSM, "drest in a little brief authority", say to these good fellows about practices that were as old as the line itself! Besides, when I was travelling with the district officer one day in a first-class compartment (allowable when with an officer holding a first-class pass), he leaned out of the window at one wayside station and called to the porter, "The signalman promised me pea sticks this week. Tell him I'm ready for them now. Thanks."

When in the country, one supposes, it's 'do as the country does' – within reason, unless you prefer to be an outcast. It's trivia really. There are worse ways of living.

However, one thing struck me at country stations: the staff seemed proud to be working for the railway and were respected in their own communities. Their loyalty was touching. They gave passengers, farmers and merchants unstinted help and were usually courteous in their country manner. I did not seem to meet any duodenal ulcers, nervous breakdowns or work stress.

Most kept their stations clean and tidy. They tended the shrub and flower beds as their own. I remember what a keen gardener the stationmaster was at Brackley. When a small circus came to the town, an elephant arrived in a specially large van. The routine was for the van, when empty, to be scrubbed out with lashings of water. Just in time, the stationmaster stopped the porter with his first bucket.

"Hang on, Joe. Look at all that marvellous manure. Wait till I get my wheelbarrow!"

You would think the boss had won the pools and was cock-a-hoop as he wheeled his half-filled barrow to the flower garden behind the station house. Alas, the next morning he found his plants all sad and withered. The straw from the van, in which the manure was mixed, had been strongly disinfected, a usual practice, and naturally the flowers had registered their protest.

In earlier days, I had often noticed station porters busily cleaning windows, dusting waiting-rooms, polishing brasses, filling fire-buckets, sweeping platforms, cleaning the toilets and similar duties, never realizing that it was a programmed and monitored routine. In my job I had to see that 'domestic rosters' were posted on staff noticeboards and that all the work was done on the day shown and by the man responsible. In addition, in my station reports to Derby HQ, I had to certify that the domestic roster was up to date and being observed. At the larger stations the rosters were quite extensive.

At the smaller stations you turned your hand to anything. One dark and stormy night, a goods train stopped at Islip on the Oxford line where I was the RSM working an afternoon shift. Towards eight o'clock I had just locked up, turned out the half-dozen oil-lamps on the two platforms, and in the store-room washed my hands under the water-pump that supplied water for the station and for the stationmaster's house forty yards away.

Above the noise of the engine, the driver shouted, "Light's out on your down distant." Then he moved off. The signal, on a very tall post, was nearly a mile down the line. I should have noticed the electric indicator dial near the distant signal lever in the small 'signal lever frame' on the platform when I had locked it up with chain and padlock for the night. The indicator was needed because the signal was too far away for me to see whether the light was in or not. It was an ingenious device. If the oil-lamp in the signal went out, a small metal ring just above the flame would contract, and a gap in it, open while hot, would close; this in turn would break an electrical circuit and operate the indicator at the station. This device was common up and down the railway system.

Islip was a 'block post' for signalling purposes, like an ordinary signalbox, but the telegraph instruments were in the booking office and the signal levers out on the platform. Not quite Heath Robinson, but certainly basic. Because trains, both goods and passenger, were not frequent, the block post was open only for a few hours daily; special equipment allowed it to be switched through to Bicester on one side and Oxford on the other, with our signals placed to the 'clear' position.

The SM worked shifts with the porter-signalman, with an overlap of several hours around midday. I worked the post as would a signalman, operating signals, points and telegraph instruments, reporting train running times to Bletchley Control and, when a passenger train was due, booking tickets as well. We were also a goods depot, and I had two level crossings, not far distant, under my control. You earned your money.

Ted Marlin, the porter-signalman, had the amusing habit of adding a touch of wisdom to conversation, starting, "Confucius, he say . . ." – something he had picked up on the BBC wireless. One of his jobs was to fill and trim the oil-lamps for the signals. But he was on early shift, so on this occasion I had no alternative but to get a light in that distant signal down the line myself.

Finding my way around in the Stygian darkness and driving rain, I went to the store-room and lighted my oil handlamp. I took a spare signal lamp, just a plain container of oil, a feeder for the wick, and a carrying handle. Using an old knife, I cleaned the wick, lit it with a match to test it, then blew it out again. Outside once more, I heard the old village church clock strike eight. In heavy railway mackintosh, I walked steadily along the dark track, using the handlamp and carefully avoiding anything that could trip me over. I had horrible thoughts of falling and lying helpless in the storm all night. Grrrr! Now the March wind and rain faced me and lashed my face viciously.

By the time I reached the signal, I was breathless and soaked to the skin. I looked up at the signal post. It seemed jolly high. I had never climbed one before and did not care much for heights. Glancing round in the pitch dark, I could not even see the occasional farm light. To be alone like this gave one an eerie feeling of being the only person alive in the world, not the ideal setting for a gregarian. During a break in the howling wind, I heard the husky croak of a frog.

Leaving my handlamp on the ground, I began to climb the iron ladder up the side of the signal post, one hand on the ladder, the other carrying the signal lamp. This was a job I was not enjoying one bit. But signals are signals, and it had to be done.

No more passenger trains were due that night, but a few night goods trains would be on the move.

At the top, a protective ring of iron supported my back. Hanging the new oil-lamp on the signal, I exchanged it for the failed one. Concentration would have been easier if the signal post had stopped swaying and the screaming wind did not blow out matches so inconsiderately. Half a box of matches and many minutes later, a steady yellow flame was burning in the protective signal casing, whose designer had understood such things. And by some mysterious alchemy beyond my intellectual limits, the yellow flame shining through the turquoise glass of the signal produced a beautiful green.

Suddenly I heard a powerful locomotive. The wind had drowned the noise until it was close. Judging by its pounding beat, it was hauling a heavy goods train and was throwing up sparks from the chimney in the effort. I would know that sound anywhere, a Crewe-built 0-6-0, a tough old workhorse of which hundreds were around. I had thought of scurrying down the signal post on hearing it. But haste or loss of concentration could be disastrous. And if I was hurt, my calls for help would float away on the winds of the mysterious night.

Now the train was coming. I held on tight. Its vibrations shook the signal post. Just as it roared below me, it belched up smoke and steam, making me cough and choke violently. Simultaneously, live sparks shot up my trouser leg and made me shout with shock. Bang-bang bang-bang over the rail joints went each wagon, and by sheer habit I counted the bloody things, forty-two precisely. Finally went the brakevan. Inside, the light showed the guard in silhouette. From my reckless, swaying perch, how I envied the cosiness of that van! Imagine the surprise of the guard if he had known that a very green, rain-soaked staionmaster was clinging for dear life at the top of a lurching signal post and saying his prayers in case he could not get down again!

The red tail-light of the train soon faded from view. Gingerly I started down the ladder, gripping it grimly as greedy gusts of wind agitated to dislodge me. No man was ever less in his element. People say it is harder to get down a mountain than climb up it. They should have included signal posts.

Tired and hungry, it took me over half an hour to trudge in the drenching rain to the station. Tomorrow I must report details to Bletchley Control, essential for a faulty signal; if necessary, a technical signals inspector would search for a cause, such as defective design. From the station I walked through Islip village to my temporary lodgings in the 'Swan', dried out, put away a hot supper and went to bed to the comforting noises of the country pub.

At the station the next day Ted, the genial porter-signalman, laughed when he heard my tale of woe. He trimmed wicks and filled the containers with oil for the signals once a week. He told me, "The chap I followed in this job warned me not to climb a high signal post on a windy day when a train is a-coming." He was suddenly dead serious, and I wondered what was up. "There's an old Chinese proverb about it. Confucius, he say – 'Never cock tlouser leg over chimley when there is flire dlown below!'"

That signal post remained the last one I was ever to climb in my railway life.

# 10

# Why Trains Sometimes Run Late

From my first days in Bletchley, work often took me into the train control room itself. I did not understand the system and had no desire whatever to work there. Frankly, the place frightened me to death. It was the local nerve-centre for all train operations consisting of main lines and many branches detailed earlier.

Twenty or more district control centres were located on the LMS, and they were grouped under several divisional control centres, three of them in England – Crewe (Western Division), Derby (Midland Division) and Manchester (Central Division). Broadly similar train control systems functioned on the other three railways. At Bletchley up to six controllers of various grading worked on each of the three shifts, and the office never closed. In charge of each shift was a head controller. Most of the work was by telephone and the compilation of large train sheets for minute-to-minute records.

Among them, the controllers had a wide knowledge of railway operations. Each was allocated specific responsibilities – control of engines and enginemen (sometimes called locos and locomen), control of guards mainly on freight trains, control of main-line trains, control of all the branch lines, and a dayshift man controlling the movement of freight rolling stock. They were a mixed lot of friendly and cheerful chaps, who had to depend on each other in this pure teamwork. In overall charge of the operating side of lines, stations and depots, was the district controller, supported by his deputy and several traffic and signalling inspectors.

A key unit in the control room was a long blackboard across the wall displaying a huge diagram which delineated all the lines, crossover roads, signalboxes, stations, depots, sidings, loops and level crossings in our district. Tags in thin card containing written details, shortened, of freight trains were pegged on the board and moved along by the controllers as reports were received from signalmen and others. Any one report could throw the office in a turmoil calling for quick action.

Most of the time all the trains were on the move, coming towards you, going away from you, changing the kaleidoscopic pattern of operations every minute, nay – second. A vast amount of freight was handled, and the skill was to weave the freight trains in and out of the expresses and branch-line stoppers. Obfuscated you might be, but bored never.

Snatches of one end of a telephone conversation were intriguing if mystifying.

"Unhook, driver. Leave the wagons there and get that engine on the shed quick!"

"Relief enginemen waiting for you at the up home at North-ampton sidings."

"Where the hell's the express, Edward? I've got to shift this goods train or we'll be in dead trouble."

"No, bobby [signalman], you damn well can't close your box. Yes, I know you're on overtime, and your dinner's spoiling in the oven. You've got to wait for your relief. A man's on the way now."

"Tell your guard there's a horse-box to pick up at Tring. And he can drop it off here for Cambridge. Sure there's a connection for Newmarket."

"Ben, two wagons off the road at Blisworth. Blocking the up fast. We'll want the crane. She's in steam? Great. Tell me when she leaves. Our inspector's on the way."

He shouts across the office to the youngest in the team, "Now then, Ronnie, is that tea made yet?"

A call comes to the branch controller, "Nineteen, thirty-two, fifty-eight. Twenty-five on." So said the signalman, on the phone from Winslow. Translated into fair English, the up local goods train, numbered nineteen in the freight timetable, arrived in Winslow goods yard at 2.32 p.m. for shunting purposes and departed at 2.58 p.m. with a load of twenty-five wagons.

It just goes on. "Down Glasgow express delayed at you eight minutes, Tom. Give us a ring soon with details for Crewe Divisional. They're playing bloody hell about it!"

"OK, so the Bedford's fifteen late. No, we can't hold up the

London express for that party. Sorry, makes no difference if it's a hundred. They'll have to catch the next."

"Hallo, Crewe? We'll want forty fitted vans for Potton veg tomorrow and sixty common users for the Bedford line brick-works on Wednesday."

"Hallo, Buckingham. Sammy, when are you going to send me that bushel of potatoes?"

It was, I suppose, to be expected after my few years at Bletch-ley, including the work as a relief stationmaster in the district, that I would be a candidate for promotion to the control room. Branch-line controller was my new label, and the prospect, though exciting, did give me butterflies. One or two chaps I have known have had to give up train control work because of the strain. Anyway, I was allocated three weeks' training – one on each shift in the usual forty-eight hour week. Part of this time I spent at main establishments, including engine sheds, at North-ampton, Oxford, Banbury and Cambridge. In leisure hours I studied internal (non-public) timetables for passenger and freight trains, empty carriage journeys, shift-work rosters for drivers, firemen and guards.

For some weeks after I took charge, I somehow had disturbing dreams – the 'Royal Scot' derailed in Bletchley station, a shunter killed by a moving wagon in the sidings, several main-line expresses delayed by a goods train I had failed to hold back on the Bedford line. When I told colleagues, I found that they had all suffered similarly – and still did! To survive in this tense and exciting and crazy business, two characteristics seemed vital – self-composure and anticipation.

Around four o'clock one morning, the main-line controller was having a shouting match on his telephone.

"Driver, you can't just stand there on the up fast line. I've got the night sleeper from Scotland coming up behind you in half an hour. And we want you out of the way quick!"

It was a Coventry driver bringing a coal train from the Mid-lands, speaking from a signalbox south of Rugby. He and his fireman had been promised relief at Rugby by Rugby Control, but there had been a slip-up. He claimed they had been on duty for nine hours and had run out of food and drink. Not a happy situation.

The driver had shouted, "If we don't get relief, we're going to drop the fire!"

A dead train on a main line? That would have been calamitous. For such an extreme a driver would have to be desperate. But the threat was enough to make the controller change his tune.

"Now look, old chap. Bear with me. If you'll bring your train to Bletchley, I'll have two relief men ready. Then I'll stop the down express parcels to get you home to Coventry."

Immediate crisis over. What's next? The motive-power controller then arranged for a 'call boy' (a man really) to cycle to the homes of a driver and a fireman in the 'special link' to report for duty as soon as possible.

A small proportion of drivers, firemen and goods guards in the 'special link' had no regular shifts but worked as required by traffic needs. When a special link man signed off duty, he was handed a small printed form instructing him to be available for his next turn of duty after his 'rest period' of twelve hours. If the controller failed to call him for work within eight hours after the twelve hours had elapsed, the man would be entitled to a full day's pay as though he had worked it, and the controller would have some explaining to do to the district controller.

In turn, we all suffered our panics, usually having a good laugh afterwards to relieve the strain. On the morning shift one day, I sweated blood and endured a churned-up stomach for half an hour as I grappled with a ridiculous unforeseen mix-up.

A routine call came from the signalman at Oxford, "Up goods ready. Can it come now?"

"What's the loading?"

"Sixty. All rough."

'Rough' meant wagons for various destinations (as distinct from a train of wagons all for one final destination). They were bound for Bletchley marshalling yard where they would need shunting, backwards and forwards, into other trains for another stage in their journeys. A passenger train, due to leave Oxford in under an hour, was scheduled to connect at Bletchley with a north-bound express and a south-bound stopping train. Therefore I must not delay that Oxford passenger train. Otherwise, trouble.

At that moment I had two options – hold back the goods train at

Oxford for nearly an hour until the passenger train had left or let the goods train come now and hope it would not delay the passenger train. If I allowed the goods train to come now, I would have two choices – have the train run into the loop line on the Oxford branch just before entering Bletchley station so as to allow the Oxford passenger train to get by into the station, or arrange for the goods train to come into Bletchley, cross over the up and down fast lines and the up and down slow, then run into the marshalling sidings. The main-line controller would have to find a 'path' for the goods across the four main lines, always tricky. I had checked that the goods train would take over an hour to cover the thirty-two miles to Bletchley and that the loop would hold sixty-three wagons. I told the Oxford signalman, "Let him come!" For a while I got on with other work.

My next move was to phone Bob Bedley, the Bletchley marshalling yard inspector: "A train of sixty rough in about an hour, Bob. Can you take it?"

Bob's voice was loud and raucous from shouting against clanging wagons and roaring, whistling engines. "No room. Can't come in the yard. We're chocka."

"I've got to shift it soon. The Oxford passenger will be behind it shortly."

"Sorry, not a hope. We've got to shift some first. Eh, why not drop it in the loop?"

"Yes, I'll have to. Thanks, Bob."

Next I phoned the signalman controlling the entrance to the loop at the Bletchley end, instructed him to run the goods train in there when it came and told him why. Meanwhile I was juggling operating moves on other branch lines. It was a busy period, and my colleagues were grappling with their own problems. I could have consulted the head controller, but as the branch man it was my responsibility. Secretly I was enjoying the situation and felt master of my tiny little empire. It was rather like playing toy trains on the grand scale, but for real, and I was often reminded of a little tin model train with a circular track that I had one Christmas.

Then came a nasty shock. The signalman controlling the entrance to the loop line phoned, "Goods in the loop . . ."

"Great, Harry!"

"It won't all go in. Guard says nothing can be done. Eight of the wagons are long bogies. Three wagons and the brakevan are sticking out on the branch line."

"Oh, blast and bloody hell!"

That signalman at Oxford should have said, "Sixty on, equal to sixty-six in length," the normal procedure. But a wiser controller would have double-checked. This time the butterflies fluttered even more wildly. The Oxford passenger was on the way and could be held back, delaying the main-line connections or miss them altogether. That lot would get me a helluva roasting.

Unhappy phrases raced through my mind: 'Not found suitable as a train controller . . .' 'Fails to seek advice in a crisis . . .' I wondered how much my colleagues suffered as I did at this moment but without batting an eyelid. Sweat was damp on my forehead, and my respiration had quickened. That passenger train from Oxford was getting nearer and nearer . . . My next hope was to have the rear of the goods train drawn clear into the loop, then to have the engine take a few wagons across the four main lines, then into the marshalling yard: I would need the main-line controller to find a 'path' over his four main lines, and Bob Bedley to find room in his marshalling yard.

I rang Bob. Yes, he could manage up to ten only ". . . to get you out of trouble . . ." I asked the main-line controller. Yes, he would try to find a path very soon, but had I a brakevan to put in rear of the ten wagons? No, I had no van available. Ordinarily a goods train is not allowed on running lines without a goods brakevan in the rear and a guard inside. Fear must have rummaged in my confused sub-conscious mind, for suddenly I recalled that a special local instruction allowed a goods train of up to ten wagons to cross the four main lines without a brakevan in rear providing that the guard rode on the engine and that the last wagon carried a red flag (light at night). This I arranged with the signalman controlling the entrance to the loop line, who told the guard, who had to walk up the train to tell the driver. Meanwhile, that train from Oxford . . .

Next, I phoned Bletchley No. 1 box, and the signalman said, "It's got to have a brakevan."

"No, Bert. Quick, page 49 in the Appendix."

Agonizing seconds later: "You're right, mate. Never seen it afore. Okay, we'll do it."

Then the same process with the bobby in No. 5 box, even trickier. At last. Everybody knew exactly what to do. We might just make it. I went out onto platform eight just as my little train of ten wagons, with a red flag on the rear, trundled through. Leaning from the engine cab, the guard shook his fist at me but grinned good-naturedly. He understood it all, I'm sure. Another goods guard, Ron Challis, a good friend of mine, stood by me, puzzled. "What the hell's that?"

"That, my dear Ron, has saved my bacon with one minute to spare! I'll tell you sometime."

"I can't wait!"

On the far side of the station I saw my Oxford train run into platform one and watched its passengers cross the bridge; some caught the north-bound express and some the up main local. What a moment of relief! No doubt thousands of similar train-juggling, nail-biting manœuvres were putting grey hairs into the heads of train controllers throughout the railways of Britain that very minute.

As I turned to go back to the control office, I spotted a friend of mine from the Bletchley tennis club, making for the Bedford train. Leg-pulling as usual, he called, "Eh, Frank, old boy, why aren't you in your little office playing trains?" I could have bashed him on the head with his tennis racquet.

Panics of this nature were quite frequent. Our total aim was to keep the trains moving, generally giving precedence to passenger trains.

Within the day-to-day operations was the supply of various types of empty wagons – from a simple coal wagon to an eight-wheeled bogie well wagon for carrying a huge industrial boiler. We supplied trade and industry in our own district, two main users being brickworks and agriculture, and empty wagons were accumulated on our territory to send to the coalfields and to industrial areas.

Aside from regular passenger trains, there were frequent 'specials' for race meetings, exhibitions, bank holidays and the like. And though regular goods or freight trains ran on a printed timetable basis, it was difficult to maintain their punctual running. Every day, special goods trains were scrambled together – engines, men, wagons, brakevans – in fast time to meet the continually changing needs of industry and trade. Wriggling this lot in between local and express passenger trains could be quite hair-raising, and you had to know how to get rid of a goods threatening the path of a passenger in double-quick time – shunt it into a siding, a lay-by, a loop line, a private siding or through a crossover road onto the opposite line – all by phone!

In a jam one day with one of my branch lines, I instructed a signalman to shunt a goods train from the path of an expected passenger train into a short, double-line siding. For me it was a desperate move and one I had not made before. Two hours later Harold Waller, an elderly goods guard, came to sign off duty, and he stormed, "Why in blazes put me down there?"

"Harold. The local passenger was behind you. I had no option. Sorry, old lad!"

"It's dangerous! Heavy falling gradient, so I had to pin down handbrakes on many wagons. And I had to split my train on them two short roads. At my age. How long you bin in the Control now, Mr Ferney?"

"A few months."

He smiled wryly. "I forgive yer. No controller's never done that afore!"

And this controller never did it again.

Relief arranged by the controllers for trainmen mainly concerned freight trains southbound, to or through London. Details of such trains came by telephone from Rugby Control Office which we wrote on small tickets in coded colours; the tickets, placed on small pegs, were inserted in holes on the huge diagram board, to show the train's last reported position; the pegs were moved along the board as the progress of the trains (freight only, we were supposed to memorize the passenger trains) was reported by signalmen and others on the line. Minute to minute, the pattern changed.

Ticket information included the engine number, home base and time of starting duty of driver, fireman and guard, the number of wagons on the train, with a note of anything special such as livestock (animals might need feeding or cows milking during the journey), and the title of the train. Here is an example – '6p Tn Wn E6245 D 655 G6.30 Nm 60 C1'. In plain English: 6 p.m. train Toton to Willesden, engine number 6245, driver and fireman booked on duty at 6.55 p.m., the guard at 6.30 p.m., all three being based at Nottingham, and the load was sixty wagons of coal. It took a newcomer time to learn the jargon and to know the power, type and class of a locomotive by its number.

From the pegs on the diagram, each controller could see at a glance the position of trains. Regular reports were received by telephone to show in advance the running of the principal express passenger trains. If, say, an up Glasgow is half an hour late, the controller must visualize the effect of this on other trains and what action he or others need to take to keep everything on the move.

I learnt early in the control office that drivers and guards worked trains, either passengers or freight, only on the routes for which they had been trained. Their 'route cards' were kept in the office, each man having to sign for each separate route. When you earmarked a man for a train, you had to check with his route card that he 'knew the road'. Knowing the road meant being familiar with all the signals, signalboxes, stations, yards, depots, level crossings, sidings, bridges, cross-overs, tunnels, junctions, line-side telephones and main gradients. On any type of train, the guard was in charge. He, as well as the driver, needed to know the railway track in darkness or dense fog, heavy rain or snow-storm. In any emergency he had to know exactly where to go and what to do. It is this kind of attention to detail, long established as railway tradition, that has always maintained a high standard of passenger safety on our railways.

By the way, in the country a smart goods guard would also know where to snare rabbits and to pick mushrooms.

Along with other operating men, the goods guard, for example, had to know intimately a large number of rules for his work, including a wide range of emergency procedures. Every two years he was examined verbally by a traffic inspector for up to an hour, more if necessary: a gruelling test that would earn rebuke if he was weak, and a second chance when justified. Earlier the guard would have been a porter, then a shunter or other grade bringing operating experience.

The control office was one of several offices on platform eight at Bletchley, ancient brick structures erected in Queen Victoria's days. It was a long office, the large diagram board on one side and windows on the other, looking out onto sidings where clanging wagons were usually on the move.

We had a network of 'circuit' telephones, the wires for which ran alongside the railway lines with telegraph wires. Our own technical staff maintained them. A post-office telephone was used, but the railway lines took the bulk of the work.

Our circuit telephone system was one in which many signal-boxes, stations and depots were linked on the one telephone line. On the Cambridge branch, for example, any one of the twenty-five places could be obtained; each place had its own calling code of long and short buzzes. And when I pressed my ringing button for three shorts and a long, though it would be heard at twenty-five places, only the signalman at Bedford, whose code it was, would lift his receiver to answer it. If any one of those twenty-five wanted to call the control office, he would press his button marked 'Control', and it would light a small bulb (one of a dozen) on my desk. There would be no sound, and the light would remain on until I answered that call. But if I were talking to Beford, any of the others could lift their receivers and 'listen in'. By listening in, signalmen and others could learn what was happening to the trains and pick up some gossip as well. If anyone lifted his receiver to 'listen in', local background noises could be heard; some were so strong and distinctive that you knew which signalbox it was without the signalman announcing himself.

On nights one week, the number nine light came on at my desk, and before the caller had a chance to say, "Is that Control?" I answered, "Hallo, Fred?"

"How the blazes did you know it was me?"

Fred Turner, the young signalman at Bletchley No. 4 box, half a mile along the Cambridge branch, and I knew each other by voice but not by face. We had never met.

"A mini-TV screen on my desk. I can see that pimple on your nose."

"Come off it, Frank. Besides, there ain't no pimple. Night goods away at twelve-ten with twenty on. I'll find out how you do it."

Among other calls, two hours later I picked up my handset and said smartly, "Hallo, Fred?"

"Marvellous! It could ha' been anybody on this line."

Several times that week the pattern was repeated. He said, "I'm going to find out before the week's out. You'll see!"

"You've found out. I told you. This little screen . . ."

Three o'clock on the Friday morning, and I answered a caller, "Control here. Hallo? Who wants Control? Hallo?"

Raucous laughter nearly split my ear. It was Fred.

"Told you I'd find out. It's very clever!"

From a shelf by his telephone he had removed a loudly ticking clock.

On my Sundays off from control work, Inspector Johnson persuaded me to lecture about the rules to local railwaymen in the Mechanics Institute. He himself revelled in the rules and nurtured me with the proselytism of one who has discovered a joy he feels impelled to pass on. Lucky was I to be blessed with such a mentor.

Among my audiences were drivers and firemen, fitters and cleaners, guards, shunters and signalmen. Essential researches taught me more than I taught them! Lecturing appealed to me, and I was determined to master the techniques. I enjoyed keeping the sessions on a light note, stimulating participation and encouraging the fellows to tell amusing railway stories.

One old main-line driver named Jimmy Oldfield, with a great bald head and an outsize snowy moustache, had only to say, "Let me drive your Baby Austin" and the place was in an uproar. His favourite story was about another express driver who was taken for a ride in the country by his daughter in her sparkling new red Baby Austin car. He said to her, "Let me have a drive, dear."

"Dad, you can't drive a motorcar!"

"Look here, I'm used to driving five hundred people on a five-hundred ton train at seventy miles an hour. So move over!"

She did. Her dad got in the driving-seat, put the car in gear and drove off – smack into a tree. He had forgotten to steer.

Whenever I saw Driver Oldfield in the 'Railway Arms', someone was sure to call, "A pint for you, Jimmy, if you'll tell us about that Baby Austin!" It always made the fellows laugh.

Somehow, in our rules classes we could not find a lot to laugh at. But the men enjoyed having things explained to them in simple terms, especially those relating to accidents and other emergencies. Drivers and guards especially liked to be reassured about their precise responsibilities and exactly what they, individually, had to do. In this I had found in myself a natural propensity.

Young chaps in the 'uniform grades' seeking promotion found the standard operating rules tedious to read and the complexities difficult to grasp. That is why voluntary classes were run in all parts of the LMS, supplementing the various official training courses. So difficult had I found the rules in my early twenties that I wrote them out in my own words and tried to distil the underlying principles. But not until I had worked on the line, been in signalboxes and marshalling yards and hobnobbed at close quarters with various types of trains and railwaymen did the rules begin to make real sense, to come alive and to be stimulating. And with your own kind, you could natter about the rules for ever!

# 11

# The Signalman, the Blonde and the Baby

In summer 1939 at Bletchley we were busy co-ordinating a programme for the evacuation of children and the elderly away from the threatened dangers of London to the safer countryside. War with Germany seemed inevitable. Our local effort was only a small part of a massive operation that started in July and finished on 8th September, five days after war had been declared. By that time the first air-raid warning sirens were curdling the blood.

In that crucial period of mass evacuation, well over two thousand extra trains in many parts of Britain had been run. Women and children, the aged and infirm migrated to the comparative safety of the countryside – in the north, the Midlands and the west. Meantime, the railways conveyed into the London area from various parts of Britain tens of thousands of Anderson and Morrison air-raid shelters, for use mainly in people's back gardens.

On 1st September, two days before that fateful day, twenty-eight loaded trains passed through Bletchley. Declared an evacuee reception area, the town that day received some eight hundred, mostly children, to make a new life in the quiet countryside. Suddenly fast-delivered Cockney accents were mingling with the more leisurely Buckinghamshire drawl.

When one through train stopped in Bletchley station, I spied a wide-eyed little girl leaning from a window. Suddenly she began to scream blue murder. Unsuccessfully her mother tried to comfort her, for it was discovered that she had dropped her Teddy onto the platform, and it had slipped down to the track. I was about to get down between the train and platform edge to perform a miraculous rescue act before their very eyes (not my first time, and safe if under the guard's eye) when a young porter beat me to it. As he handed Teddy to its owner, the little girl smiled happily. But the tears fell again when she noticed one of its beady eyes was missing.

"Never mind, love," the guard said gently. "He's lost an eye, but we saved his life, didn't we!"

In later years millions of people of all ages would have their own 'evacuation' stories to tell about their radically altered way of life. Youngsters were seeing real lambs and farmyards for the first time, and country people were trying to understand the Cockney humour. Youthful jokes were cracked about farm life – such as the little fellow who, when he saw two milk bottles on a doorstep, shouted to his friend, "Look, Pete, a cow's nest with two eggs!"

For the period of the war the railways were taken over by the government as part of the total strategy. Few people escaped dramatic changes in their way of life. With a colleague I travelled to Bedford for a 'medical'. He looked thin and pale-faced, while people had always told me I had a healthy, ruddy mug. After tedious hours of doing the rounds of the medical specialists, I was shocked when he passed 'A1' and I was rejected 'C111', unfit for the Armed Services. The reason seemed to be that my two recent operations meant attending a London hospital regularly for out-patient treatment (nothing too serious; they said I'd live). I was never called upon again because the railway registered me as an 'essential worker' in railway operating – what became known as a 'reserved occupation'. Long hours of hard work in the 'black-out', duties in the Civil Defence Volunteers – later Home Guard – and fire-watching at strategic railway establishments formed the routine. When railway lines were bombed, work in the control office was harassing, but at least we were not being shot at.

In the following year a modest promotion from control work took me to Mansfield, again as a district relief stationmaster. After surviving a gruelling verbal examination at Derby on operating rules and regulations, I was finally 'approved' by the great L. F. Rowlandson himself, the LMS staff superintendent.

In his private office he asked, "Are you ready to move soon?"

"As soon as you wish, sir."

"Good. Married, I see. Any family?"

"A baby son, two weeks old."

His stern face softened momentarily. "We'll postpone your transfer for three months. Give your wife time to get on her feet." And he marked my file.

He added, "You will be my personal representative, as you were at Bletchley, like all my relief stationmasters. Report to me, personally, anything you find wrong, anything . . . unsatisfactory."

As I left, two thoughts struck me: first, probably the post at Mansfield was not going to be vacant anyway for three months; and second, I did not really want to be a snooper. Not my style. Besides, I do too many unorthodox things myself! When in a January snowstorm we moved home to Mansfield, I found that the post had indeed been vacant for three months. So much for my suspicious mind!

At Mansfield there were engine sheds and, as we were in former Midland Railway territory, a host of locomotives of various types and classes, fresh to me, were to be seen.

Different problems were to be faced in this new district during the several years I was there. One station I did not care for was Ambergate on the Midland main line, a triangular station with three separate routes converging on it, served by several signal-boxes. As 'relief', and there only for short periods, I never felt quite sure of my bearings and hoped nothing would go wrong, especially during the night.

Trent, between Nottingham and Derby, was unusual in that trains could travel both north and south from either of the two island platforms, with unusual routings. It stood on the main line between London (St Pancras) and Sheffield. Until I had mastered the local railway geography, including all the signalboxes, sidings and crossover roads, I kept in my office out of sight while passengers were around! Going through old files in the safe in the private office, I came across a letter signed with a flourish in vivid green ink by a stationmaster who had worked there many years ago: L. P. Briggs, the very man who had interviewed me at Stoke station for my first post on the railway. It gave me an eerie feeling.

On my first day at Shirebrook, deputizing for the regular stationmaster on annual leave for two weeks, gossips were busy. Shirebrook stood on the Nottingham-Worksop line, the junction signalbox controlling a branch line to local collieries. Staff consisted of a few clerks, station porters and signalmen. Apart from passengers, coal trains were despatched from the nearby pits in this busy Nottinghamshire coalfield.

Station tittle-tattle, it seemed, focused on the woman porter, an attractive honey-blonde in her mid-thirties, said to be having an affair with the signalman, David Aidley, a personable fellow, fair-haired and broad-shouldered, around forty. Mr Proctor, the elderly chief goods clerk, an acid man, tall and thin, with a lantern jaw and a bowler hat always worn dead straight, was incensed. His office, two hundred yards down the line, was opposite the junction signalbox.

Sourly, he informed me, "She's married, you know. Husband in Burma fighting for her country. And suffering heaven knows what out there! And she messing about with another man behind his back!"

Conscious that he was old enough to be my dad, I chided him gently. "Steady on, Mr Proctor. I'm a stationmaster not a marriage guidance counsellor."

"Yes, but even off duty, like now, she goes up to his box to make his tea. He's married as well, you know. Two kids. It's not good enough. Not on a public station, or in a private signalbox. Everybody's talking. Even the passengers."

"I've seen nothing wrong. What am I supposed to do?"

"Tell her to keep out of that signalbox for a start."

"Will that stop them being in love?"

He dabbed his face with a red spotted handkerchief. "Love fiddlesticks! You're just like our regular boss. Do nothing!" Chuntering and disgruntled, he strode off to his little brick office in the goods yard opposite the signalbox.

Next morning he telephoned me. His voice was urgent. "She's just gone up the steps to the signalbox. If you go now, you'll catch 'em at it!"

"Catch 'em at what, Mr Proctor, drinking tea and pulling signal levers?"

But he had hung up. He had boxed me in, and I had to act. So after a while I donned my uniform cap and from my office walked leisurely down the platform and along the line, crossed the tracks and climbed the wooden steps up to the junction signalbox. On the door a metal plate proclaimed, "Strictly private. No admittance".

Thankfully, the signalman was alone. "'Morning, David."

"'Morning, sir. Nice to see you again."

We chatted amiably and I signed his train register book, adding the time of my visit.

When there was nothing on the 'block' (no trains signalled), I asked, "Is your rule book handy?"

Looking surprised, he produced it at once from his locker. "David, will you read Rule 72, please. Aloud?"

He began hesitantly, "Signalboxes must be kept strictly private, and signalmen must not allow any unauthorized person to enter."

"You broke Rule 72 this morning."

"Now, Mr Ferneyhough. There's a lot of mischievous gossip buzzing around the station, and I . . ."

"I'm not interested in gossip, David. I'm concerned only with the safety of this railway. It's a junction here. You have to keep your wits about you. You know, any distraction could be dangerous."

"Yes, but . . . It's this way . . . Let me explain, in confidence. I . . ."

"Look, if you caused only a trivial irregularity, and an unauthorized person was in your box, you'd be in dead trouble. And so would I."

He answered a bell code on the telegraph instrument and pulled a lever for an empty wagon train. "I understand, sir. It won't happen again."

For the rest of my fortnight there, not another word of gossip did I hear, and everyone, including the pretty blonde porter, got on with their work. Even Mr Proctor's sour face threatened to crack into a smile. "Well, you seem to have done it," he conceded, "though I don't know how!"

It was some months later, in the refreshment rooms on Nottingham Midland station, that I met fellow relief stationmaster Pat Regan. We were great mates and enjoyed a good old chat about people and places we both knew.

"I was at Shirebrook last week," he told me as we drank coffee. "You remember that woman porter there? A real looker. Honeyblonde. She's been transferred up the line to Mansfield. It's nothing like so convenient for her, of course."

"Oh, why the move?"

"One of her close relations works at Shirebrook. As you know, the district office people frown on that. She hadn't let on at her interview for the job. And when they found out, they didn't like it at all. Hence the quick shift."

"This relation, who was she?"

"Not a she, a he. A signalman at the junction box. He's her brother."

Near tragedy struck one Saturday afternoon when I was in charge at Elmton on the Nottingham-Worksop line. A quieter station you could hardly imagine, though it sprang to life briefly at morning and early evening peak times, and on Saturdays for shoppers north-bound for Worksop and Retford, and south for Mansfield and Nottingham. Set in the coalfields, the station saw a steady flow of empty wagon trains into the nearby collieries, and loaded trains for various destinations. A line branched off to Chesterfield, giving passenger connections for Sheffield and the north. Elmton village consisted largely of miners' neat, modern houses.

On our Saturday afternoon 'down' train, which connected at Worksop for the north via the London & North Eastern Railway, I had reserved in advance a third-class compartment for a small party of RAF cadets and their officer. I greeted them on arrival and explained that I would see them to their reserved seats, their train being due soon.

But I never did.

At about the same time an 'up' train for Nottingham was almost due to arrive on the far platform opposite. In the absence of an overbridge, passengers crossed the line at either end of the platforms, where it had been made level to the rails with timbers, a common arrangement. In the booking office, Mrs Goddard, the woman porter, was issuing tickets to the passengers, and porter Bill Tomkins had gone across to the far platform to await the Nottingham train. By now the nearside platform was becoming quite crowded with waiting passengers.

First the Nottingham train steamed into the far platform, and while it was standing there, the train for the nearside platform was drawing near.

Suddenly into view came a young man, running wildly along the platform and pushing a large pram, turning and twisting his way to avoid colliding with other passengers. I knew at once that he was aiming to go over the timbered crossing, away on the left to the far platform for the waiting Nottingham train, before the other train approaching the near platform would come in and block his path to the far platform.

In his frenetic scramble, he misjudged and the pram tipped over the edge of the platform at a sharply oblique angle and hung there, right in the path of the oncoming train. Women screamed. Men shouted. I glimpsed a young woman nearby, panting and distressed and hitting the back of her hand on her forehead, thespian-like as in some Victorian melodrama. White with shock, the young man was squatting on his haunches, hanging on grimly to the pram handle. My first blind impulse was to dash to the pram and grab the baby. But the tiny mite was securely strapped in. The steaming locomotive was now only yards away, and I caught a vision of a wild-looking driver working frantically at his controls. I grabbed at the pram handle and threw my whole body backwards in a great, muscle-wracking heave, pulling the pram on top of me. That very instant, the locomotive struck the under-carriage of the pram and severed it from the bodywork. The baby screamed, but she was safe.

My uniform cap had rolled along the platform. Passengers helped me up and replaced my cap. The father of the baby was still squatting on his haunches as the train slowed past him. I helped him up, and his drawn face told of deep shock; someone took his arm and led him away. Scores of passengers still hung around the platform, talking anxiously. Finding enough breath to blow my whistle, I called out, "Join the train, *please*. We must get moving!" Doors opened and banged shut as people reluctantly climbed aboard. Then, another scream. A young woman by an open door was crying and holding her hand. It had been trapped in the door. On three fingers the skin was broken and blood flowed profusely. Her mother was binding it with a handkerchief and trying to console her. Heavens, what an afternoon!

"You'd better come to the office, my dear, and we'll bandage it up for you," I suggested. All stations kept a fully kitted first-aid box.

"Oh, no," the mother wailed adamantly. "We've just got to go on this train."

"As you wish, madam. I'll ask the guard to get his first-aid box ready at the next station."

Closing the carriage door carefully, I blew my whistle once more and raised my hand to the guard. He in turn waved his green flag to the driver. The train began to move with great surging noises and masses of steam, and a middle-aged man leaned from a carriage window, waved an arm and shouted, "You deserve a bloody medal, mate!"

From the far platform the Nottingham train had now departed and the station was silent once more. Against the office wall lay a very battered pram body, and nearby its twisted underframe and wheels. Everything had happened so quickly.

Glancing down the road, I watched a young woman, with a tiny baby clutched to her breast, walking slowly along, her husband's arm protectively round her shoulders, and I shuddered at what might have happened.

Motherly Mrs Goddard, the porter, came to me. "Come and sit down in the office, Mr Ferney, and I'll make you a strong cup of tea."

"Yes, please. I'd like that."

Walking with shaking legs, I found myself cold and trembling. My trousers were badly torn below the knee, and warm blood trickled down one leg and into my shoe. Porter Bill Tomkins put the kettle on the gas ring while Mrs Goddard washed and bandaged my leg and stitched a temporary repair of my trousers. That evening I was glad to get home to my wife and baby in Mansfield. My mind kept returning to the near tragedy as I thought about that poor engine driver. For an instant he must have suffered agonies. I never came across him again.

In the autumn a month or so later, I spent another week at Elmton, and on the Saturday the usual shoppers arrived for the early afternoon trains. After both had departed, a man in his late twenties came to the office. His face seemed familiar.

"You must think I'm terrible," he began.

"Oh, why, sir?"

"That Saturday afternoon in the summer. My baby . . ."

His voice broke and tears came. We gripped hands warmly.

"My wife's only just getting over it. And we didn't even say thank you!"

"Not to worry, my friend. I do understand."

He placed a small package on my desk and hurried away. After he had gone, I opened it. Fifty Players cigarettes. A kind thought. It seemed almost a pity that I had given up smoking three years earlier.

Being in charge of staff is not always easy on a working railway. One difficulty I met with was that of discouraging men from taking unnecessary risks. When you are a relief man, a flitting shadow, here today and there tomorrow, your reputation, whatever it is, follows you around. But personal popularity is immaterial when a life is at stake.

In Blidworth sidings in Nottinghamshire, a locomotive was shunting back and forth, under the hand signals of the goods guard who was assembling loaded wagons into a train. And what I saw I could scarcely believe. The young fireman stood on top of the tender, raking coal to the front, a routine task to save time when firing. But not on a moving engine! Each time the engine went under the footbridge, the fireman ducked. I had ghastly visions of him being struck by the bridge, knocked off the tender, crashing to the ground and cracking his skull. I would have to rush to the office for the first-aid box, tend his injuries, telephone for an ambulance, get him to the hospital and have the unhappy mission of telling his mother.

"Driver," I shouted above the noise of the engine. "That boy is taking an awful risk."

"Bugger off! We've got to get this train away. We're half an hour late already!"

This angered me. "You trying to kill your fireman?"

"He's used to this job. Nothing to it."

"Better to delay the train than run such a risk."

"You tell that to Nottingham Control. They're creating merry hell about the delay."

"Driver, there's absolutely no argument. I'm ordering you to stop. That boy is somebody's son. But I'll bet he's not yours!"

Swearing to himself, the driver called to his fireman to come down off the tender and back to the footplate. He then carried on with his shunting. From my experience, that driver's behaviour was exceptional. But I'll bet they did exactly the same risky routine the next day, and the next . . .

When deputizing for the yardmaster at Hasland marshalling yard, which served several collieries near Chesterfield, I saw a goods guard riding on his shunting pole which he had jammed in the underframe of a wagon; he was 'shunting out' his train. Some guards rode on their poles to save walking back and forth as the shunting processes went on. Certainly a little time could be saved, but the sight of it gave me the shivers.

When the guard was near enough, I thought that, instead of proselytizing, I would try shock tactics.

"Tell me, guard, where d'you live?"

He looked at me suspiciously. "Basford near Nottingham. Why?"

I produced pencil and notebook. "And your address?"

"Eh, what the bloody hell is this?"

"If you slip off that pole, and your foot goes under the wagon and gets cut off, I'll have to get a message to your missus smart!"

I thought he was going to punch me. "You lousy bugger! What you trying to do to me?"

"Why ride your pole? You know it's dangerous." It was also, of course, against the company's rules.

He growled. "You oughta see them shunters in Toton Yard. Them all do it. Else they'd never get through the work."

I stopped myself from saying something like: Indians travel on carriage roofs, but many get injured. "Look, guard, I can't turn a blind eye. When I worked in the accidents office at Derby HQ, we had reports every week about guards and shunters falling off their poles." He blew his whistle to signal the engine driver. "Nobody wants you to ride on your pole, only yourself. And who's going to say thank you for getting your train away on time if you lose a foot?"

He drew his hand across his mouth and muttered, "I s'pose you're right, Guv'nor. It's a daft thing to do."

He was smiling, so I pummelled his ribs. "I guess you're somebody's dad, eh?"

"Aye. Three of 'em. All young monkeys!"

While travelling around Nottinghamshire as a peripatetic station-master, living among engines and carriages and wagons, in signalboxes and marshalling yards, and enjoying the railway life, dreams about another career gave me no peace. I found my work so absorbing and varied that I felt an irresistible urge to write about it.

For years I had longed vaguely to become a writer but the odds seemed formidable. At the age of twelve I had sold *Evening Sentinel* newspapers on the streets of Hanley after school. I left school (elementary) at fourteen, then was a butcher's boy for two years before joining the LMS Railway. Some 350 boys and girls attended our village school on the edge of the town. Throughout, I was fortunate enough to be at or near the top of my class and spent the last two years there with a small group to study English, Latin roots, algebra, French and Pitman's shorthand. For the final year I was head boy. We respected our marvellous teachers, who worked us hard with a firm, but kind, discipline. Of the several school prizes I won, one was in a district competition for an essay entitled (as mentioned earlier) 'The Effect of Temperance on Character'. (Drunkenness was common then. Even railway stations had their share. Perhaps the authorities thought they would get at the dads through their lads and lassies.) For a decade I attended evening classes, read avidly, joined in debates, swotted in libraries, listened to learned lectures and helped to fill a corner in my academic vacuum. Before I was married, I spent short holidays in different countries in Europe and incidentally saw some impressive steam locomotives, express trains and magnificent stations, all excitingly very 'foreign'. Amateur attempts at writing from the age of thirty stimulated enormously my interest in railways, and I sought to learn more and more from my knowledgeable colleagues – in permanent-way work, signals, telecommunications, bridge and tunnel maintenance, locomotive maintenance, carriage and wagon servicing, timetabling – the list is endless.

After one year of tunnel-vision concentration and accumulating numerous bits of paper known as rejection slips, I began to sell my articles. Though in time I wrote articles on many non-railway subjects, most early efforts dealt with locomotives, station working, traffic controlling, work in a booking office and much about new rolling stock and equipment.

Railway managements forbade railway staff to give interviews to journalists or to write public articles concerning railway policy;

such work was the responsibility of the railway Press departments: in my view, rightly so. Too many minefields strew the
path for amateurs. Managements also required any railway staff
writing about railway subjects to submit a draft to their superior
officer (immediate boss). When a new circular was issued from
HQ, reiterating these instructions, my erstwhile chief in London
called me to his private office.

"I understand you write for the Press. You might care to study
this circular."

I read it. "I never send my articles to HQ for approval."

He blinked. "You realize that could bring you trouble?"

"Yes. I'd welcome that."

"Whatever for, Ferneyhough?"

"They might offer me a job in the Press department."

He laughed. "Making the tea? You're more likely to get the
bloody sack!"

But I took the subject more seriously than that. For example, I
was scrupulously careful in checking and re-checking facts, and I
avoided controversial subjects and was loyal to the company that
paid my wages.

Meantime, the ghastly war years had passed by, and people
everywhere wanted to start again with renewed hope and pur-
pose. When VE Day and VJ Day of 1945 brought the long agony to
an end, all the four railway companies worked desperately to get
back to normal. Steadily restaurant-car services resumed, sleeping-cars were re-instated and the famous travelling post offices
from London to Penzance and to Aberdeen went back to work.
Railway camping coaches (converted carriages), for family holidays at seaside and country sites, were seen again. It was good
news for many that some of the famous 'named' trains were to be
restored.

In a public statement the four main-line railway companies
jointly committed themselves to their immediate task: "They
were determined to regain and surpass their peacetime standards
of public service. Their intention is to equip their properties and
train their staffs so as to enable the finest railway service in the
world to be offered to the British public. That, in a nutshell, is
their post-war plan."

Other people had plans too. In the general election of 1945 the

British people rejected war-time leader Winston Churchill in favour of Clement Attlee, whose party political mandate had included nationalization of large sectors of British industry, including the railways.

Soon after, I received another modest promotion to district relief stationmaster based at Chesterfield, another new and promising territory.

# 12

# Dark Terror Strikes
# in the Tunnel

At one extreme, iron and steel works and collieries; at the other, the rolling hills of the Hope Valley leading to Manchester – that was my new territory. And a long tunnel under the Pennines offered its own challenge.

Finishing duty as yardmaster at Hasland marshalling yard around lunchtime one showery April Thursday, I needed a lift to Chesterfield station, several miles away, to get home. In the main-line signalbox I asked the signalman, "Anything Chesterfield way?"

"Yes, light engine just coming. It's tender first, so you'll get wet! I'll peg him at the down home board."

Plodding through heavy rain, I went along the track and saw an engine approaching. What a dirty old beauty! A Midland six-coupled goods with open-type driving-cab and not the best weather for tender-first running. It must have been 1910 vintage. And the whistle – its cracked old sound jerked me right back to boyhood days.

Climbing up to the footplate, I made myself known to the driver and fireman. Another engine crew followed me up the steps. Five on this tiny footplate was a crowd, and running tender first was rough. Rain drove in fiercely as we gained speed, and I gripped the brim of my brown felt trilby hat, new only a week ago. The enginemen passed rude remarks about this old tub – enough to make the dear old lady blush. Hissing steam burst out at every joint with arrogant prodigality, and just easy running strained her every rivet.

At the next signalbox, we stopped to pick up a bowler-hatted operating inspector, bringing our number up to six. He twitted us, "Didn't you see that circular about overcrowding footplates? We'll all be getting a Form One!" This was a disciplinary form that has given many a railwayman a sleepless night and a day's suspension.

On the skyline I could see Chesterfield's famous crooked church spire. The engine was now slowing down, and our driver said, "I'm stopping at yon end of the platform, chaps. Then you can nip off."

As we ran into the station, the inspector suddenly shouted, "Duck down, lads!"

He bent himself double, and some of us quickly followed suit. I knew he would have a good reason, and it was the presence, on the platform, of the district officer himself. I peered cautiously out of the cab doorway, and at that very second a mischievous gust of wind snatched at my hat and skimmed it with gay abandon into the steam-laden slipstream.

"Oh, blast!"

The others chuckled.

Walking to Chesterfield bus station for a bus home to Mansfield, driving rain soaked my hair and trickled icily down my back.

In the Hasland office the next morning, I answered my telephone. It was the district officer. "I believe you lost your hat yesterday."

A little apprehensively, I answered, "Yes, I did indeed, sir." I wondered how he knew it was mine.

"It's here in my office. I understand you're coming to Sheffield this afternoon. You can pick it up then."

It was a relief to know it had been found.

That afternoon his secretary duly ushered me into the inner sanctum, and the chief handed over my hat. He commented casually, "It seems to have been run over by a train!"

What a mess, my lovely brown trilby, battered and filthy with grease and rust. I laid it on a chair and sensed trouble.

"I really called you in to remind you about the circular from my office. Too many people riding on footplates."

Oh, so that was it. But how did he know?

"I understand, sir. Sorry about that."

"Quite! First, you have no loco pass. Second, six people on an engine is risky. And third, I expect my stationmasters to uphold official instructions. Not to flout them."

"I do take the point, sir."

As I moved towards the door, leaving my useless hat, he

grinned slyly. "Don't forget your hat. Good job your name was in it!"

The district officer had several district inspectors on his staff; they were about my own grade or a little higher. Though the inspectors wore bowler hats to show their authority, they did sometimes miss out on catching reckless staff bending the rules or taking unnecessary risks. If a bowler hat was seen strolling along the line, keen-eyed signalmen in their boxes or shunters in their bothies would telephone to warn their mates, "Bowler coming your way, Bill!" Presumably on the principle that you hang together or hang separately.

A district inspector, accompanied by his immediate chief, a young assistant district officer (still wet behind the ears) with a university degree, travelled by car to several signalboxes on a branch line. The young officer put a pet question about the operating rules, confident that each man would give him the wrong answer. Wisely the inspector, with dry ears, kept mum. The question was: "When one of two lines is blocked, as in a derailment, would you set up the single line working procedure immediately?" The first signalman said, "Yes." But the officer told him, "It's not necessary immediately if the next two or more trains on the route are travelling on the clear line in the right direction." At the next box, the signalman got the right answer, and at the next, and the next, and the next . . . The officer was surprised. But the inspector, who had once been a signalman, was not.

Years ago I thought inspectors' bowler hats were company issue. Not so. Braided peaked caps were issued but seldom worn – possibly because they were not sufficiently distinguished from the headgear of their subordinates. So there ought to be an accumulation of vintage braided peaked caps, untouched by human head, in attics up and down the country, which could earn a pound or two at the railway hobby shops.

On the second day of my two weeks' stint as stationmaster at Grindleford, I had a sudden urge to walk through the tunnel. At a little over three miles, burrowed beneath the Pennines, it is the second longest on Britain's railways (the longest is the Severn Tunnel which runs under the Bristol Channel for nearly 4½ miles). That challenging tunnel – Totley Tunnel, linking Grindleford and Dore & Totley stations, is some five miles from Sheffield on the Hope Valley line of forty-five miles to Manchester, one of the most scenic lines in England. Many of these attractive country stations had pretty gardens from spring to autumn.

In my tiny office, I had already talked with Bert Hopkins, the permanent-way ganger; he was responsible, with his two or three men, for the daily inspection and maintenance of the track in the tunnel.

"It be no job for a worrier, sir," he told me in his slow Derbyshire speech. "You has to keep your mind on your work. Them trains, they comes through that fast! And mek sure to get in them funkholes smart like."

"Oh, yes, the alcoves or recesses. You like the job in the tunnel?"

"Suits me. Done it for years. P-way Inspector, he goes through regular. And betimes we has the officers' inspection train with our chief engineering man."

Short tunnels I had walked through often enough. But nothing like this one. I told Bert Hopkins, also the signalman and the booking clerk, of my intention and that I would return from Dore by train.

Bert warned, "Take care, sir. And don't hurry."

Soon after ten I lit an oil handlamp and set off. Within a few minutes I had stepped out of the blazing June sunshine into the diabolic depths beneath the green hills. The lamp illuminated my path only a few yards ahead in the 'cess' on the right-hand side of the double track, facing oncoming traffic. Allowing for a steady pace and taking refuge in the recesses while any trains passed, I estimated my walk would take about an hour and a half. When my eyes had adjusted to the darkness, I walked with more confidence. On my face, the air was cool. The dank smell of the tunnel was tinged with the odour from my oil-lamp and the remnants of sulphury smoke from a recent train. My footsteps echoed eerily in the mysterious depths. Occasionally I kicked a stone which clattered like a great fall of rock.

Now that I had lost the faint light from the tunnel entrance, a feeling of loneliness depressed me and stimulated my imagination. In this alien ambience I felt vulnerable. Perhaps a large lump of coal would fall off a tender, strike me on the head and knock me cold. I could even be scalded to death by a furiously steaming engine or have my clothes set alight by sparks from the chimney. Supposing I tripped and struck my head on the rail? I could easily be decapitated by a passing express. How I wished I had never worked in the accident office at Derby HQ. And I really must stop reading those official reports about railway disasters.

In the dark silence I asked myself - why the hell do such a stupid thing in the first place? Experience. Experience? What good will it do you? If something goes wrong, how will you explain to your masters your unnecessary presence in the second longest tunnel in Britain? Yet in my job I had to become familiar with everything on the section of line that happened to be under my temporary jurisdiction. I was expected to cope immediately with any kind of emergency. Oh, yes. That's my alibi. I needed to know this tunnel, man to man.

On rare occasions in history, terrible disasters had happened in railway tunnels. I could only hope that on this particular day, in this particular tunnel, no history would be made.

I glanced up at the two bare wires running alongside the tunnel wall, which had a matching pair on the other side. Even without leaving his engine, a driver on a train in trouble had only to make the two wires touch, and he knew that the signalmen in the boxes at each end of the tunnel, where danger warnings would be given in sound and vision, would slam their signals to danger. In no time at all emergency services would be set in motion.

As I strode steadily along, my mind ranged over the relevant rules that would do their best to protect me. Rule 11 – employees whose duties compel them to be on the lines of railway must, when possible, face the traffic. Reckless exposure of himself to danger is an offence . . . and he will be punished accordingly (if recklessness brought his death, wasn't that punishment enough?). Rule 15 – employees are expressly prohibited from walking upon the line unless they are required to do so in the execution of their duty. Yes, my case for being in the tunnel seemed less flimsy but more risky.

Rule 126 – the driver and fireman must see that coal on the engine is not stacked too high and that the coal, fire-irons and tools are so placed that they will not fall off when the engine is in motion. When passing through a tunnel, they must refrain from throwing out fire or cinders, also hot water, *as far as practicable* (Ouch!).

Rule 127 – the driver must sound his engine whistle when entering and emerging from tunnels and frequently when passing through long tunnels. I could only hope that any enginemen sharing the tunnel with me this morning would be well up in their rules and realize that this tunnel came in the category of 'long'.

But supposing, I thought, that two trains passed me at precisely the same moment? Not to worry. Rule 234 tells me what to do: men passing through or working in a tunnel when trains are approaching in both directions must, if unable to reach any recess in the walls, lie down either in the space between the two running lines (gosh, that would be an 'experience'!) or between the line and the side of the tunnel until the trains have passed. The width of the space, continues this Rule, depends upon the construction of the tunnel, with which every man must make himself acquainted, in order that he may select the place which affords the greatest safety. I reflected that not many railway rules actually instruct you to lie down on the job; most tell you to get up and go.

You know, if people like Stephenson and Brunel had not invented such things as tunnels, I would not now be enjoying this self-inflicted misery like a true masochist. Yet I consoled myself with the happy thought that this unique experience would be marvellous – in retrospect.

Because of roof leaks, it was a wet and muddy tunnel. That day I happened to be wearing my newest uniform suit, complete with brass buttons, clean blue shirt, maroon tie and gold-braided peaked cap. So I did not at all fancy being forced to lie down in the tunnel mud just for a train. At one point a stream of cold and dirty water quite thoughtlessly showered icily down my neck, just by way of introduction and to show that a railway tunnel is no respecter of persons.

Suddenly a nerve-shattering shock stopped me in my tracks

and set me trembling. With a thunderous noise, a train had whooshed into the tunnel behind me. Displaced air rushed past like a furious hurricane. The piercing whistle of the engine shrieked like ten thousand agonized devils in a Wagner opera, leaving my agitated nerve-ends fluttering. I had never known a fear quite like this. I shook all over till every muscle in my body quivered. I scrambled to an alcove and waited. Louder and louder swelled that deafening noise. The whistle sounded frequently. The title of a Dorothy Sayers novel – *The Nine Tailors* – rushed horribly into my mind, in which the victim, imprisoned in a church tower belfry, was killed by the overwhelming sound of the ringing bells.

That train. Never before had I realized the terrifying impact a powerful goods engine hauling a train of wagons could make in the reverberating confines of a long tunnel. The walls seemed to scoop up the imprisoned roar of the train and fling it at my head with deafening enormity.

As the engine roared past in an ear-splitting crescendo, a quick flash of intense heat scorched across my face. Again the engine whistle screamed. Clang-clang-clang shouted the passing wagons, their wheels squealing on the metals. Finally the brakevan with its red tail-lights passed, then faded into the distance, leaving a deathly, ghostly silence broken only by the drip-drip-drip from the roof and my own disturbing heart-beats.

After the peak of semi-delirium came an odd feeling of exhilaration. I had shared a tunnel with a raving monster and survived. I continued walking, my swinging handlamp picking out ghoulish shapes from the earth's strata on the tunnel walls, my lungs coughing painfully from the acrid stench of the sulphur from the engine chimney which still hung heavily in the air.

Expected soon was the mid-morning local passenger train from Sheffield to Manchester Central. A distant whistle warned of its approach, then a whoosh of air, followed by a roar that increased in volume every second. Into the safety of an alcove I scuttled, like a rabbit to its burrow with a terrier close on its tail. As the lighted train flew by, the roaring reached a spine-shivering, ear-popping climax. Then I heard a loud explosion like a bomb, followed by the sound of smashing glass. When everything was quiet again, I sought the cause. Some thoughtless person had thrown an empty beer bottle through the carriage window. One supposes it seldom occurs to passengers that railwaymen are working there to keep the hidden track safe for their journeys deep under the hills.

Plodding along, I became aware of a tiny spot of daylight at the end of the tunnel, a thrilling moment and a reminder that, after all, the real world was still going on out there and that maybe the tunnel roof would not cave in. Then a horrible thought sprang to mind: instead of a spot of daylight, it could be the headlamp of a mighty express hurtling inexorably towards me. It is strange but down there, deep under the Pennines, enveloped in mother earth, the overwhelming concept of 'tunnel' seemed to disorientate my thinking processes and inflame my imagination. I thought of all those navvies of the last century who had hewn out these great rabbit holes for humans to plunge through at incredible speeds; those men, working with pick and shovel by tallow light, some to their death, had far more than I to be frightened of; how many screams of mortal terror had echoed to these walls before daylight was seen at each end of the tunnel?

At last, the relief! I was blinking to dazzling daylight and enjoying the short walk from the tunnel mouth to Dore & Totley station. The stationmaster saw me to the local train, and he asked, "Did you enjoy it in there?"

"Not really! Have you walked through?"

He deflated me with his reply. "Oh, yes, quite a few times. Good-day!"

Back through the tunnel to Grindleford we steamed, a twelve-minute run in the comfort of an upholstered, electrically lit carriage.

On the platform at Grindleford I was greeted by the grinning young booking clerk and the middle-aged porter. The porter said, "Anybody would know where you been, sir!"

Back in my little office, the mirror told me why. I was filthy.

Late in the afternoon Bert Hopkins arrived. His pallid face bore deep lines, and I guessed he was nearing retirement. But he looked contented enough, puffing at a short clay pipe.

"The SM at Dore said he'd walked through the tunnel a number of times."

"Never! He were pulling your leg. He wouldna go in there to save his life. I knows him." He tapped his pipe out in my empty iron fireplace. "This morning," he said, "we went afore you. And we came out after you, about three o'clock."

"Everything all right in there?"

"Pretty good, sir. Just a few loose keys as usual and a slack chair. It's good track in yonder. Enjoy going through?"

"Well, now, Bert. It was an experience! I don't know how you fellows do it."

"When I landed that job fifteen year ago, I had nightmares for a month. The first time a train went through and me there, I nearly died o' fright. Hard to explain. And I'd got this fear of closed-in places . . ."

"Claustrophobia?"

"Summat like that. I didna tell nobody, only the missus. Or I wouldna got this job, see?"

"As you said, Bert, no job for a worrier!"

"Aye. Suit me alright, sir. Tell you what, though. That tunnel. She be warm in winter and cool in summer. That she be."

Just before the bank holiday, I was required to assist in the enquiry office at Derby. A girl clerk and I at the counter, armed with a pile of timetables and masses of holiday leaflets, faced the verbal bombardment of the travelling public: What's the return fare from Leicester to Lancaster? What time for the boat from Holyhead to connect with the Irish Mail? Is there a dining-car on the afternoon train to London? Can I send my luggage in advance to Jersey? Are there any tunnels on the line to Crewe – they frighten my mother? What's the best train to Hereford in the morning and where do I change? Do I need a ticket for my cat? What's the best way to Scotland? Are there any trains in Ireland? What happens if you pull the communication cord? Can I go engine spotting on platform two? An elderly lady for Scarborough changing at York asked for the arrival and departure platform numbers at York. We did not have such information, and she was such a dear old thing I could not have teased her with 'The driver's name is Tom Cobley, and he's married with three children.'

Sometimes the small office was full of enquirers, and in between helping them the strident telephone would ring commandingly. It is a wonderful instrument for jumping the queue.

His pencil poised, a businessman asked for a morning service, somewhat complicated, from Belper to Baschurch. Immediately I ripped off – "Leave Belper 9.50, arrive Derby 10.6. Leave Derby at 10.22 and arrive Birmingham New Street at 11.22. Walk or take a taxi nearly half a mile to the Great Western station at Snow Hill, and depart 11.56, arriving Shrewsbury 1.04 p.m. Leave Shrewsbury at 1.40 and arrive Baschurch at two o'clock."

You should have seen the fellow's face, and for a moment I basked in the warm glow of his unstinted admiration. Finishing his notes, he grinned appreciatively. "Marvellous! You must know every train in the timetable, young man. Here, have a cigar."

"Thanks."

"How long have you worked here?"

"Three days."

"Incredible!"

I leaned forward confidentially. "It's absolutely easy, sir. Nothing to it."

"There must be a secret. What is it?"

"Fifteen minutes ago I worked out a service for a lady from Belper to Rednal, five miles beyond Baschurch. I'll have forgotten it by tomorrow."

He seemed really disappointed, then smiled, "Wish you hadn't told me. It's spoilt the illusion!"

Next came a short spell in Derby booking office. Booking offices were very private. A passenger could peek in only through the ticket window when the wooden slide door was raised. He might see railway ticket racks and dusty shelves of record books. When no trains were due, we would pull down these slide doors, and passengers could not see what we were up to. You could drink tea, eat a bacon sandwich or a chunk of fruit cake and put your feet on the desk, unless, of course, the chief clerk or the stationmaster was around. Then there was always a bit of horseplay, or flirting with the lady clerk.

Between train times we made up our books, recorded tickets

issued, counted the money and any free travel vouchers, hoping that the one (debit) would match the other (credit). A 'float' was kept for giving change. Any cash shortage was recorded in the 'loss' column, and any over in the 'surplus' column. We were not required to pay in any loss or pocket any surplus. But your reputation was at stake. A good booking clerk could balance nearly every time, unless some smart passenger had slipped him an Irish shilling or a French franc in the rush.

One afternoon Yorkshireman Claud Greeves, the middle-aged clerk on the Matlock and Manchester window, was angry. And every few minutes he grew angrier. A gentle draught from the booking hall, which happened when the wind was in a certain direction, blew through the booking-office window and wafted passengers' one-pound and ten-shilling notes onto the office floor.

A passenger would say, "Return to Buxton, please," and put a pound note down on the counter. Then, he would exclaim, "Oh, it's gone!"

Claud would stoop down, pick up the note from near his feet, place it firmly back again under a paperweight by the window and say, in a controlled tone through clenched teeth, "Hold tha note, mister!"

Next a lady would ask, "Single Matlock, please," put down her 10 shilling note, watch it flutter out of her sight and giggle, "Whoops, it's vanished!"

A few more like this and Claud was going up the wall. Meanwhile his queue was still growing. I sat at a table behind him doing my books and felt sorry for him. I watched for floating notes that flew to the floor and picked them up for him. His usually pale neck at the back was turning as red as an engine furnace. Any minute now, I thought, he would explode.

His last passenger was now booked, and through the window I could see the Matlock and Manchester train just leaving, hauled by a Stanier 4-6-0 'Jubilee'-class locomotive. Claud slammed his window down so fiercely that it made Arthur Macdonald at the next window jump in surprise.

On Claud's counter was a large cash bowl overflowing with piles of paper money from his takings. He began to sing in a high-pitched tenor, to the tune of 'On Ilka Moor ba'at 'at': "Oh hold your note, your note. Oh hold your note, your note. Oh la-dy, hold your note!" He laughed recklessly, grabbed two fistfuls of notes and flung them over his head. As they fluttered to the floor, he sang his ditty again, and we all three fell about laughing like a bunch of louts. Recovering our breath, we carefully picked up the money and placed it in Claud's cash bowl.

"Thanks, chaps. I'd got to sing, or go mad!"

Half an hour later he had completed his books and found he was a shilling to the good.

As in most other businesses, imponderables abound in the railways. How many extra trains should be run on bank holidays; where should trains start and finish; how many carriages on each train, and what proportion should be first class. (And the passenger department is only one of many.) Holiday business can be influenced enormously by the weather alone. Somebody has to make the decisions. No one has yet devised a magic formula, and the LMS employed no magicians.

Rough estimates had to be used, based on previous years' records, coupled with the long experience and judgement of management officials, leavened by local events, plus that mystical something called flair. Then there was that cunning device – which could bring wanton waste or piles of profit – known to us railwaymen as 'Q' trains; these were 'standby specials', complete with trainmen, carriages and engines, already alight and loaded with coal and water. If unexpected crowds surged to the station, quick co-ordinated action by stationmaster, station inspector, passenger manager and traffic control would throw that 'Q' train into the traffic stream in no time. Yet, with all the techniques, you could still end up with some empty trains and others bulging at the doors with gasping passengers.

My interest in all this came about by another modest promotion – from district relief stationmaster based at Chesterfield to area passenger salesman located in the district passenger manager's office at Sheffield. Drumming up new business, mainly parties, was my main task, in Sheffield and in the Hope Valley. Occasionally I had to lend a hand on a special project.

And that is how I came to be counting passengers on Sheffield station on a wet Easter Saturday. Mr Larry Cooper, our passenger chief, handed me lists of the north-to-south trains, regular and special, that would call at Sheffield. My able and friendly colleague, Harry Jacobs, was to take the south-to-north trains. This job was new to me, and Harry gave me useful wrinkles, the most important being how and where to snatch that hurried snack and steaming hot tea. Our job was to do a head-count of passengers in the trains, and Harry showed me how to arrange the forms on my clipboard.

Sadly for holiday-makers, it was both wet and blustery. Violent gusts of wind scudded engine steam and smoke and swept through the old Midland station like a miniature hurricane, flinging random litter high in the iron roof and mischievously removing the occasional hat.

The job itself was a slog. Up and down the platforms among scurrying passengers, over the footbridge and back, clutching my clipboard and forms against the persistent wind, peering through train windows and frantically trying to count separately first- and third-class passengers while each train remained briefly in the station. It was complicated by passengers getting both on and off the trains. Also required on my records were estimates of children travelling, the proportion of first- and third-class accommodation on each train, and its actual – as distinct from its booked – time of departure. Surely there was a better system than this!

Between times I managed a sustaining cup of tea and snack from the station refreshment rooms. Adding to the miseries of aching legs and feet, driving rain at the ends of the platforms just beyond the protective awnings had steadily soaked me through to the skin. Throughout the day some splendid engines had come through the station, especially on the long-distance expresses to the far West Country, but I did not find time to enjoy a single one. Soon now my colleague Clive Keane would take over from me.

About four o'clock, in came the last train on my shift; then I would take my records back to Mr Cooper in our office near the station. This train was from Newcastle and would steam off to call at Derby, Birmingham, Gloucester and Bristol, with connections down to Paignton. Who would want to go to Devon in weather like this? (You could get just as wet in Sheffield.) Many, it seemed, for the train was jam-packed.

It stood in the platform several minutes before departure, giving me comfortable time to do the counting and to complete my forms. Noisily the engine was blowing off steam, all fired up and roaring to go. I could see the driver, head inclined against wind and rain, awaiting the starting-signal from the guard. Whistles blew. The green flag was waved. And the great train vibrated the ground under you in its thrusting energies to start. Standing at the front end, I watched the old Midland three-cylinder compound 4-4-0 flex her iron muscles and turn those gigantic seven-foot driving-wheels.

A young man charged down the overbridge steps to catch this train. Instead, he caught me. I toppled base over apex like a circus performing clown. Clipboard and record forms came loose, and all my precious papers flew in fancy-free abandon upon the blustering breeze. They danced and floated along the platform like fairy nymphs in a Tchaikovsky ballet, away down the line and into limbo. Not wishing to miss such frolicking fun, my trilby hat joined in the chase.

Somewhat dazed, I picked myself up. The scurrying passenger had dived into a moving carriage and slammed the door behind him. He did not even say goodbye. Two schoolgirls, pigtailed and straw-hatted, stood nearby, holding their hats against the wind with one hand and stifling their giggles with the other. Frustrated and furious, I brushed myself down. Then came a ray of kindness. A middle-aged lady wearing pink approached. She had retrieved a handful of my forms, and my sagging faith in human nature was revived.

Delighted, she said, "I saw it all, young man. And I just managed to rescue these for you."

"Thank you, lady. I really am most grateful."

A porter had saved my hat, so I was able to raise it to her in the style to which she was no doubt accustomed. Smiling, I took the forms she had handed me, and as she walked away I looked down at them. They were all blanks. You could have knocked me down with a paperclip. It is too boring to repeat what my chief, Mr Cooper, said to me in his private office that afternoon. But during my remaining time with him at Sheffield he never assigned to me a similar project again.

# 13

# £50-Worth of BR for Each One of Us

That telephone call froze my blood. It was at Heeley station, near Sheffield, where I was deputizing as stationmaster, when Mr Ernest Wright, staff superintendent at Euston HQ, rang.

"Ferneyhough, I understand you write for the Press."

A call from on high about my writing activities had been a constant anxiety. What awful gaffe had I committed in print that such a big man should phone me direct? I answered his call in a strong, confident voice. Might as well go down fighting.

His invitation was breathtaking. "Will you come to London and write a textbook for me?" He did not mention the subject. But who cares! It's writing about railways.

"Nothing I'd like better, sir. When can I start?"

"We'll see. I've read your articles about locomotives and titled trains. Now, you know the passenger station business quite well. I want a teaching volume about booking and parcels office clerical work and accounts."

"I understand, sir."

"We've never had one before. And I'd like it written in a popular and readable style. Does it appeal?"

"Very much, Mr Wright. Soon as you wish."

"That's good. I'll arrange for you to see me next week."

Even he had to go through the proper channels, via my district officer.

Within weeks, off I moved to London and slogged hard in Room 173, St Pancras Chambers, that massive architectural pile of extravagant Victoriana that fronts St Pancras station. In just over a year the textbook (anonymous) was in use. With it went a long-established two-year lecture course which I revised, and a new correspondence course which I also wrote: all leading to official internal examinations and graded certificates of merit. The whole training package was designed mainly for young clerks and adults seeking promotion to senior clerk, stationmaster or other supervisory post. Regularly brought up to date by others, the textbook was in use in the railway education department for well over twenty years, when the system was changed.

By the time I had written a fresh correspondence course for the second year, the railways had been nationalized. The 'appointed day' was 1st January 1948. Most of us in the railways wondered anxiously what would happen. Nothing did, at least not immediately of any significance. The trains still ran. Locomotives still chuffed, and ticket collectors clipped the tickets. Changes could come only slowly, and the immediate impact was sure to be far greater in the management structure than at stations, depots and works.

In theory, the people of Britain now owned the railways, but they still had to pay fares. I divided the statutory capital value by the total population and found that every man, woman and child owned a bit of railway to the value of £50. That would have been worth a couple of timber sleepers, half a wheel or a gross of peas for guards' whistles. Though all of us owned it, none of us could sell it. Such absurdities offered rich literary and verbal sustenance to the polemical.

Some experience of State control had been evident during the two World Wars when the railways had been 'taken over', and this paved the way for the Transport Act of 1947. A large proportion of the inland transport services came into public ownership.

Take the railways. Just imagine the complexities of welding four powerful and individual railway companies into one national, unified system! Apart from creating new management structures right down the line, there was the formidable task of communication among the large numbers of staff. What about the old loyalties? Of all the four railway companies, loyalty was undoubtedly the strongest in the old Great Western Railway: a family business if ever there was one. It was alone in the amalgamations of 1923 in retaining its famous and historical name (listen to me, an old LMS man!) from the company's inception in 1833. But on 1st January 1948 this much-loved line, which has been aptly described as "the fine old English gentleman of Britain's Victorian Railways", was, after 115 glorious years, redesignated 'Western Region'. Brunel and Gooch must have shuffled uneasily in their resting-places.

'British Transport Commission' (BTC), basically a policy-making body, was the name of the organization heading the several nationalized transport undertakings. The board managing the railways for the BTC was termed the 'Railway Executive'; its chairman, Sir Eustace Missenden, was formerly general manager of the Southern Railway. Missenden had begun his distinguished career as a clerk on the old South Eastern Railway. Though few clerks rose to such dizzy heights, to my personal knowledge a good number of clerks, station porters, engine cleaners and works apprentices progressed to quite good positions in railway management. You did not have to be somebody's blue-eyed boy, a privileged apprentice, a management trainee or a nephew of a high-up at HQ, though these things helped sometimes.

While still working in St Pancras Chambers, I was one day handed by the head of the textbook section a staff newspaper, *Transport News*. "This is just up your street," was his comment. Its eight pages were loud and vigorous, in the *Daily Mirror* mode. It was a popular version of the BTC's first annual report, the 'heavy' version having been presented to Mr Alfred Barnes, the Minister of Transport. This was September 1949. The front page invited readers to comment. I fell for it. My written comments were under two headings: 'brickbats' and 'bouquets'. My rather harsh criticisms could hardly have pleased the editor. My letter ended with a brief biographical note, and I named a few of the publications (there were over fifty by that time) to which I had contributed: *Life & Letters Today, London Opinion, Railway Gazette, Good Housekeeping, Sunday Chronicle, Daily Mirror*, the textbook and a book about railways of the world.

By return, from the editor came a two-line, cautiously casual letter: When you are passing this way, please call and see me. I did, having first sent him a selection of my published work. 'The editor' turned out to be the very distinguished and highly qualified chief publicity officer for the BTC, with a large, thickly carpeted private office and a huge desk to prove it. This was high up in 55 Broadway, HQ of London Transport in Westminster. On his desk were lots of important-looking files and an exquisite calendar – one that you turn up daily to the date and day – in beautifully grained oak. It all made me feel very remote from steaming locomotives and bustling stations and sleepy branch lines. Yet I supposed there was a connection – somewhere. Given time, I would find it.

On my second interview with him, he appointed me to a temporary position as a writer "for a few months to see if you like it". So off to London I did go.

In my new job of writing mainly for staff publications, I confess to suffering some sleepless nights. At times it all seemed a little beyond me, and I felt I might have to pull out of what was a marvellous opportunity: being well paid for my two hobbies – railways and writing.

I was trying to write short articles to briefs I received from higher up. But they were not right for print, and nobody was satisfied. Most disconcerting. After a few weeks of travel and interviewing people, I suddenly decided that I would write what, in my own judgement, was the sort of thing we ought to be propagating. It worked, and my confidence leapt to a new plateau and stayed there.

But I could not be finally appointed yet, if at all. Under State ownership, such positions at management level (a low rung, mark you) had to be advertised internally throughout the entire inland transport network – railways, road transport, London Transport, provincial and Scottish buses, hotels, docks and inland waterways. Unbelievably, 247 people applied. Imagine my joy when, after the interviews had been held, that coveted letter of appointment arrived: six months after my temporary appointment. The suspense was over. A private office, handsome rise in pay, management status, first-class travel and aged thirty-nine.

Christian Barman, the chief publicity officer, my chief, was, I found, a man of many talents. Author of books, he had edited 'quality' magazines, was a BBC broadcaster on the arts, held four professional qualifications, had worked in the USA, had been an adviser to the government and had held top publicity appointments with the former Great Western Railway and the London Transport Board. He held membership in distinguished London clubs and had a sizeable entry in *Who's Who*. He had written much about railways, particularly station architecture and passenger amenity. No wonder a cloud of provincial inferiority descended on me in his presence! Yet he was modest about his accomplishments. Civilized and courteous, he delighted people with his subtle wit. For example, when he received an internal memo dated 1st April with some misconceptions, from the head of a department who was a little bumptious, his reply began, "Thank you for your memo written on April Fool's day . . ."

He was a dapper man, short and thick-set, and was popular and well-liked by everybody. How fortunate for me to work for such a master. From him I learnt much about writing and literature and acquired new insight into the skill and art of dealing with people of all kinds. As a writer I had to interview people of every level in many parts of Britain.

In this post I had access to board minutes, internal files, departmental reports and many other documents and sources which I scoured for 'story leads'. Travel took me all over England, Scotland and Wales, and I was fortunate to ride on many crack expresses and inspect closely some of our finest steam locomotives, which might otherwise not have been possible. For my work I selected most of my own story leads, chose my own places to visit and was able to interview top managements or the lowest grades in any of the BTC undertakings. It was a freedom and independence I treasured, but it had to be earned continuously by producing the required written material. Above all it gave me an intimate knowledge of management thinking and policies. I found my way around, under and through this monolithic bureaucracy, enjoyed its ambient complexity and on the whole enjoyed the people I met. And fortunately I could always find far more material than we could ever hope to print.

Of the many draft typescripts I placed on Christian Barman's desk for approval, few were criticized. Much must have been mediocre dross, but he concentrated on the parts he thought good. Because of his encouragement, I worked twice as hard for him as I would have done for a carping critic. In his small team he built up strong loyalties, so effective for creative work. If one of us produced something worthy of notice, he passed the credit from above to the individual; and if any committed an embarrassing or costly error, he would go into it fully with the chap concerned but carry the blame himself.

Once settled in London, I chose St Albans for my home and decided it was a wonderful place in which to put down roots and bring up our children. In time we were to become so involved in the local community that to leave it was unthinkable, promotion or not. Also, by a fluke my wife and I were to start a retail office-equipment business there, employing four or five people and selling out after twenty years.

Now back to the railways. Dramatic changes were taking place as unification progressed. Geographically there were now six regions, each with its own management structure.

Take just one aspect of unification – locomotives. Forget about Gresley; don't worry about Bulleid or Stanier or Collett. Standardization – that was the new word in locomotives, and many other things as well. It's cheaper, more efficient. Who can argue against that! Hats off to them, the new team created a beauty in the great steam tradition. But first there had to be a top man, and as a member of the Railway Executive (the board), he was right at the top, the great R. A. Riddles himself. In an earlier book of mine, my biographical entry noted his birth year, 1892. (I was to be with him at a London railway function in 1981, and he made a lively speech, with the media in liberal attendance.)

Under Riddles' guidance, a locomotive standards committee was formed. (A satirist once claimed that a camel was a horse designed by a committee.) Eight prototype principles for building new steam locomotives were established; they were mainly old faithfuls, well proven in the locomotive world, but refined and embracing the best practices also from private enterprise:

1) maximum steam-raising capacity
2) simplicity, the least number of working parts all readily available
3) each new class to handle a wide variety of mixed traffic
4) high standard of bearings
5) simplified shed preparation, by wide use of mechanical lubricators and grease lubrication
6) more rapid disposal, self-cleaning smoke-boxes, rocking grates, self-emptying ashpans
7) high factors of adhesion to minimize wheel-slipping
8) high thermal efficiency, through large grate areas, high degree of superheating, long-lap valve gear

At first six new standard classes were undertaken and four

others planned. It was difficult for those people not closely involved with the steam-locomotive business to visualize the enormity of the task. For example, Riddles was saddled with a legacy of about four hundred types of steam locomotive. Some were thirty to forty years old, themselves legacies from the old railway companies of pre-1923 vintage: Midland, London & North Western, North Eastern, Caledonian, South Eastern, North Staffordshire, Furness and scores more, famous names steadily fading from living memory.

For me, as a writing man, all this made wonderful writing 'copy' and kept me abreast of what was going on.

With the Railway Executive firmly behind him, Riddles planned his building programme from 1951 as follows:

| type or class | wheel arrangement | axle load in tons |
|---|---|---|
| 7 | 4-6-2 | $20\frac{1}{4}$ |
| 6 | 4-6-2 | $18\frac{1}{2}$ |
| 5 | 4-6-0 | 19 |
| 4 | 4-6-0 | 17 |
| 4 | 2-6-4T | 18 |
| 3 | 2-6-2T | $16\frac{1}{4}$ |

The four additional types to be introduced, in later years as required, were:

| | | |
|---|---|---|
| 4 | 2-6-0 | $16\frac{3}{4}$ |
| 3 | 2-6-0 | 16 |
| 2 | 2-6-0 | 16 |
| 2 | 2-6-2T | 13 |

Even the tank engines, which do not have fuel tenders, were to be 'mixed-traffic' types, along with others, for hauling both passenger trains and goods or freight; this would make for greater versatility in daily operation. Improved wagons would enable freight trains to run at higher average speeds and would be able to share main lines with express passenger trains with less interference. I can assure you from my Bletchley train control experience what a help this would be.

In January 1951 the very first British Railways standard locomotive was ready to steam, and it went into service on the 30th. Named appropriately 'Britannia', it was a 'Pacific'-type 4-6-2 wheel arrangement, with 6-feet 2-inch drivers and a boiler pressure of 250 pounds. I had to write a piece about it from one of the BTC publications and saw Alfred Barnes, the Minister of Transport, name it at a ceremony in London. Numbered 70000, it hauled mainly express passenger and fast freight trains serving East Anglia. Fifty-five of the class were built at Crewe.

These new standard types were to become the workhorses and were to see the nationalized railways through to further stages of development. Apart from the versatility, such routine work as servicing, maintaining and overhauling would be much simplified. Many old engines had to be scrapped. After the war much of the railway system was clapped out and needed renewing anyway.

As with locomotives, the numerous types of carriages just had to be ruthlessly reduced. Riddles and his team settled for twelve different body styles for corridor trains, from the countless types still around:

third-class corridor
third-class corridor brake
first-class corridor
composite corridor (first and third)
composite corridor brake
third-class open, fixed seating
third-class open, loose seating (movable chairs)
first-class open, fixed seating
first-class open, loose seating
kitchen car
restaurant car with kitchen and loose seating
passenger train brakevan

Down the line, 'composite' is seldom heard: only 'compo', one of the thousands of terms that were bound to bewilder the trepid newcomer.

Riddles also devised a massive programme for wagons. Various departments were busy re-organizing signalling, telecommunications, permanent way, structures and a massive range of administration to match. What a lot there was to write about! Yet I really missed the homely chaps at the local stations and engine sheds and marshalling yards, the friendly passengers and traders and, above all, the passenger and goods trains steaming in and out of your station or yard every day; you felt you were part of the real railway. I could only hope that my writing would interest people about what was happening on the railways under new ownership.

Travelling around in search of 'stories' brought its own fun. On Leeds City station one morning I stood chatting with the assistant stationmaster, Harry Bostock, who had worked with me at Hanley station in teenage days, when a train from York came in and would soon depart for Swansea. When porters were busy unloading the guard's van, a crate of large live lobsters fell off a platform barrow. The crate door burst open, and soon the monster creepy-crawlers, vicious claws threatening, scrambled randomly along the platform. Some went down to the track under the train. Frenetic porters made chase, reluctant to handle them. Anxious to get the train away, Harry ordered, "Never mind the lobsters. Shut those doors and let's be moving!"

Doors banged, whistles sounded, steam hissed and the train was about to move. Just then a young woman screamed and, grabbing at her skirts, jumped onto a platform seat. A lobster had climbed onto her suitcase, and she perhaps felt that her legs were vulnerable. A passenger shunter, who wore thick protective gloves for his work, gave a hand, and it took fifteen minutes to get the truants back into their crate after their brief encounter on the busy station.

In the afternoon I travelled back to London in a reserved compartment with a VIP party that included W. P. (Bill) Allen. A former locomotive driver who rose to general secretary of the railway drivers' union, Allen was a member of the Railway Executive board, responsible for personnel matters. His pale face was adorned by a waxed moustache. This likeable and popular character, with steam deep in his veins, hob-nobbed with distinguished fellow board members, including V. Barrington-Ward, Robert Riddles, General Sir William Slim and General Sir G. Daril Watson. They must have learnt a little more about locomotives

The 'Centenary Express': 6000 'King George V' leaves Hereford on 15th September 1975, for one of several journeys with vintage vehicles to mark a century of dining cars.

A wintry dawn: a steam-train at Taplow.

The Glasgow portion of the 'Royal Scot' climbing to Beattock in 1928.
The 'Royal Scot's locomotive is a 4−6−0 no.6113 'Cameronian'.

Above: The 'Mayflower' near Teignmouth on the Plymouth—
London line, in 1959. The train carried the name from 1955 to 1965,
when many names faded from view. Below: British Rail's 'last steam
train' storms out of Liverpool's Lime Street station on Sunday 11th
August 1968, to make way for the diesels and electrics.

Top: Built in 1838, 'Lion' is the only surviving original working loco of the L&MR resident at the Merseyside County Museum. Above: The 'Cornwall', no.3020, built (and now preserved) at Crewe in 1847 for the L&NWR. Below: GWR's 'King Edward VII' 4−6−0 no.6001.

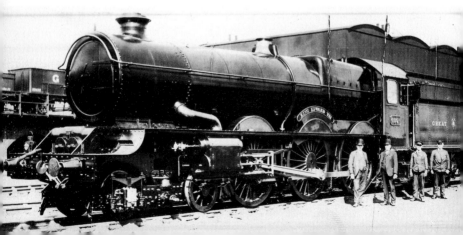

Top: The Midland 1000, built in 1902 and worked until 1951. Above: The LMS 'City of London', a class 8P 4−6−2 'Pacific'. Below: The 'Royal Scot' class 6P of 1923 which made a tour of the USA in 1933.

A driver prepares his steam locomotive (here he is oiling the crosshead) at Polmadie, Glasgow, before the loco leaves the depot.

In view of the acute post-war coal shortage, in 1946 the GWR converted passenger locos from coal to oil-burning. The absence of the usual coal fire in the driver's cabin is noticeable here — and it resulted in a considerable reduction in the work of the fireman.

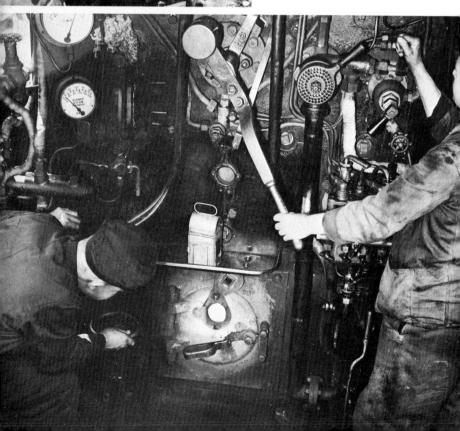

No old-time railway man could care for a loco more lovingly than these 1980 enthusiasts cleaning a 5690 'Leander' (ex-LMS) for the (preserved) Severn Valley Railway.

One of the survivors: an ex-LMS 5000 'Black Five' leaving Arley, southbound, on the Severn Valley Railway.

A perceptive railway comment from 'Ionicus' of *Punch*, used as a
Christmas card by the British Transport Commission in 1957 but
equally valid today.

from the man whose hand had progressed from cleaning-rag to firing-shovel, then to the regulator itself.

After dinner in the dining-car we played solo whist for pennies. Allen won several shillings as our train steamed along on that magnificent stretch of track via Grantham and Peterborough. I suspect he was a little conscious that I, low down in the management scale, had been privileged to see him gambling in the confines of a private compartment. As we neared King's Cross, he leaned forward confidentially and from the corner of his mouth said quietly, "A private party, lad. Just a word to the wise. Even a publicity man must know that."

Not sure whether he was leg-pulling, I twitted him, "Not a word, sir, until I write your life story – or mine!"

He grinned and winked. "Wait till I'm dead!"

I did. After a railway career to be proud of, he died in 1958, aged sixty-nine.

Yet another VIP performance of a somewhat different character. An old friend of mine was involved as a public relations man. Barry was always a bit fly and tended to take chances.

Picture the scene: a large London station in those remaining few halcyon years before railway nationalization. Picture the old-style general manager of one of the big four railway companies, with his entourage, alighting from his special inspection train – a piece of real old-world mobile luxury – on a sunny afternoon after inspecting a main-line route, replete following an excellent lunch that ended with coffee, brandy and cigars.

The GM (I got to know him in later years) fancied himself as a man with the common touch, and we remember that in railway circles, before egalitarianism had set in, the GM was second only to the deity. As they approached the ticket barrier, he turned to his personal public relations man and asked discreetly, "Do I know this ticket collector?"

Barry was on the ball. "He's Dawson, sir."

"Do we know anything about him?"

Smart PR men always know everything about everybody. "Wife just out of hospital, sir, after an operation."

When the party reached the barrier, the ticket collector obviously knew that he was in the presence of the mighty, and he touched his cap in respect if not in awe.

Grandly the GM called out, "Well, Dawson, my man. How's your wife now?"

Clearly taken aback, the ticket collector stuttered, "She's f-fine now, s-sir. Thank you, sir."

"She's over the operation?"

"Operation? Oh, yes, the operation. She's fine now, sir." He touched his cap again. "Thank you, sir."

Barry, the PR man, hung back awhile as the party went through the barrier. He noticed the ticket collector push his cap back absently and scratch his head. The collector turned to the porter standing by. "What about that then, 'Arry? Ever heard anything like it in your life?"

"Never, mate. Fantastic! The General Manager hisself. Just think, mate."

"I am thinking, mate. Our GM is either nuts or he thinks I'm some other bugger. And me a bachelor all me life!"

Then Barry quietly moved off. I wondered if this incident had anything to do with his later removal from the job.

Pete, another publicity colleague of mine, was a natural showman, produced worthwhile results and would do anything for a laugh. An exhibition was to be mounted on Waterloo station concourse in London to promote important trains starting there, including the 'Atlantic Coast Express'. Several titled trains were still being re-introduced after withdrawal during the war years, and in the 1950s Pete was in charge of the Waterloo project and similar schemes. He phoned me. "Come along about mid-morning on Thursday. It'll give you something to write about." He would say no more.

When I arrived on the Waterloo concourse, a fair number of journalists and Press photographers had assembled. Pete, always a natty dresser, looked particularly smart. Familiar station sights and sounds were evident – loudspeakers announcing the trains, excited passengers scurrying around, porters pushing barrows of luggage, tea trolleys offering a quick cup of tea. Curious onlookers had gathered around the exhibition stand, brightly decorated by three pretty girls.

Now comes the big moment. Pete suddenly rushes off. Across the concourse I see a camel being led by its white-coated handler. Pete joins him. So this was it. A camel. The most tatty, mangy specimen of a camel you ever did see comes loping into view. Pete, a happy smile lighting his round face, announces to the Press boys, "Meet Saudi Sammy, the famous circus camel, a great performer!"

In these noisy and unfamiliar precincts the poor animal is obviously terrified, and his handler seems worried. Press cameras flash. An engine whistle screams. Suddenly Sammy stands still, splays out his legs, lifts his haughty head and lets out an almighty roar-cum-howl of roof-shattering volume. Startled onlookers back away. Even Press men look alarmed. Then Sammy groans "Ah-ah-ah" with relief as he begins to empty his bladder, the capacity of which would surely have equalled that of a sizeable GWR tank engine. Pete, standing dangerously near, jumps back too late to avoid his immaculately creased trousers getting a thorough splashing.

Plaintively, he turns to grinning Pressmen. "What's my wife going to say if I tell her a camel peed on me on Waterloo station!"

Chuckles rise to ribald laughter as the upset animal raises his tail high and empties his innards of everything he has eaten for a week and deposits the largest steaming pile of top-quality garden fertilizer that has ever been seen outside a circus. Now Pete is really suffering. He must wish Sammy back on the arid desert of Saudi Arabia, and he tries to laugh it off. But wait! Sammy has not finished his performance. He emits another "Ah-ah-ah" of sublime relief, sinks gently to his knobbly knees, then rolls over and over in the vast, smelly ocean he has just created.

Sammy's distressed handler gets the animal on his feet, and the filth drips thickly down his shaggy coat. When, dog-like, he shakes himself, the nearby panic is comic. Pressmen and onlookers have already backed away to escape the pungent effluvium assailing their nostrils. Much of their laughter is at Pete's evident discomfiture. He grabs the handler viciously and hisses through clenched jaw, "For God's same get this filthy beast off our bloody station fast!" Within minutes porters are working furiously with buckets of water and long-handled brushes. Soon the concourse resumes an orderly pattern once more.

For months afterwards Pete's friends ragged him. "Next time, let's have a camel train", or "Like to hear another filthy story?" or "How's that pet camel of yours?"

"Like me," he would grin. "Still got the hump!"

Since the 1920s the main-line railway companies had been running their own staff magazines, good-quality glossies that had a good reputation. They all had to end when nationalization came, and by January 1950 the first issue of the new British Railways magazine appeared, with six regional editions. The HQ editor was Bill Brudenell, a former publicity man from the LMS. A few years later I became his assistant, and before his retirement in 1960 I was to take over as executive editor.

On my transfer to Marylebone HQ on joining the magazine, one of the amenities was to lunch in the waitress-served management dining-room with chaps from various departments. In the early 1950s heated discussions, both private and official, centred around a proposal to change the standard braking system from the long-established vacuum brake to air brake. Some defined them as the 'suck brake' and the 'blow brake', similar to a domestic vacuum cleaner. In the dining-room you really did get to know what was happening and what the thinking was in high places.

In the top echelons of management much lobbying went on. Systems overseas were studied. Understandably, cautious top brass favoured carrying on as before. More go-ahead people were for change. On the relative merits of the two systems, experts were sharply divided, and our lunchtime discussions generated more heat than light. Being out of my technical depth, I stirred the pot with a big spoon and enjoyed the fun.

It was in 1955, under chairman Sir Brian (later Lord) Robertson, that the vacuum brake won, for all vehicles – locomotives, carriages, wagons. Certainly the air brake was already in use in Britain on the growing number of electric and diesel multi-unit trains, but total conversion throughout British Railways to air braking would have taken many years, the Board explained, and it would have cost an additional £20 to £30 million. Changeover, as I can assure you, would also have created immeasurable operating difficulties and delays by working the two systems during conversion. The BTC decision confirmed that the vacuum brake would continue for all freight and for all passenger rolling stock (except of course for diesels and electrics).

How intriguing to have sat under the boardroom table at the

'Kremlin' (as it was called) in the discussions! Board members and departmental officers would be, to some extent, prisoners in their own professions – mechanical engineer, electrical engineer, financial, investment, operating, commercial and industrial relations chiefs. Yet such a conclusion, after all the arguments and information had been considered, could be only a corporate one – a committee decision. The die had been cast. Managements down the line were informed and instructed accordingly. Waiting anxiously in the wings were those manufacturers and suppliers to whom the decision could influence millions of pounds of business. Whispers drifted along the corridors of power that it was a wrong judgment, especially in the long term. Some sections of the Press hotted up the controversy, to the embarrassment of the Board, and could well have been fuelled by shrewd and secret lobbying. As a writer, my job at HQ was to report policy decisions and their likely effects, to state the facts objectively and not to reason why – except across the confidential lunch table.

# 14
# Steam Takes its Last Brave Gasp

After all the publicity razmatazz about the great 'Britannia' locomotive and the plans of 1951 to build large numbers of the new standard types, I was amazed to hear on the grapevine the following year that this massive building programme was doomed. And early in 1953 it became obvious that dear old steam would have to go. More modern motive-power systems were rapidly gaining favour, and before the year was out, thirty-four multi-unit diesel vehicles had gone into service, some in Cumberland and some in the West Riding of Yorkshire.

When I travelled to Derby Works to write about the diesels, I learnt that an extensive programme for building them in prodigious quantities had already begun.

This national change of direction, and a lot more besides, was made public on 24th January 1955. General Sir Brian (later Lord) Robertson, then chairman of the British Transport Commission, announced, with a panoply of trumpet blowing, a £1,200 million plan for the modernization and re-equipment of British Railways. "The next fifteen years," the statement claimed, "were to witness the greatest revolution ever seen in modern times on any railway in the world, eventually to put Britain in the lead in wheel-to-rail transport." One of the main features was for far more electrification.

In his public statement Sir Brian paid a tribute to the pioneering part that steam had played, adding, "Many factors indicate that the end of the steam era is at hand – the growing shortage of large coal suitable for locomotives; the insistent demand for a reduction in air pollution and for greater cleanliness in trains and stations; and the need for better acceleration." It was, I recall, also increasingly difficult to find young chaps who would clean and stoke the engines.

Surprisingly many new railway preservation societies were formed that very year. Suddenly steam – now to be the underdog

– enjoyed an unexpected surge of nostalgic interest that spread far and fast throughout the land. To this phenomenon we will return shortly.

Meanwhile I was kept busy with the railway staff magazine. Such a lot was going on. The editor, Bill Brudenell, wrote the popular monthly leading article signed 'The Man on the Line'. When he became publications officer, and I served as executive editor, writing that leading article luckily fell to me. To deal with commitments in addition to the magazine, I headed a small team in a post I was to occupy for some years. Proof-checking was a tedious but vital monthly chore, and an item we almost let through at the last minute on the staff news pages read, "Retired people are requested to complete the above form and return it to the Editor as soon as possible. News of retired members of the staff who have died will also be particularly welcome."

Leisure activities occupied several pages. Under the highly successful British Railways Staff Association, every spare-time interest was catered for, from golf and angling to pottery and marquetry. Amateur drama was strong in all six geographical regions. The ancient fever of dressing up to "strut and fret one's hour upon a stage" had seeped into the blood of many starry-eyed Thespians. Local, regional and national competitions were held, always supported by top people in railway management and judged by professionals.

Highly popular also were various sports. When the two winning regions met to play off their cricket finals at Raynes Park, the Southern Region pitch in South London, the trophy was to be presented by General Sir Brian Robertson CB GCB CBE KCMG KCVO DSO MC. And if he had hit me over the head with his military baton at the peak of the ceremonial, no one would have blamed him.

My boss, cautious Bill Brudenell, had warned as I left the London office, "Sir Brian likes everything to go with military precision."

"Even cricket?"

"Even cricket. Especially the trophy presentation."

I attended to report the match for the BR staff magazine and took with me a professional photographer. It was a glorious sunny August afternoon and evening. And the sight of the players in immaculate whites, the crack of leather on willow, the clapping and applause of wives and sweethearts, relations and friends, a real family occasion in a traditional, peaceful English setting, prompted me to exclaim, "It's a great life on the railways, even if there isn't an engine in sight!"

As usual on such special occasions, regional general managers and some of their officers were there – I spotted Gerry Fiennes, H. A. Short, J. W. Watkins, W. P. ('Bill') Allen and Charles Hopkins – from both the competing regions, the LMR and the NER, some of them with important traders as guests. At the zenith of the railway cricket season, people of all levels mixed and chatted freely. Even Sir Brian's rather forbidding and autocratic aura had slipped a little. During the season teams had played their various heats through districts and regions. Today the two giants were to bat it out for the coveted 'Mitchell-Hedges' Trophy, a beautiful silver cup made in 1784 and donated by F. A. Mitchell-Hedges, explorer and author, for railway sports.

After hours of splendid cricket, the North Eastern, captained by Harry Laidler, were the winners. Off we trooped to the pavilion where we had earlier taken tea and nibbled tasty snacks. Now for the presentations. My number-one photograph, I had told Mike the cameraman, was to be of Sir Brian presenting the cup to the winning captain. Indoors, flash would be needed. After a brief speech about *esprit de corps* and similar traditional sentiments, Sir Brian, posing with his best smile for the picture, shook hands with the captain, and with the other hand held the trophy. Both men smiled into the camera. Mike pressed the shutter. A click, but no flash. Tragedy! What about my best picture? Mike looked at me. "Sorry. Can we do it again?"

Neither Sir Brian nor the captain was aware that the photo was a flop. They stood there chatting, Harry Laidler clutching the trophy proudly as the audience looked on. Only one thought commanded my mind. That picture. The railway cricket picture of the year, to be cherished by the captain, his team and his family and admired by his friends and the regional manager himself.

I approached Sir Brian. "Sorry, sir. The flash failed. Would you do it again, please?"

Everybody was watching. Silent. He glared at me from beneath those fiercely bushy eyebrows. His brindled moustache bristled ominously. It was his will against mine on really a mere triviality. A tense moment. Forcefully, as though to a delinquent subaltern who had dropped his rifle on the General's big toe, he spat out, "It spoils everything to do it again. You should have had it right the first time!" Turning to the captain, I gave what I hoped was a disarming smile. Gently but firmly I wrested the precious, shining cup from his surprised grasp and thrusted it pointedly into Sir Brian's unwilling hands, nodded to the cameraman, then smartly nipped out of the General's vision. I could not bear to watch, just in case of a repeat flash failure. Smiling broadly, with his mouth if not with his eyes, Sir Brian mechanically went through the motions, with the captain, of the presentation of the cup again. To my relief the flash flashed, Sir Brian flashed his most dazzling smile, and the applause was deafening.

In due time Bill Brudenell sent a copy of the magazine personally to Sir Brian. It had the most delightful picture of him I had ever seen. Let's hope that when the Great General sees it, he will pardon me from 'jankers' and restore my pips.

It was two days later that Sheila, Sir Brian's secretary, telephoned. "He's away today, Frank. Come over and look in his private office."

There, propped up on the mantelpiece, was the magazine, open at the cricket page. I sighed in relief. "How nice!"

"Sir Brian would like a print, ten by eight. Can you arrange?"

"My pleasure, Sheila."

Ever since the railways were nationalized in 1948, each change of government has brought changes in railway policy and investment that were influenced more by contemporary political expediency than by proved economic and commercial criteria. Furthermore, each change has brought large increases in costly administration without necessarily carrying one extra passenger or package of goods. Enough Ministers of Transport to form their own club have laid their indelible fingers on the railway management. And few Railways Board Chairmen have exceeded their original contracts of five years.

How permanent can a permanent-way be!

As each new chairman arrived to a fanfare of sounding brass and tinkling cymbal (we in mass communication became inured to the paradigm), Bill Brudenell, my chief, would say his usual little piece. Bill had joined the publicity department of the London & North Western Railway in 1915 at fifteen. "Sir Josiah Stamp", he said, "came from the ICI with a fantastic salary to the LMS in 1926 to improve the finances. They keep coming. Each man thinks he's going to make the railways pay. He'll fail like the rest of 'em!"

And so it came to pass that yet another willing victim strode along the permanent way, also temporarily, reigning for a mere four years and two months from March 1961. (I had to clean my typewriter keys and start afresh, again.) Dr Richard Beeching, a former director of ICI, was a big, round, heavy man with a pear-shaped face. He carried lots of techni-academic qualifications, starting with PhD. Made me feel really ignorant, which I was. Still, I could run a nice cosy little branch-line station, couple up wagons, work a small signalbox. Could *he*? But the thing about Beeching that really bugged me (as I, as a young stationmaster, must have bugged others) was that at forty-eight he was two years my junior!

His brief from Transport Minister Ernest Marples was fairly general – make 'em efficient, make 'em competitive, make 'em pay, and he had a fairly free hand. Assembling a small team at HQ, he had detailed records made (mainly from only one average week) of how much all the stations and lines were actually being used. Some of the chaps working on them sat with us at the lunch table, and they could not stop talking about it.

The Transport Act of 1962 abolished the British Transport Commission, changed the top administration of its various boards and wrote off millions of pounds of losses.

Beeching's salary, £24,000 against Sir Brian Robertson's mere £10,000, was good 'copy'. The good doctor had only to clear his throat in public and the headline would run: "Dr Beeching £24,000 Railways Board Chairman Coughs at Euston". A BRB chairmanship was a guarantee of instant public recognition. Every newspaper reader and televiewer knew that genial, kindly, pear-shaped face like a brother's.

Another promotion came my way, head of features section, writing and placing key articles in the Press and drafting speech notes for Beeching. (In my provincial ignorance, I had always thought that important people wrote their own speeches; it shows what wicked things you learn when you move up to the seething metropolis.) Though I had 'ghosted' articles before, I had never ghosted speeches. But somebody higher up thought I could, so I did. Not the easiest of jobs but challenging to the imagination. The head of the department started me off with a short brief, and my assistant, a former Fleet Street journalist, shared the work. In building up a speech, I was free to seek information at the Railways Board directly from any source, such as chief officers, departmental files and records and occasionally from a Board member.

Unexpectedly, an old friend in banking invited me to attend the luncheon at which the very first speech I worked on was delivered. It was at the Hyde Park Hotel in the presence of a large and distinguished audience. Sitting there smoking an after-lunch cigar, a large one just like Beeching's, when he rose to speak it was odd to hear some of one's carefully concocted phrases being trotted out. For a crazy, fleeting second, I felt like a ventriloquist operating a remotely controlled, oversized, pear-faced dummy.

After my assistant and I had worked on about a dozen speeches, I was overcome with the idiotic desire to draft a spoof speech to be delivered at, say, the Albert Hall with a large audience and masses of media men. (I still have a copy at home). In the office we had a good chuckle over it, and I should then have destroyed the typescript. Unfortunately I left it out on my desk, and in my absence it disappeared. Then came a phone call from Bob Barton, a bit of a wag, from the marketing department on the next floor.

"Buy me a large scotch in the station buffet at half past five, and the incriminating document is yours. If not, it goes anonymously to Chairman B!"

He'd do it too! Over the drinks that evening the typescript was safely in my hands. As we prepared to go our separate ways home from Marylebone station, he grinned, "Reckless of you, Ferney, to leave such dangerous, incriminating material unattended on your desk." Then he added wickedly, "I'll make sure I don't do the same with my photocopy!"

Though Beeching was best known as the 'axe man', he brought many improvements and developments, injected new blood into middle and top management to fertilize new ideas and applied fresh thought to stale problems. "A seat in a train," his new marketing men proclaimed, "is more perishable than today's newspaper or this morning's fish. The instant a train has left with an empty seat, that seat has perished."

One of Beeching's new men appointed to the highest level, when confronted at a big meeting with plans for new signalling schemes costing many millions, suggested, "Can't we cut out all this new signalling and take out more insurance against accidents?" The senior signalling officer was shocked. "It's impossible to insure against railway train accidents, sir. The premium would cost billions, and the railways would go bust in a week!" Encouraged by the grins round the table, he added for good measure, "Besides, we are talking about life and death!" Of course, if they wished passengers could insure against train accidents, and customers could insure their packages or merchandise for carriage by either passenger or freight train, against damage or loss: a long-established facility.

During the speech-writing period, another fascinating task fell to me – giving public talks to 'opinion-forming bodies' about the Beeching Plan. Beeching himself had asked for someone to do this. Such talks were often reported in the Press, extending their propaganda value. Speaking-engagements took me east to Norwich, west to Dartmouth, south to the Isle of Wight, to central Wales and many other places between. Audiences included Rotary Clubs, Round Table, Lions International, business and professional clubs, chambers of commerce, women's organizations, political groups and universities. (A long chapter would be needed to accommodate the amusing things that happened.)

For my public talks – 'The Beeching Plan' – each basically the same, I used one postcard of notes and delivered 'off the cuff'. It is monotonous to read a speech, and some people are inclined to doze off. Because it was repetitious, for each occasion I worked out something lively to stop *me* from dozing off. I liked to begin with about four amusing stories, and in the office we collected new ones and added our own twist. In beginning a talk, after four good laughs I would say, "I have twenty more funny stories. Or would you prefer to hear all about railway goods yards?"

In giving many talks, I was surprised at the range of knowledge people had of the railways, their keen interest in steam locomotives and how much the local railway station meant to them. Many quoted youthful anecdotes ("I well remember . . .") about trains and stations and seemed far more interested in the nostalgic past than in the technological future. The whole subject seemed to be charged with sentiment and emotion of considerable depth, and I always tried to handle discussions with sensitive understanding.

After the shortest reign of any Railways Board chairman except Raymond, Beeching departed in 1965, to be followed in turn by Raymond, Johnson, Marsh and Parker. During the 1950s and 1960s steam was being rapidly run down. Thousands of beautiful steam-engines were going to the scrapyard. Lots of stations, depots, works, marshalling yards and little-used lines had been closed. And then it happened to me. When I heard in the office that the little branch line of my childhood, between Stoke-on-Trent and Leek, that took us to see our country grandparents, and our little station at Bucknall had been finally closed, I don't mind confessing to being choked up. Something inside me died a little. At that moment I experienced deep feeling about the Beeching closures and knew better how others felt. In my heart a diffused sadness. But in my reasoning a recognition of the inevitability of it all.

Meantime I would continue propagating the new, while holding in my affections the achievements and greatness of the old and the part that the steam locomotive had contributed in building up for over a century the prosperity of Britain. The new would be my bread and butter, the old my hobby. Thank heavens for the railway societies and all those marvellous people who run them.

In the 1960s steam, before my very eyes, was quickly fading from the railway scene. And of course there had to be a 'last day'. Sunday 4th August 1968 was the day that the very last scheduled train ran with a steam locomotive at its head, the stopping train to all our yesterdays.

Proving that someone high up at British Rail was perceptive enough to combine business with sentiment, the following Sunday a nostalgic 'Farewell to Steam' special train ran on the London Midland Region, a commemorative event full of sweet sorrow. The train was packed with cameras and tape recorders to capture, in vision and sound, by amateur and professional, a sad moment in our railway history.

Running from Liverpool to Carlisle, its route was through Manchester, Blackburn and Hellifield, through busy town and beautiful countryside, returning the same way. 'Old Faithful' had served the nation well for 143 years since those great pioneering days of George Stephenson's first public steam-locomotive railway, the Stockton & Darlington.

# 15

# The Fabulous World of Great Steam Locomotives

Some folk say to me, "I can't understand all this fuss about steam locomotives. They all look alike." But, as every railway enthusiast knows, the opposite is true. They differ just as beautiful women do, and their vital statistics are always fascinating. Equally each one has its own individuality and its own stimulating story to tell. And most enthusiasts have their own favourites.

Forget for the moment those majestic machines such as Gresley's A4s, Bulleid's 'Merchant Navys', Collett's 'Kings' and Stanier's 'Black Fives'. Take the Class 4 0-6-0 freight. Though these unnamed, unglamorous workhorses rarely receive their share of glory, they were busy in the mundane but essential role of humping the country's goods about. Serving Britain's trade and industry, their business was vital.

On my travels for many years I noticed Fowler's ubiquitous 0-6-0 types on the LMS system. I often rode on the footplate or in a goods brakevan hauled by one. I saw them on many routes pulling coal trains, empty wagon trains for collieries and steel-works, and trains for mixed goods, and shunting in marshalling yards. And I could identify their thrusting, throbbing beat a mile off!

Just after World War II I sometimes travelled on one on a regular run in the Sheffield and Rotherham districts and got to know Bob, the driver. In the Rotherham signalbox Bob told me that his favourite Fowler six coupled had been scrapped. He said, with a tear in his voice, "You know, I loved that old engine. We'd had our ups and downs and our happy times together. And we've had to coax her on occasion. Cross me heart, if she was a woman, I'd marry the old girl and make an honest engine out of her!" Bob was typical of many steam drivers I knew, a special breed of railwaymen. Sometimes they could be proud and stubborn. Invariably physically strong and robust, they were of independent character which was nurtured by the personal responsibility of driving trains – passenger or goods – day or night, in fine weather or foul, year in and year out. And whether the regulator was manipulating a glamorous 'Royal Scot' or a Fowler six coupled made no matter.

Fowler's 0-6-0s first appeared on the LMS in 1924, when this railway was only a year old. Up to 1941 580 had been built. Five more were produced for the Somerset & Dorset Railway which ran through undulating country between Bath and Bournemouth. Driving-wheels of 5 feet 3 inches diameter were designed for pulling-power rather than speed; the two inside cylinders were 20 inches by 26 inches, and boiler pressure was 175 pounds – all contributing to a tractive effort of over 24,000 pounds.

In locomotive circles Sir Henry Fowler (whom I had seen briefly on the overbridge at Derby station in 1930) had been the chief mechanical engineer of the former Midland Railway. His LMS 0-6-0 improved freights followed the pattern of his earlier designs for the Midland and had been the catalyst that had proved so successful. From 1911 to 1922 the Midland had built 192 of this class. Simple lines and solid strength. No. 43924, built by the Midland at Derby in 1920, was not withdrawn by British Railways until 1965. The dear old lady was soon off to the Barry scrapyard in South Wales to join many other old-timers. However, by 1968 she had still not been sold or broken up. Then the Midland 4F Preservation Society got their loving hands on her for posterity. I saw her on one of her occasional runs, recalling happy days, on the Keighley & Worth Valley Railway, her proud owners.

Fowler's LMS 'Royal Scot' class 4-6-0 No. 6100, mentioned earlier, visited America and Canada in 1933 on a goodwill mission and covered 11,194 miles over their railroads; luckily George Stephenson's influence in the 1820s had resulted in the North American rail gauge being the same as the British. I remember all the excitement about this trip when I worked at Derby.

No. 6100 was reconstructed in 1950 with a taper boiler and other modifications. She was withdrawn from service in 1962 and restored to LMS livery. Several times I had seen this fine specimen hauling expresses through Bletchley in the 1930s. She is now at Bressingham Hall near Diss in Norfolk where, for a small charge, I rode with other excited visitors on the roomy footplate. We travelled little more than walking pace on the short length of track, and she emitted only gentle puffs through the blast pipe, giving no inkling of her enormous latent power.

Much information is conveyed about locomotives by their wheel arrangements. Railway engineers and others have bestowed on some of them an identifying name. 'Pacific' and 'Atlantic' seem the best known, followed by 'Mogul' and 'Baltic'.

Here is a short list:

| | | | |
|---|---|---|---|
| 2-6-0 | Mogul | 4-4-2 | Atlantic |
| 2-6-2 | Prairie | 4-6-2 | Pacific |
| 2-8-0 | Consolidation | 4-6-4 | Baltic |
| 2-8-2 | Mikado | 4-8-2 | Mountain |
| 2-10-0 | Decapod | | |

Cylinders, a key to power and movement, have passed through various stages. Stephenson's 'Rocket', an 0-2-2, had two cylinders, both outside. From the late 1830s engineers sometimes placed them inside the frames, out of sight, yet less accessible. Many locomotives had three cylinders: for example, Bulleid's 'Battle of Britain' and 'Merchant Navy' classes. The LMS 'Coronation' class were fitted with four. On three- and four-cylinder machines, two are placed outside. I remember in the 1930s coming across three-cylinder types for the first time at Waterloo in London and was intrigued to notice the exhaust blast coming in a rhythm of threes instead of fours. Some years later, intrigue turned to surprise when I learnt that Stephenson and Howe, as early as 1846, had registered a patent in London for a locomotive design incorporating three cylinders.

Boiler pressure for the 'Rocket' of 1829 was fifty pounds to the square inch. Through the century, larger locomotives brought higher pressures. In 1905 the Midland built one with a pressure of 220, tremendous for its day. In the 1920s and 1930s 250 was common, some of Bulleid's on the Southern Railway being as high as 280. Development of tractive effort in pounds, the usual measure of power for steam locomotives, also reflects the pace of change. The four-ton 'Rocket' was 825. By the turn of the century 17,000 was common. GWR 'King George V' (still steaming around) was 40,300, and 'Evening Star' 39,667.

Among my personal fancies is 'Cornwall', the locomotive I

spotted in July 1937 in Bletchley off to London town for the centenary of the London & Birmingham line. And I had had a quick peep at this machine in Crewe Works in 1927 while working in the offices there. Knowing of my interest, a senior clerk had said, "There's an old engine in the paint shop. Like to see it?"

"Oh, yes, please. How old is it?"

"Built here in 1847. It's a beauty, but a bit neglected."

We had hurried into the Works and there it was, in the paint shop, a 2-2-2 with those enormous driving-wheels. We could not stay long because it was in working hours. The senior clerk told me that she had served for pulling an inspection saloon for the company directors and was now retired.

Though originally built as a 2-2-2, two more wheels had been added, making it a 4-2-2. But in 1858 John Ramsbottom, chief mechanical engineer of the L&NW Railway and a clever inventor, rebuilt her completely, reverting to the original 2-2-2. She ran in ordinary services until 1902, was temporarily withdrawn, then in 1907 the directors had taken a fancy to her; it must have been those enormous drivers at 8½ feet diameter and their encasing splashers that had such an attractive design. Altogether lovely on the eye. In an aesthetic mood, Brunel had said of another stylish locomotive, Stephenson's 'North Star', that she was "ornament enough for a drawing-room". After languishing alone and neglected in the Crewe paintshop for many years, she had a face lift and was powdered and painted for display to admiring eyes in the Clapham Transport Museum in South London. Recently she was restored at the Severn Valley Railway, with the intention of running in live steam, along with others of the steam-world nobility, at the re-enactment of the Rainhill Trials near Liverpool in 1980. To the disappointment of the hundreds of thousands of spectators, she was not ready in time.

Another fine specimen I have seen – this time in the Glasgow Museum – was the 'Gordon Highlander'. You could expect a romantic name like that for an engine designed for expresses serving the romantic Great North of Scotland Railway. A 4-4-0 built in 1920, she turned out to be the final express engine for an outpost railway formed in 1846 to get a line from the comparatively rich city of Aberdeen to Inverness. The Aberdeen line gave access to Ballater, the station for Balmoral Castle, residence of royalty, remote among the wild Highland mountains, to which Queen Victoria and her family frequently travelled. Links were made with Peterhead, Fraserburgh, Banff, Elgin and Lossiemouth on the Moray coast, birthplace of Ramsay Macdonald, the first Prime Minister from the Labour Party.

On examining the 'Gordon Highlander', you can see that the fine lines are enhanced by a sweeping curve from the driving-cab, a curve picked up by the arc of the wheel guard. Tidiness is achieved by straight, simple lines and inside cylinders. For the period when boilers were getting larger, the chimney and dome are somewhat high. Appropriate for those Scottish expresses, driving-wheels are 6 feet 1 inch in diameter, cylinders 18 inches by 26 inches, boiler pressure 165 and tractive effort 16,185 pounds. A product of the North British Locomotive Company, Glasgow, she was withdrawn from service in 1958. Considering the rugged territory of her schedules, thirty-eight years was a commendable working life. After being restored to working order, she achieved a number of special runs and looks resplendent in the GNSR livery of green, with red and yellow lines.

Like many other steam enthusiasts, I was astonished at my first sighting of a war-time austerity locomotive. Several of us from the control office stood on the platform to watch. She was trundling through Bletchley station with a long train of goods wagons loaded with military materials. As she progressed through the covered platforms, she rumbled and roared and echoed like some great angry gorgon monster, steam and smoke billowing all around to show her mood. She looked naked, uncared-for, unfinished. At 4 feet 8½ inches, the driving-wheels of this 2-10-0 version were small, geared for muscle power rather than dashing speeds. Incidentally, they matched exactly the driving-wheels of the 'Rocket' and the standard gauge of the track. Cylinders were 19 inches by 28 inches, boiler pressure 225 and tractive effort 34,215. Designed by Riddles and built by the North British Locomotive Company, 150 were produced in 1943–5 for service in Britain and overseas. Initially, WD 3651, the second of the class of 1943 vintage, went to the railway training centre at Longmoor in Hampshire. In 1952 her new number was 600 and her name 'Gordon'. Acquired by the Severn Valley Railway, she showed her paces in 1975 with many other great steam locomotives of the day at Shildon when the 150th anniversary of the Stockton & Darlington Railway was being celebrated.

All told, many hundred austerity locomotives of different types within the basic design were built, including a batch in America. The North British worked closely with Britain's railways and the war-time Ministry of Supply. For obvious reasons of economy, their design ensured a minimum of tooling and casting in the workshops and avoided using scarce materials. Many served overseas – in Europe, Iran, Palestine, Egypt and the Western Desert areas. Shorn of all ostentatious fal-de-lals, windshields and other extravagant frippery, their naked austerity caught the roving eye and gave an impression of throbbing power, as though they had taken off their jackets to get down to business.

An austerity 0-6-0 Q1 class, with the simplest exterior lines, not unlike a child's toy engine, prompted William Stanier to twit its designer and his old friend Oliver Bulleid, "Where's the key?" From 1942 forty were built at Brighton and Ashford Works. This type was so naked as to be almost vulgar. But though unconventional, matching Bulleid's character, they were highly efficient and attained maximum power with minimum weight. Some people thought they were the ugliest ever designed, but they epitomized the perid. So that posterity can judge what austerity can do, BR No. 33001, withdrawn in 1964, has been preserved, and I spotted her recently on the Bluebell Railway in Sussex, where she was on loan.

Some austerity types were constructed at Vulcan Foundry at Newton-le-Willows in Lancashire.

About 450 of various austerity types were lent to British Railways before shipment overseas from October 1944, and many hundreds did service in the UK before transfer to the War Department. A large number of austerity 2-8-0 types were built in America and entered Britain by different routes for security purposes, through docks at Cardiff, Birkenhead, Manchester, Hull, Glasgow and London. We saw several American versions in Nottinghamshire and Yorkshire. They looked less tidy than their British counterparts, for they exposed to view far more detail – piping, running-gear and stays; and they had bar-type frames and a high running-board, giving easy access to sand-boxes and other equipment high on the boiler barrel.

Locomotives find their way to the preservation societies by diverse and devious routes. A WD austerity 2-8-0 No. 79257 built at Vulcan Foundry in 1945 went to the Dutch State Railways as No. 4464. It was sold to the Swedish State Railways as No. 1931 and can now be seen at Haworth on the Keighley & Worth Valley Railway.

In the Midlands during and just after the war, a locomotive type that gave me no peace was the Beyer-Garratt, Garratt for short. I longed to get aboard that footplate. Sometimes I saw them hauling enormous coal trains of well over a thousand tons from the vast sorting sidings at Toton near Nottingham to North London. What monster fellows they were! Literally two engines in one, with a wheel arrangement of 2-6-0+0-6-2, though there were several wheel notations. In fact, they often saved a train being double-headed by traditional engines, and they pulled trains of enormous length.

Then the opportunity came. I had been working in the yard-master's office at Toton and had to get to Trent for a passenger train home to Mansfield. The yardmaster told me, "Coal train just leaving. Hop on the engine." And there it was, all steaming to go. A Garratt! And I knew the driver.

"How far you going?"

"Trent, Albert."

"That's not far," he grinned. "Come to Cricklewood and have a real ride!"

The Garratt magnet was strong, but home pulled even more.

Though October, it was hot on the footplate, and the fireman was shovelling furiously to feed this great hungry monster. In that short trip, it was my most exciting ride. The feel of thrust and the roar of power were quite overwhelming. I learnt from my reference books later that the tractive effort of this class was terrifically high at well over 45,000 and that the huge water tanks held 4,500 gallons.

When I was promoted to the British Transport Commission as a writer, I was to see many highly important characters in the world of steam railways. One of them, a folk-hero of mine, was R. A. Riddles. Then fifty-eight, this eminent locomotive builder was on the board and at the peak of an illustrious career. He was British Railways' highest authority not only on locomotives but on carriages and wagons too. I sometimes passed him in the corridor. Slim of build, with a military bearing, he would be marching along determinedly to a board meeting clutching a fistful of papers. He had little time, people said, for those who failed to give their all. But he was amusing and had a sense of fun, a characteristic he let loose in his public speeches.

No budding engineer could have started lower down the ladder. At seventeen, he was apprenticed at Crewe in 1909 for a four-year course. An aura of magic reigned over the Cheshire Works, and many able engineers trained there have been proud to call themselves 'Crewe Men'. During World War II he had been mainly responsible for the range of austerity locomotives. And at the LMS he had risen to vice-president before moving to British Railways Marylebone headquarters on nationalization. By the time Riddles retired in 1954, he had set the pace for the new British Rail standard locomotive fleet but was ready to welcome the changes in basic motive power.

Six years later the very last steam locomotive to be built was launched. Evocatively named 'Evening Star', she was built at Swindon Works and was the last of 251 in this class. Numbered 92220, she had a 2-10-0 wheel arrangement and was classified 9F (Freight). Other details are: driving-wheels, 5 feet; cylinders, 20 inches by 28 inches; boiler pressure, 250 pounds; tractive effort, 39,667; weight, 139 tons. She was fitted with a wide Belpaire firebox, Walschaert valve gear, double chimney and double blast pipe like Gresley's memorable A4s, and a new-pattern spark arrester located between blast pipe top and the chimney petticoat. She was one of the best class of steam-engine ever to work on Britain's railways and designed in a traditional but beautiful style: English right down to her flanges. There had to be a 'last one', and this was it, embracing the best traditions of the master-builders of steam. With such a magnificent specimen, steam did not go out with a whimper but with a proud and mighty roar of unsurpassed power. However anyone can look at this machine without a tremendous thrill, I shall never know.

Welcome evidence that a warm heart and not a diesel engine was still beating in the breast of British Rail top brass came when it was decided to give a razmatazz send-off on the day of her naming ceremony – 18th March 1960. Keith Grand, the last larger-than-life personality to have matured on the Great Western, at that time a member of the Railways Board, performed the naming ceremony in traditional Swindon style in the presence of a large company and in a setting of historical locomotives. As I stood there with old friends and colleagues, I could not help looking over my shoulder in case the ghosts of Brunel or Gooch, who built Swindon Works, might be drifting around. It was moving to be standing there, reflecting that Gooch had opened the works in 1843 when he was only twenty-seven and was already totally committed to his master, Brunel, ten years his senior.

During her short working life, 'Evening Star' busied herself on main lines hauling weighty freight trains, her ten coupled driving-wheels of five feet diameter making light of the heavy work. Her end could easily have been in a scrapyard, but some percipient person rescued her. For a short spell she was on loan to the Keighley & Worth Valley Railway, located in picturesque Yorkshire countryside. She showed her steam power at two famous anniversaries – Shildon in 1975 and Rainhill in 1980. She had already been destined to her rightful and permanent home, the National Railway Museum at York, opened by the Duke of Edinburgh in 1975.

At the crowded Shildon Exhibition I was interviewed by a BBC television personality named Fiona Johnston from the Newcastle studios. It concerned a book I had just published to mark the celebration.

Fiona said, "Where would you like to stand?"

Glancing round at the various locomotives, I spotted my target. "By the 'Evening Star', of course!" And I explained why.

Meanwhile, an arc of onlookers gathered round to watch, as the camera team took up their positions. A lady in the crowd near my wife said to her husband, "Ay-up, George, who's yon whiskery old gent wi' Fiona?" Nothing like the media for cutting you down to size.

Another splendid specimen to be rescued was a 'Britannia' class 5 standard locomotive 4-6-2 No. 70000, designed by Robert Riddles in 1951. It was acquired by the Britannia Locomotive Society formed in 1969 and is steamed on occasion on the Nene Valley Railway near Peterborough.

Riddles himself was at long last honoured in a very special way on 19th May 1981: a main-line electric locomotive was named after him at Euston station in London. Friends and colleagues came to witness the unveiling, and I attended as a guest of the London Midland Region. On the busy platform radio, television and Press men swelled the ranks.

Host James O'Brien, general manager of the LMR, said, "Robert Riddles is the last of a long line of eminent locomotive engineers. One of his greatest achievements was to design the famous austerity locomotives – over a thousand were built for home and overseas – for war work. Among them, his 2-10-0 was superb for the times – easy to maintain, would run on the roughest track, burn the poorest fuel and haul the heaviest loads. Yet he was an early supporter of electrification."

In an excellent and witty speech Riddles talked about past glories and gave lively interviews to media men. Chatting informally afterwards, he said to me, "When I started as an apprentice in Crewe steam locomotive works, I never dreamed that over seventy years later I would have a massive electric locomotive named after me!" All but ninety and still going strong. What a splendid man of the iron road, and what a privilege to know him!

Among the best known and most versatile locomotives ever produced in Britain were the Stanier LMS 'Black Fives'. You saw them here, you saw them there, you saw them steaming everywhere. In the late 1930s I spotted many on the Nor' West main line, and a little later on the Midland route through Leicester, Derby and Sheffield and on to Manchester, Leeds and Glasgow. Sir William Stanier (1878–1966) was the engineer responsible. Formerly of the Great Western, he became chief mechanical engineer to the LMS 1932–44 when he developed his 4-6-0 class 5MT (mixed traffic – passengers or freight). In so doing, he turned a traditional locomotive into a legend.

'Ubiquitous' is a fair adjective, for the number of 'Black Fives' roaring along the LMS metals totalled 842, built between 1934 and 1950. Minor modifications on some of them included Caprotti valve gear. Driving-wheels were 6 feet, cylinders 18½ inches by 28 inches, boiler pressure 225 pounds and tractive effort 25,455 pounds. So well did the robust 'Black Fives' stand up to their fast passenger and express freight work that, when the new standard locomotives were being built after nationalization, Stanier's 'Black Fives' formed the basis of the British Railways Class 5MT 4-6-0 types of 1951; the Stanier had built up a great reputation for free steaming and reliability. The fame of these engines is likely to live long, because about a dozen have been preserved by societies and museums.

Stanier's LMS maroon-liveried 'Jubilee' class 4-6-0s with 6 feet 9-inch drivers for long-distance expresses added to the engineer's reputation. Of the several restored, 'Leander' is probably the best known and one that I have seen several times in recent years. In the 1950s I sometimes spotted a 'Jubilee' on the LMS express titled train the 'Midlander' on the Wolverhampton-Birmingham-Euston route.

Though I am an old LMS man and was brought up to regard the LNER as one of our hated rivals (only in the business sense, not *real* hate), I have long admired the work of their engineers, particularly that of Sir Nigel Gresley (1876–1941). His paper qualifications were dazzling. Apart from his knighthood and CBE, his professional notations read – DSc, MInstCE, MIMechE, MIEE, MInstT. Few railway engineers indeed had earned full professional status in the three main branches of engineering. This son of a church minister was the Great Northern engineer responsible for locomotives, carriages and wagons between 1911 and 1922 and chief mechanical engineer of the LNER 1923–41. Some later critics have sought faults in his workmanship, including his locomotives; one of my chiefs with a propensity for philosophizing was prompted to remark, "The critical faculty of the human intellect is often far more highly developed than the creative one. The talkers and the doers. The ranting windbags and those who quietly get on with the job."

An exceptional output must rate Gresley one of the world's great steam-locomotive designers, whose 'Mallard' A4 streamlined 'Pacific' number No. 4468 brought him everlasting fame by creating a world record. On 3rd July 1938 this locomotive hauled a train of seven coaches near Peterborough at 126 m.p.h. He also designed articulated carriages, twin sleeping-cars and triple dining-car sets.

But his locomotives – you cannot help being stirred by them.

His 'Flying Scotsman' (there is charisma in that name), built at Doncaster in 1923 to haul the inaugural non-stop train of the same name between London King's Cross and Edinburgh, was his first of 'Pacific' design with 4-6-2 wheel notation. After its withdrawal from British Railways service in 1963 in Beeching's time, Mr Alan Pegler, a businessman, purchased it, and in 1969 he toured it extensively in America and Canada. A great railway enthusiast, highly popular and widely known, a friend for several years, Alan told me the traumatic story of the ups and downs on that exciting but costly trip and of the locomotive's return to the UK in 1973.

This famous locomotive is now owned by Mr William McAlpine and Flying Scotsman Enterprises; she is based at the Steamtown Railway Museum in Carnforth, where George Hinchcliffe, the managing director, showed it to me recently, bearing that famous number, 4472.

# 16

# Famous Trains from the Days of Our Youth

Why give trains their own special titles? Exciting names such as 'Flying Scotsman' and 'Red Dragon', 'Cheltenham Flyer' and 'Irish Mail' seem to snatch instantly at the memories of youth. Why were there so many in the 1920s and 1930s and so few now? Various reasons are given. With the closing of many branch lines and the consequently smaller network, plus the higher average speeds of today, it is uneconomical to allocate the same sets of coaches, including dining-vehicles, to be labelled and used on three or four single or return runs on the one day. Coach versatility would be reduced. To involve many coaches in titles would also require the carriage name boards – some of them long and cumbersome – to be transferred from one set of coaches to another: not so convenient in the highly concentrated and tightly scheduled operations of today. Modern trends require high-quality services in terms of speed and comfort for all trains, making it less easy to pick out trains of a much superior quality to justify a title.

The vogue for bestowing titles on top-quality trains was particularly prevalent between the two World Wars. Then competition, that great motivator of the human animal, was nudging in various directions. Nothing concentrates the mind of private enterprise like the loss of business. Inter-railway competition was strong, for example, between the LMS and the LNER in their fight for the lucrative Anglo-Scottish business. The LMS and the GWR were fierce rivals for traffic between London and Birmingham and on to North Wales and Merseyside. The GWR and the SR battled aggressively to win superiority between London and the West Country. On top of all this, increasingly devastating inroads into the railway passenger and goods business revenues were being made by buses, cars and lorries. And in the 1930s the newest vehicles of transport – aeroplanes – were rapidly opening up an internal network. In self-protection even the railways invested in the internal airline business, but their brave adventure was ended by the war of 1939.

Nonetheless, some few trains bearing official titles do survive to this day. Undoubtedly, a train with a name is a public attraction and acquires an aura of romance such as that which made the steam railways so fascinating. For the passenger there is something of a secret pride, or at least of pleasure, when he tells a friend, "I went on the 'Royal Scot'," rather than, "I travelled on the 10.45 a.m. from Euston." (Those thrusting whiz-kids in mass-marketing skills have long shown the commercial advantages of the brand-image name.)

Perhaps in the railways someone some time with perception and imagination will devise a means of creating a personality in some of our best trains in much the way that naming individual ones did, and the skill to persuade the decision-makers that it would be of real value. In a more general way, the HST 125 trains have carved themselves a niche, and one often hears friends say, with some pride, "I took the 125 to Bristol" – or Newcastle or Edinburgh. As in any other sphere, the element of novelty can usually be depended on as a talking-point.

From various sources I have compiled a list of titled trains (as distinct from named locomotives), well-known trains that are so much an intrinsic part of our railway heritage. Many will jog the memories of people who have travelled on them, seen them fly through their local station or photographed them for private collections.

| | |
|---|---|
| Aberdonian | Cambrian Coast Express |
| Atlantic Coast Express (ACE) | Capitals Limited |
| Birmingham Pullman | Capitals United |
| Blackpool & Fylde Express | Cathedral Express |
| Bon Accord | Cheltenham Spa Express |
| Bournemouth Belle | Cheltenham Flyer |
| Bournemouth Limited | City-to-City Express |
| Brighton Belle | Comet |
| Bristol Pullman | Cornish Riviera Express |
| Bristolian | Cornishman |
| Broadsman | Coronation |
| Caledonian | Coronation Scot |

Day Continental
Devon Belle
Devonian
East Anglian
Elizabethan
Emerald Isle Express
Executive
Fair Maid
Fast Belfast
Fenman
Flying Scotsman
Golden Arrow
Golden Hind
Grampian
Granite City
Heart of Midlothian
Hebridean
Highlandman
Hook Continental
Hull Pullman
Inter-City
Irish Mails
Irish Mail via Fishguard
Irishman
John O' Groat
Kentish Belle
Lakes Express
Lancastrian
Lewisman
Liverpool Pullman
Mancunian
Man of Kent
Manxman
Master Cutler
Mayflower
Merchant Venturer
Merseyside Express
Midday Scot
Midland Pullman

Midlander
Night Ferry
Night Limited
Night Scot
Night Scotsman
Norfolk Coast Express
Norfolkman
North Briton
North Eastern
Northern Irishman
Northumbrian
Orcadian
Oxford Pullman
Palatine
Peak Express
Pembroke Coast Express
Pines Express
Queen of Scots
Red Dragon
Red Rose
Robin Hood
Royal Duchy
Royal Highlander
Royal Scot
Royal Wessex
Scandinavian
Scarborough Flyer
Shamrock
Sheffield Special
Silver Jubilee
South Wales Pullman
South Yorkshireman
Southern Belle
St Mungo
Sunny South Express
Talisman
Tyne-Tees Pullman
Thames-Clyde Express
Thames-Forth Express

| | |
|---|---|
| Torbay Express | Tynesider |
| Trans-Pennines | Ulster Express |

Most of these titles are now extinct. Other trains of individual character, or having their own special story, acquired unofficial titles or nicknames, the better known ones being easy to identify from this short list:

| | |
|---|---|
| Blackpool Club Train | Paddy |
| Corridor (for Midday Scot) | Ports to Ports Express |
| Limited | West Coast Postal |
| Llandudno Club Train | Windermere Club Train |
| North Country Continental | |

Some groups of trains acquired their own unofficial names, among them the Cambridge Buffet expresses and the Manchester Club trains.

In addition, numerous trains, especially local ones, were known by favourite nicknames by both railway people and the travelling public. You are bound to recognize some: the School Train, the Milk Train, the Colliers' Train, the Race Train, the Horse Train, the Workmen's Train, the Push-and-Pull, the Shuttle, the Boat Train, the Newspaper Train, the Mail Train, the Works Train, the Cattle Market Train, the Stockbrokers' Train, the Theatre Train, the Ghost Train, Daddy's Train.

At Newark the 11 a.m. train from Lincoln to Nottingham was known as 'Charlie's Train'. When I was doing relief work there in 1946, the station foreman told me that many years ago a porter named Charlie Branson had loaded a barrow full of parcels into the guard's van for Lincoln instead of for Nottingham, delaying the train about ten minutes in sorting things out. The next day it was 'Charlie's train' . . . and the next, and the next . . .

It was during the 1930s, while working first in London then in the Bletchley area, that I saw and travelled on a good number of titled trains. This brought a new and fascinating interest in the great trains of the day. Details were plethoric – the types of carriages, the class and technical features of the locomotives, the speed and running times, the routes, when the train or its title was first introduced and any other special characteristics. A name or emblem on the smokebox door of the locomotive, nameboards proudly borne on the sides of the carriages, and sometimes a decorated design and name above the ticket barrier at the entrance to the platform, all contrived to create an individuality, a personality that was memorable, out of a mass of timber and iron, glass and upholstery.

What more stirring sight was there than the 'Royal Scot' in LMS maroon and all its finery hauling its great train, steaming and roaring through the foothills of the Lake District, or the chocolate-and-cream of the GWR 'Cheltenham Flyer' tearing through the green and placid hills of Wiltshire! Such a remembered vision of elegance and speed evokes that sigh of mingled joy and sadness which heaves silently in the breast of the true and unashamed enthusiast for steam railways.

Before World War I a fair number of crack trains already bore titles, some dating back to the previous century. But during that war only four retained their official names: the 'Night Scotsman', the 'Aberdonian', the 'Flying Scotsman' and the 'Cornish Riviera Express'. When peace came, the old names re-appeared and many new ones were created, especially after the 1923 amalgamations. To justify a title, a train needed quality to face the glare of the public spotlight, which could be even more fierce if something went wrong on the journey. Creating star quality for specific trains and bestowing on them an exciting and recognizable identity tended to give the railways as a whole more glamour and style, made them more talked about and encouraged railway employees to take a greater pride in their company.

Pride certainly gripped me when, in my early twenties, I made my first journey on the 'Mancunian', a London-Manchester train which served my home and birthplace, Stoke-on-Trent. On that occasion, it was hauled by a maroon-liveried 'Jubilee'-class 4-6-0 built by Stanier, heavier locomotives being restricted from the Stoke route. Leaving Euston at 4.10 p.m., a three-minute stop at Bletchley enabled a portion of the train to be hauled by a waiting locomotive through to Northampton, while the main train went on to Rugby and Lichfield. We reached Stoke 'on time' at 7 p.m. Further stops would be made at Congleton, Macclesfield and Stockport, to arrive in Manchester London Road station at 8.5 p.m. The southbound 'Mancunian' left London Road at 9.45 a.m.

for a 3½ hour journey. Average speeds of over sixty miles an hour were often achieved by a 'Royal Scot' class locomotive, and in later years by a 4-6-2 'Pacific' type.

Useful for train spotting, our office at Euston House was just across the road from the old station. When I had to take files to the general offices built around the Great Hall, I timed such visits to see a titled train. I saw away at 10.45 a.m. the 'Royal Scot', decorated with its tartan nameboards on every carriage and bound for Glasgow; and the 12.5 p.m. 'Mid-day Scot', and at 1.20 p.m. the 'Emerald Isle Express' bound for Holyhead to connect with a ship to Dublin. In the evenings a colleague joined me, and we saw such crack trains as the 'Ulsterman' bound for Heysham in Lancashire with ship connection to Belfast. At 7.15 p.m. it was the 'Royal Highlander' off to Inverness. Then at 8.45 p.m. we could see away the 'Royal Mail' to Holyhead, connecting with a ship for Dublin. The excitement of those romantic nameboards set off in me a longing to explore some of those far-off places that I had not yet seen.

According to the timetables and train nameboards, she was officially the 'Cheltenham Spa Express'. But she was known and loved as the 'Cheltenham Flyer'. This train started modestly as an afternoon run from Cheltenham and Gloucester to Paddington, eventually earning world acclaim. In the 1920s some main-line railways had achieved notable runs which earned much valuable prestige. Leader in the field was the North Eastern Railway, which in 1923 became part of the LNER and had scored mightily with a forty-four-mile run from Darlington to York in only forty-three minutes. And what a beautiful stretch of permanent way it was too; still is.

On the GWR, a splendid race track of 77½ miles lay between Swindon and Paddington. Beautifully aligned, it was almost level, a tempting section for GWR operating men with a penchant for a flash of speed. Speeds increased the competitive pressures, and in 1929 the GWR cut the time of its star runner on this fast stretch to seventy minutes. That raised a few eyebrows because, at an average of just over sixty-six miles an hour, it catapulted to the top as the fastest regular run in the world. It was only natural that a train with such a dazzling performance should earn the accolade among its admirers of its own nickname, the 'Cheltenham Flyer'. Though the epithet became more popular than the official title, it never received official blessing. But with such a brilliant and acclaimed success on the world steam-railways scene, who cares!

In 1932 the run from Swindon was down to 65 minutes, lifting the start-to-stop average to 71·4 miles an hour. To maintain so high an average, incredible bursts of speed had to be made. And how rewarding, not only for drivers and firemen but for guards and travelling ticket-collectors, those backroom men in the operating office and many others, to be pedestalled in triumph by 'the fastest train in the world'.

Many envious eyes had been cast towards the Flyer of the West, and soon the glory was to be wrested from the proud hands of the GWR. But first a look at the train itself and the classic GWR locomotives that made such records possible. Usually the main train consisted of a third-class brake, corridor composite, restaurant car, corridor composite, third class, and third-class brake – a six-coach set; the compos included both first- and third-class accommodation. Departing from Cheltenham at 2.40 p.m., the train ran into Gloucester, picked up a through composite brake coach which had left Hereford at 1.15 p.m. as a stopping service, reversed and hooked on to the locomotive. With stops at Stroud and Kemble, it was timed to reach Paddington at 5 p.m. Both the locomotive and the coaching stock of this train went down from Paddington daily at 10.45 a.m., making a semi-fast train that was nothing to write home about. A 'Castle' locomotive generally did both trips. I had seen the down train leave Paddington but had never travelled on it in either direction.

For the history books, the best journey of the 'Flyer' was recorded in fine detail on 6th June 1932, when speed was in the atmosphere, and I read about it afterwards in the railway magazines at Derby. Between Swindon and Paddington the figures were: 77·3 miles in 56 minutes 47 seconds, to average 81·7 m.p.h. Champing at the bit for this epoch-making journey was that famous locomotive 'Tregenna Castle', No. 5006, a 4-6-0 with four cylinders, an engine of Charles Collett design that was the Great Western tradition personified. Ordinarily the 5 p.m. 'Cheltenham Spa Express', with testing gradients to tackle, was no headline stealer, but on this great day it had a good run – not surprising, for up front was 4-6-0 'Manorbier Castle' No. 5005.

Though some good timings on this important route were achieved after World War II, the famous 'Cheltenham Flyer', clad in the familiar chocolate and cream, that had revelled in a brief sojourn of world renown, never came back. Yet this wonderful train (like many others), must still remain in the memory of countless people around the world.

Back again to the 1930s: it had to be another really great train with a notable track record to climb onto the pedestal labelled 'Britain's Fastest Train'. And the honour was bestowed on the LNER 'Silver Jubilee' streamlined train in 1935. On its best run between King's Cross and Grantham, the train reached 112½ miles an hour, a record for Britain. This piece of history was made on 27th September, which happened to be exactly 110 years after George Stephenson had driven his 'Locomotion No. 1' on the opening day of the Stockton & Darlington Railway. That was really when it all began. The 'Silver Jubilee' has another claim to history: it was the first train in Britain to be streamlined throughout from locomotive to guard's van. Its *raison d'être* was the silver jubilee of the reign of King George V.

Starting its regular service on 30th September 1935, this new train's 10 a.m. departure from Newcastle Central was balanced by the 5.30 p.m. from King's Cross. In both directions the non-stop runs were scheduled to take four hours. Gresley built four locomotives to handle the trains: 'Silver Link' No. 2509, 'Quicksilver' No. 2510, 'Silver King' No. 2511, and 'Silver Fox' No. 2512. All were Class A4 'Pacific' 4-6-2. The train was finished in a livery of silver-grey throughout, with stainless steel fittings. In 1937 I watched this train flash through Hatfield station, one of the most spectacular railway sights to cross my vision. When war broke out two years later, this beautiful train was withdrawn, never to run again.

My friend Kenneth Wheaton tells me about the journeys of his father, Sydney, on the 'Bournemouth Limited', starting in 1929. Mr Wheaton managed a large emporium in Bournemouth and travelled to London one day most weeks with two other businessmen. Departing smartly at 8.40 a.m. the 'Limited', a noted punctual runner, reached Waterloo at 10.38 a.m. Then on their separate ways to the City and the West End they did go. They met again at Waterloo in the restaurant car of the return 4.30 p.m. 'Bournemouth Limited', due to reach Bournemouth at 6.38 p.m.

Habitually they stayed in the restaurant car throughout the non-stop journey and took afternoon tea. This was usually a light meal which might consist of buttered toasted teacakes, thin bread-and-butter and strawberry jam with a pot of freshly made tea. Sometimes there was ham, salad or cucumber sandwiches and a slice of rich fruitcake. Fred, the senior steward, knew exactly their individual personal foibles. Mr Meeham wanted to start his tea punctually at 4.30 p.m., just as the train steamed out of Waterloo; Mr Wheaton liked his at precisely 5 p.m., as the train was roaring through Woking; and Mr Chapman preferred his at 5.15 p.m., as the train approached Basingstoke. Says Kenneth, "There was time for a genteel service in those leisurely days of railway steam when gentlemen were gentlemen."

Though the title was not conferred on the train until July 1929 when formed of corridor stock, a non-stop had first run on this route of 108 miles in 1899 in London & South Western days. No really serious gradients exist to impede good speeds, but on the up journey a gradient averaging around one in 250 runs for a trying 16 miles beyond Winchester; and on the down journey the pull from Waterloo for about 50 miles is, in equestrian terms, .'against the collar'.

Introduced largely for the Waterloo-Bournemouth non-stoppers were Dugald Drummond's splendid four-cylinder 4-6-0s with six feet seven inch driving-wheels. First built in 1905, they were simple, sturdy and consistently reliable, like battle-ships, and were at that time the largest locomotives in Britain. Later to this route came Richard Maunsell's famous 'King Arthurs' and 'Schools', cutting the best journey schedules to 116 minutes. In the late 1930s the normal formation of the 'Limited' was eleven bogie coaches. When war came, this notable train was withdrawn, ending for ever the daily non-stop running between Waterloo and Bournemouth. I am glad to be able to re-call just one journey to Bournemouth I made on the 'Limited' in the summer of 1935.

When my neighbour Ernst Bamberg told me that one of his

boyhood ambitions was to ride in the driving-cab of an express locomotive, I knew exactly how he felt. He was captivated by the railways, and as the managing director of a small local firm, he was a railway customer.

Because I worked in the public relations department of British Rail headquarters, he bestowed upon me more power than I could claim. He said, "You're more important than Dr Beeching, because you can get me a ride on a loco and he can't." Plausible, to be sure. However, Ernst is persuasive, and I am a sucker for steam-lovers, so I secured permission for him to travel the eighty-four miles from Waterloo as far as Salisbury on the locomotive of that famous train the 'Atlantic Coast Express'. After this, it was even more difficult to convince him that I was only a diminutive cog in a massive bureaucratic something or other. I knew how the cogs worked, that's all.

We travelled together from St Albans. At Waterloo a colleague escorted us beyond the platform and onto the track to the giant locomotive. Lucky for both of us, it was 'Channel Packet', a Merchant Navy class 4-6-2, No. 35001, of 1941 vintage; it was a Bulleid product with three cylinders, and the first British locomotive to be lighted throughout by electricity.

I had arranged for a railway photographer to be there, for we might want pictorial evidence in case Ernst did something madly rash and dangerous. Later the picture appeared, together with a brief news item I wrote, in a Hertfordshire newspaper; this was *my* professional reward – presenting the nationalized railways with a human face.

Ernst had a far rougher ride than he had expected. He had to be careful to dodge the fireman's busy shovel, hold on to a handrail so as not to fall onto the track, avoid touching any scorching hot metal and stand back from the fierce heat of the furnace when the firebox doors were open. And when the driver sounded the engine whistle, Ernst jumped so much that his hat fell off. Otherwise, he said, he enjoyed it immensely, an experience he would never forget. Travelling first class on his return from Salisbury, he luxuriated on real, well-sprung upholstery.

Several things surprised him – the amount of coal the fireman fed into that hungry furnace, the frightening oscillation under his feet between the tender and the engine, the casual and confident way the driver handled the train and read the signals, the deafening scream of the engine whistle, and the thunderous roar as they plunged through stations and under bridges. Some time later, when he was president of the local Rotary Club, he invited me to give a talk to members about railways, which brought a little more publicity for the 'old firm'.

Before the 1923 amalgamations, the London & South Western had run an express leaving Waterloo around 11 a.m. But not until 1926 was it given its title 'Atlantic Coast Express', an exciting name with adventurous overtones and irresistibly abbreviated to 'ACE'.   It was a unique train because in its heyday it ran in nine different sections or portions and served many places on and off the main route – Ilfracombe, Torrington, Padstow, Bude, Plymouth, Exeter, Exmouth, Sidmouth, Salisbury, Seaton and a few more! (As a young man in the operating department, if I had a train in even four portions, I had to check and re-check my paperwork, to avoid scheduling a couple of coaches to the wrong station.) In later years, the portions of the train were steadily discontinued; and 1964 saw the end of this most un-usual multi-destination service. Among the well-known engines that worked the train were Bulleid's 4-6-2 'Merchant Navy' class, including his 'Belgian Marine', No. 35017.

Another famous train, one of the greatest, engaged my atten-tion during my days at the Railways Board. My chief asked me to visit Hornsey carriage sidings, some four miles from King's Cross, the nearby locomotive sheds and the station itself. He wanted, for a small illustrated book the department was to publish, a fully descriptive chapter about the preparations of staff, train and locomotive of the 'Flying Scotsman' itself. The train was due to depart, as it had done since Victorian times, at ten in the morning.

What steam man could wish for a better commission!

Every tiny detail had to be investigated: preparing the locomo-tive, including greasing and oiling, stocking up with fuel, testing the brake pressures, the driver collecting from the shed offices any instructions that might apply to the journey of 393 miles to Edinburgh Waverley. Water, soap and towels would be needed in the train toilets; the guard would check his personal, first-aid and emergency equipment and his train brake pressure; cylinders of gas would need to be fitted underneath the kitchen car for cooking; and victualling of the restaurant-car set would be required for meals served on the journey. A carriage and wagon department man ('wheel tapper') would check the wheels, the undercarriages and the electric, heating, coupling and braking connections between the carriages. High in her eyrie the train announcer will be checking her script as the train is being hauled into the platform by a shunting engine, myself riding with the guard. Finally the locomotive is on the train; the platform duties are finished; then the station inspector's whistle signals the train to start. After about two hours of research, talking to various staff, scribbling shorthand in my notebook, then being there on platform eight at that dramatic moment when the great train began to move, it brought a thrill of spectacle that remains vividly in the memory.

It was a more mundane train that brought a sequence of operating oddities that were unbelievable. Alf Duncombe, the guard, who told me the story, brought the 8.55 a.m. 'Merseyside Express' from Euston, Liverpool bound. Up front was a 'Coronation' 4-6-2 'Pacific', of a class that Stanier had made famous in the 1930s.

Famous or not, it developed engine trouble as the train approached Crewe. At Hadmore, as the fireman lowered his scoop into the water trough at speed, the firebox brick-arch collapsed. Then, every driver's ultimate fear, the engine 'dropped a plug', the last defensive line against a boiler explosion, an emergency often created by a low water level in the boiler. The lead plugs having melted in the intense heat, water is spurted onto the fierce fire in a great cloud of hissing steam. On this occasion railway telephone lines buzzed and soon a locomotive to assist arrived from Crewe to haul the failed locomotive and its train to Crewe for attention. This assistant locomotive was also a Stanier – a 'Black Five'. The intention was that the assistant locomotive would haul the failed machine and train to Crewe and take the 'Coronation' off the train, and for the 'Black Five' to take the train the remaining thirty-five miles to Liverpool.

But it never reached Crewe. On the way the vacuum brake pipe on the assistant locomotive failed, depriving the whole train of automatic braking. Passengers found themselves stopped 'in the middle of nowhere'. Puzzled heads popped out from carriage windows enquiringly. In their compartments frustrated passengers would be trying, fruitlessly, to unravel the mysteries of lengthy delays to important trains apparently without any reason whatsoever. They could only conclude that a bunch of stupid idiots were trying to work this complicated railway system, something quite beyond their simple minds. While the waiting passengers fumed or joked or relaxed, along came another fine big locomotive rolling along the rails to assist. And would you believe it – another 'Black Five'! Railwaymen at Crewe witnessed this extraordinary sight of an express train being headed by three Stanier locomotives. In Crewe station the train was uncoupled; the leading 'Black Five' shunted the two lame ducks out of the way, then took the train to Liverpool, somewhat late, but safe.

Probably the passengers were told nothing, but someone was sure to tell Sir William Stanier.

# 17

# Life After Death in the Engine Graveyards

In the 1950s, when British Railways had decided to phase out steam to make way for the new diesels and electrics, we in the HQ public relations department were encouraged to play down steam and to build up the new types of power. To promote the new image meant placing articles, news items and illustrations in the BR staff magazine and massively among the media of publications and every kind of broadcasting.

For years we had been glamorizing steam. That was now to stop. Understandably. It was sensible to propagate the new systems, to explain how they work and how passengers, traders, industrialists and railway staff would be affected. After all, millions of pounds of public money were being invested.

But when you have been a steam man from your cradle right up to your mid-forties, you cannot let it blow away just like that. I doubt whether some top officials appreciated how deeply millions of people, both public and railway staff, were attached to steam railways. Several senior people of my close acquaintance at HQ, though heavily involved in the technical changeover, secretly nursed their long-felt love of the traditional system and on occasion enjoyed a steam trip with one of the many societies. To keep in touch, some took society membership but did not shout about it.

Not until steam had been gone on BR for some years did the management begin to realize the commercial value of continuing with some steam-locomotive journeys. Then the passenger department started to initiate their own steam-railway excursions on a viable basis, jointly with preservation societies and others who owned steam locomotives. Increasingly too British Rail have given the societies backing for private steam runs on British Rail public routes. By 1974 BR had approved over one thousand miles of the line for this, an arrangement that will continue at least until the mid-1980s. After that, renewal will be considered for a further period. The length of route so approved represents about nine per cent of BR's total route mileage. No railway enthusiast, surely, should grumble about that!

Here is a list of the main routes approved:

| ENGLAND AND WALES | miles |
|---|---|
| Birmingham (Moor Street)/Saltley – Didcot | 77 |
| Tyseley – Stratford-on-Avon | 22 |
| Hatton/Lapworth – Stratford-on-Avon | 9 |
| York – Leeds (via Harrogate) | 39 |
| York – Leeds (via Church Fenton) | 25 |
| Leeds – Carnforth | 64 |
| Carnforth – Barrow – Sellafield & Dalton<br>Junction Curve | 64 |
| Hull – York (via Goole) | 62 |
| York – Sheffield (via Pontefract) | 46 |
| Guide Bridge – Sheffield | 40 |
| Middlesbrough – Sunderland – Newcastle | 48 |
| Settle Junction – Carlisle | 73½ |
| Newcastle – Carlisle | 60 |
| Chester – Newport (via Shrewsbury and Hereford) | 136 |
| Chester – New Mills South Junction/Woodley<br>Junction (Special dispensation is required<br>for this route) | 60 |

| SCOTLAND | |
|---|---|
| Edinburgh – Aberdeen (over Forth and Tay Bridges) | 130 |
| Dundee – Stirling – Edinburgh | 90 |
| Dalmeny – Winchburgh Junction | 4½ |
| Circular: Dundee – Ladybank – Thornton –<br>Dunfermline – Cowdenbeath –<br>Thornton – Dundee | 91 |

Because some of these routes overlap, it is not possible to make an accurate total of miles quoted. For the 1980 celebrations of the Liverpool & Manchester Railway, British Rail approved three additional routes for steam running: Liverpool – Manchester, Hellifield – Blackburn – Manchester, Guide Bridge – Manchester, a total approaching ninety miles.

In co-operation with the societies, British Rail keep an updated record of steam locomotives which may be considered for steam running over BR lines. Arranging a run depends on the condition of the locomotive, a detailed examination, approval by BR's regional chief mechanical and electrical engineer, and specific route clearance by the chief civil engineer. At present I hold a list of over thirty 'approved' locomotives (twenty-two in 1974). Included are such famous and much-loved engines as 'Hardwicke', 'Britannia', 'Sir Nigel Gresley', 'Flying Scotsman', 'Clan Line', 'Duchess of Hamilton', 'Princess Elizabeth', 'Leander' and 'George Stephenson', plus Great Western 'King', 'Castle', 'Hall' and 'Manor' classes. Each year some are added and some removed. Many of these splendid locomotives I have been privileged to see – at Shildon, Rainhill, Clapham, Swindon and York, on view at various exhibitions, hauling trains that have been chartered by one of the societies or sponsored by BR, or standing quietly at their home depots awaiting expectantly the next call to show what they can do.

Some societies, especially those with working locomotives and large capital investment, are looking ahead past the end of the century. What trends will influence their prospects? Each year fewer footplatemen with steam experience remain. Steam working will need to be concentrated on fewer depots where enough trained staff are available. Large locomotives to haul excursions over BR lines become increasingly more costly and difficult to maintain. Indeed, many replacement parts have to be specially manufactured. As time goes on, British Rail will have little option but to apply more stringent inspection procedures. However, sufficient expertise should be available for steam working on BR lines at least until the mid or late 1980s.

Owners or operators who plan to run their locomotives over BR lines maintain proper records of each one, with dates: mileages run, hours in steam, defects and their repair, boiler washouts and boiler condition. Any alterations that may affect either the loading-gauge profile or axle weights have to be notified specially to British Rail. For the excursions, owners or operators are responsible for fire lighting, steam raising, coaling, watering, fire dropping and such chores. BR provide a driver, fireman and traction inspector. One representative of the owner or operator may travel on the footplate to observe the working of the locomotive.

The Steam Locomotive Operators' Association (SLOA) acts as co-ordinator with British Rail for all steam charters advertised to the public. This keeps the organization tidy. Located in each of the five regions of BR is a regional steam liaison officer. Steam operations in Scotland are controlled by BR's Scottish Region, which consults with other regions when trains run south of the border. Policy is controlled by the Inter-City marketing officer at Railways Board headquarters in London, two main factors being safety and commercial viability.

Steam charters are confined generally to Saturdays, Sundays and Bank Holidays from January to May and from September to December and depend upon routes and resources available. Always popular are such routes as Settle – Carlisle, Shrewsbury – Hereford – Newport and Guide Bridge – Sheffield. Insurance? Most important. Charterers have to indemnify British Rail against mishap by taking out insurance cover for more than £2 million, a figure that rises with inflation. Cover is high. The premium is not so terrifying!

Steam excursions sponsored by British Rail usually run during the summer months on mid-week days and some bank holidays, with connecting services from many main-line stations.

Societies, of course, run their own steam locomotives, alone or as specials, on their own private lines as well as on British Rail approved routes.

Since the beginning of the major revolution in railway motive power in the mid-1950s, public enthusiasm for steam locomotives and steam railways and all that goes with them has grown at an astonishing pace, and the great new surge in railway preservation, which began after Sir Brian Robertson had announced that steam must go, has matured to impressive proportions.

Official BR encouragement can be seen in the sixteen pages in the full public timetable devoted to the timetables of over twenty private companies operating around Britain. A simple map with code numbers shows their locations and the connections with the railway network. Also listed are steam excursions which run on BR lines approved for steam. Among them are two trains with titles: the 'North Yorkshireman' and the 'Scarborough Spa Express'.

Many members of the railway preservation societies have commented to me about the welcome development of co-operation with British Rail. Captain Peter Manisty RN (Retd), chairman of the Association of Railway Preservation Societies (ARPS) since 1964 and a personal friend for many years, said to me recently, "We well understand that British Rail's first commitment must be to its own customers and to the safety of the system. But we are enormously grateful for the generous assistance they give us. May it long continue."

When British Rail announce details of steam runs they are organizing, a good Press is assured. Typical is one from the *Daily Telegraph*: "The trip marks a new era in nostalgic steam journeys which British Rail will be operating to the Yorkshire coast this summer." The sight and sound of these trains capture that sigh of joy and sadness mingled which heaves silently in the breast of the true steam-railway nostalgic.

How widespread is the interest in steam railways? In Britain there are over two million enthusiasts and about five hundred railway societies; some are tiny clubs, and others own railway lines several miles long which regularly run their trains. Including museums and similar organizations, preserved equipment embraces some five hundred steam locomotives, plus carriages, wagons, track, stations, signalboxes, engine sheds and every type of railway relic that recreates the atmosphere of bygone days. Many young men who barely remember the steam trains wear engineers' overalls at the weekend to wield paintbrush and polishing rag, oil-can and spanner. Steam ventures attract people from all walks of life and in all the professions, notably parsons, doctors and solicitors. HRH Prince Philip, the Duke of Edinburgh, himself, is Patron of the Transport Trust, a leading society. Surprisingly, girls and women too are caught by the sight and sound of the steam era, dispelling the notion that it is exclusively a masculine proclivity. Membership breaks down social barriers, bridges generation gaps and fosters a tremendous fellow-feeling of affinity, reminiscent of my younger working days in steam railways.

When British Rail phased out steam, they had little option but to sell most of the locomotives for scrap. Woodham Brothers, scrap merchants of Barry in South Wales, with admirable investment foresight, bought hundreds. Of these, around 150 have been purchased since 1968 and moved from Barry to preserved railways and depots throughout Britain. So far, about thirty are steamable. At Barry, several dozen others (more than seventy in 1983) are being studied by a group of interested parties for their potential for steaming or use as spare parts, an activity co-ordinated by the Transport Trust in London. Woodhams do not expect to start cutting up these remaining locomotives until 1984 or later.

Converting a rusty old engine to full steaming might sound easy, but it takes years of sweat and anxiety, leisure time and energy, not to say finances, by enthusiastic volunteers to reach that great moment when the locomotive, now fired and steaming, actually moves along the rails all by itself! Only those who have suffered can appreciate the thrill of it all.

In 1981 the National Railway Preservation Campaign was inaugurated to boost public awareness, 1982 having been proclaimed the Year of Consolidation. Robert Adley, MP for Christchurch and Lymington, was appointed campaign president. He held a Press conference concerning the 'Barry Rescue' on 17th February 1981. This was followed six days later by the now famous Adjournment Debate in which Adley and Kenneth Clarke (Under-Secretary of State for Transport) held the floor in the House of Commons for nearly half an hour. Clarke referred to the 'brotherhood of steam' and stated he was a long-standing railway steam enthusiast and a shareholder in the Great Central Preservation Society at Loughborough. In the debate many other railway societies were mentioned.

As anyone knows who has visited the scrapyard at Barry, towards a hundred old workhorses have stood there in all weathers since the late 1960s, suffering inexorable deterioration, a sad sight for the lover of locomotives. Even now a few of special historic interest have been earmarked for the kiss of life ready for steaming in the 1980s.

Dai Woodham in 1957 was only thirty-eight when he stumbled on a gold mine. He bought a redundant locomotive to carve up and sell in pieces. This was the start of the avalanche. Other scrap merchants benefited too. In the bigger yards large numbers were whipped around by crane, carved up like carcases, acetylene torches flashing, and quickly converted to hard cash. Not at Barry. Never an iconoclast, Dai Woodham seemed in no hurry to tear them apart. Some, of course, had to go to pieces. But by the end of British Rail's steam era, the largest concentration of steam locomotives in Britain had accumulated at Barry. They rested on the rusty rails amid the oil and mud, in company with those hardy railway weeds, the colourful willow herb and ragwort that never seem to die. Hardy? Some of those locomotives had run for half a century and clocked up two million miles. Others were barely a few years old.

Published articles about scrapped locomotives inevitably pointed a signpost to Barry. Liberal details and lively illustrations tempted enthusiasts to trek to this new Mecca. Schoolboys and university dons, parsons and canons, admirals and generals: they all went. Hope and joy went knocking. Dai Woodham recalls a desperate woman. "She rang me up, pleading with me not to sell an engine to her husband. She'd discovered he'd taken out a mortgage on the house."

Barry is an open scrapyard, a living legend of dead locos. Folk wander around as they like. Poignant messages have been roughly painted on earmarked locomotives: "Please save me", "Reserved", "A bad day for steam". One had large, sad eyes painted on the smokebox door, with tears falling. A group of drivers had earmarked an LMS Stanier 'Black Five' with the hope of purchase. (How do you explain it to your wife? "Darling, I've just bought a locomotive! Where shall I put it?") 'Outsiders' rarely appreciate how much the steam railways mean to those of us who have spent a lifetime with trains, a deep sentiment that is beyond the reach of polemics.

The speed at which British Rail ran out of steam locomotives during the changeover was staggering. In the ten years to 1967, I used to see the figures in the office, year by year. Sometimes a hundred went for scrap in a week. Good-quality stuff it was, too. Dai Woodham kept on buying. "After a while," he said, "I lost count. But it must be between eight hundred and a thousand." And the brainchildren of Gresley and Stanier, Bulleid and Collett, their 'Kings' and 'Castles', the 'Coronations' and 'Lord Nelsons', those A3s and A4s, legends in their working lifetime, steamed on their last sorrowful journeys to the scrapyard. Yet some were destined to be resurrected for their 'second coming' in steam.

For preservation or otherwise, customers paid in the region of £4,000 to £15,000 apiece, the price being based mainly on weight as scrap, to save argument.

Through the post, piles of flattering, grateful, admiring, praising, fulsome panegyrics reached Dai Woodham to swell his filing cabinets. They still come. One ended, "PS. You are a giant among giants." Dai never sought fame. Fame was thrust upon him. Whether he wanted it or not, he was becoming enshrined in the history of steam railways. He has a large collection of autographed railway books from grateful authors (that gives me an idea!) who had eulogized him fulsomely in their traditional acknowledgements. On my second visit to Barry, I told him, "I'm writing a book . . ."

"Oh, hell. Not another one!"

He seems to enjoy this sort of thing more than he will admit, and his eyes crinkled up in a give-away smile.

People enjoy wandering about the scrapyard unhindered. And there are lots of them. The master of this mass of dead metal said, "Over 2½ million have been here now." Robert Adley MP claimed that Dai's scrapyard must be the biggest tourist attraction never to be visited by the chairmen of Britain's tourist boards. Around his yard Dai is tramping up to the ears in the incredible nostalgia of sentimental and stirring memories; this businessman who strides around the piles of metal, mentally converting into golden pounds the value of his rusty mounds, and who unwittingly builds up the dreams of those who would create a living, vibrating glimpse of those halcyon days of far away and long ago.

Ambling round the yard one day, quiet, except for the hissing acetylene torches and screaming gulls, I caught again that smell of railway stations and goods depots, engine sheds and creosoted sleepers that had been my life for so long.

Dai's scrapyard has been described as "a place of sad pilgrimage". Yet in other hands the lot might have been quickly broken up. In the event, much of our national heritage has been rescued and recreated for many to enjoy. Metal from the objects of men's dreams have been magically metamorphosed into an elegant Rolls Royce Camargue (replacing his earlier Silver Shadow), which many have seen parked among the rust without a blush. How could anyone envy Dai his rewards!

Yet, whatever fame and fortune he may have achieved, it is but the reflected glory of the great age of steam railways. Even so, nothing can obliterate the public service he has rendered, in keeping alive a British tradition that suffered its birthpangs in the pain of the Industrial Revolution.

Societies with their own railways usually produce their own magazines for members and glossy brochures of their services for the public. Here is a snippet from *The Knotty*, journal of the North Staffordshire Railway Company (1978) Ltd, based at Cheddleton station on the picturesque Churnet Valley line. Such snippets reflect the affection for the old railway companies, and the problems tackled. "Wanted – Dead or Alive," an advertisement reads. "To help create the right period atmosphere at Cheddleton, we need more milk churns, old enamel advertising signs, and wooden bench seats, preferably of railway origin." And another: "Help wanted to purchase one of the few remaining high-sided signalmen's chairs used in signalboxes on the NSR." Journal editor John Taylor served an apprenticeship at Crewe Works in the final days of steam.

Typical of the Society's tours is one they ran recently to Snowdonia, in Wales, a joint venture with BBC Radio Stoke.

Sometimes a member breaks into verse. Here are lines about class 4 mixed traffic engine No. 80136:

> EIGHT years plus six down at Barry she's lain
> OH, what a long time to be out in the rain.
> ONE day, she'll steam,
> THREE years from arriving
> SIX coupled wheels we want to see driving.
>
> C learly, this engine is no good in store,
> L ive steam's what we want beyond Oakamoor,
> A lton's the place, so come on, dig deep;

S upport Mr Oldfield, 'cos
S team's not cheap.

4 just a few hours of work at weekend
M akes this fine engine
T he easier to mend.

In 1980 the NSR had their first steaming locomotive. Sir Arthur Bryan, chairman of the famous potteries Wedgwood company, named the locomotive 'Sir Josiah Wedgwood' on a day of great excitement in 1981. Classed as J94, it is a saddle tank 0-6-0 austerity type, built in 1952 by Hunslet of Leeds to the design of R. A. Riddles, meeting war-time specifications agreed in 1943. Its two cylinders are 18 inches by 26 inches, boiler pressure 170 pounds, drivers small at 4 feet 3 inches diameter and tractive effort 23,780. Valve gear is of the Stephenson type, invented a century and a half ago by the genius himself. Though in good condition, it was taken out of service for an extensive work programme. Active members of other societies will sympathize on reading the work list:

Boiler washout and partial retube
Fitting of new forward fusible plug
Regrinding of regulator valve faces
Fitting four oil-supply pipes to valve spindles
Oil-box drain-holes to be drilled
Brazing of leaking injector pipe
Installation of brick arch in firebox
Fitting seats and doors
New smokebox waste plates to be fitted

Most of the work was finished in 1981, ready for steaming on the short runs at Cheddleton station, a beautiful area I have known since boyhood. Livery is in the NSR colour of madder lake, the special paint mix having been donated by a generous manufacturer. Before I even understood the word 'livery', this rich crimson of NSR locomotives and carriages was part of my young life.

Brochures published by the larger societies are usually of a high artistic and commercial standard. Take the Severn Valley Railway. This is a full-sized standard-gauge line running regular stream-hauled passenger trains serving enthusiasts and tourists between Bridgenorth in Salop and Bewdley in Worcestershire, thirteen miles long. It follows closely the meandering course of the River Severn and is punctuated by the quaint old-world charm of its eight country stations. Because roads in the valley are few, some of the lovely views are exclusive to the railway. A four-course English luncheon with wines recreates the authentic period atmosphere in the restored 1930s restaurant car. Various tourist attractions are available nearby and the line connects with British Rail at Kidderminster on the Birmingham-Worcester line.

Few paid staff run this beautiful railway, which is mainly dependent on members. On occasion, shares are offered to the public, a practice of many of the larger societies. Even the company name has a business-like ring – 'Severn Valley Railway (Holdings) Limited'. Let the figures for a recent year tell us more: passenger tickets sold – 187,000; turnover – £634,000; net profit – £62,311; paid-up membership – 10,835. Four locomotives to haul four separate sets of coaches on summer Sundays; six fully operational signalboxes and six fully manned stations. On my visit Mr M. J. Draper, one of the officials, told me, "We have an operational fleet of twelve steam locomotives and thirty passenger coaches. Probably the largest working collection of its kind on any site in Britain, if not in the world."

Few railway centres can transport you straight back to the 1920s and 1930s better than Didcot, unless it is Steamtown at Carnforth, or the Beamish collection, or the Bluebell Line, or the Keighley & Worth Valley Railway, or the . . . Such controversial comment is sure to raise hackles and temperatures here and there, just as the fight for competitive business set alight our railway forefathers. At many of the railway preservation centres we are reminded in numerous ways of the battles and glories of long ago. With Brian Minks, a member of the Great Western Society, at Didcot, it was so Great Western you seemed to get a whiff of pint-sized Brunel's giant-sized cigars and hear echoes of his arguments favouring his broad gauge. A section of seven-foot gauge has been laid in the yard for all to see.

On the day of my visit with Brian, not only was the heady

odour of steam locomotives heavy in the air but the warm sun had brought out the pungent reek of creosote from the permanent-way timber sleepers; it flashed me vividly right back to station-mastering days in the Bletchley district.

Here is an extract from the Didcot brochure: "To bring the history of railways to life, there is nothing quite like the sight, smell and sound of a steam engine in action. At Didcot . . . the Society has established a large working collection of steam locomotives, passenger coaches and goods wagons from the Great Western Railway." On my visit 'Evening Star' was there, and so was 'Winston Churchill' in the 'Battle of Britain' class, and – a rare vehicle – a travelling post office.

Didcot offers a million things. So do many other society centres. Numerous though they are, each is entirely different, each has its own entrancing story to tell. Some members belong to several societies, and they spend weekends and holidays helping in all kinds of voluntary work, making like-minded friends in the process.

Typical themes from society brochures are – "Leave 1982 behind, obtain your ticket and slow down to the leisurely pace of life long ago . . ." ". . . let us take you back to the nostalgic days when steam ruled supreme . . ." "Bring your tape recorder to make a sound recording of a famous locomotive to recapture the charisma of those great days . . ." A friend of mine has installed loudspeakers at home in two rooms downstairs and two bedrooms, and with a stereo tape recording and all the doors open, he recreates the most incredible and realistic sound of a giant locomotive hauling an express at top speed you ever heard.

Steam railways liberally stimulate the arts, and many artists are well known for their railway themes – David Shepherd and Terence Cuneo, C. Hamilton Ellis and John Wigston, to quote a few. Among the many songs and musical scores are 'Oh, Mr Porter', 'The Runaway Train', 'Coronation Scot' and Honegger's famous 'Pacific 231'. And films about railways are legion.

Now here's a funny thought. Technically trains can be driven automatically, and much has been proved on London Transport's automated Victoria Line. All the knowledge and skills required have been around for years. When driverless main-line trains arrive, interest in the railway preservation societies will surely soar. Long-term investments are bound to pay off!

# 18

# Celebrating the Great Stars of Steam

By their massive public pulling power, two events in the affairs of steam have, in recent years, astonished the pundits in the railway world. Each celebrated the 150th anniversary of a historic railway opening. In 1975 it was the Stockton & Darlington staged at Shildon, and in 1980 the Liverpool & Manchester at Rainhill. During each of these two years I published a railway book to coincide with the celebrations and consequently became deeply involved in what went on.

Built by George Stephenson and opened in 1825, the S&DR was certainly the world's first public steam locomotive railway, but it was mainly to link the coalfields of Durham with the estuary at Stockton-on-Tees. As the catalyst of a revolution that rapidly spread throughout the civilized world, the little railway was celebrated widely throughout 1975 in the grand style. The celebrations were the longest, most imaginative and spectacular of their kind ever presented.

British Rail's Shildon Works was the setting for a week-long exhibition, 24th–30th August 1975. A most impressive collection included sixty steam locomotives and forty carriages and wagons; some engines were well over a century old. In sharp contrast, modern rolling stock was also displayed. Stalls run by railway societies from all round Britain, and other supporters, sold a kaleidoscopic variety of railwayana. All week the area was crowded with masses of people.

Jim Palm, an old friend of mine, a BBC radio staff man, told me of a little girl who gazed up, bewildered, at one of the steaming giants, clutched her father's hand and asked, "But Daddy, what are they *for*?"

A major attraction was a full-sized working reproduction of Stephenson's 'Locomotion No. 1' of 1825. In Shildon Works it ran to and fro along the track and made the most fascinating steam machinery noises from its two cylinders, in a rhythm you wanted to dance to.

George Hinchcliffe, managing director of the Steamtown Railway Museum at Carnforth, planned and co-ordinated the movements of all the locomotives and vehicles from all round Britain in a complicated project that took a year or two to plan. Some locomotives travelled under their own steam and needed scheduled coaling and water facilities on the journeys; others were hauled 'dead' on the railway; several were transported by road.

On the evening of the opening, 'Evening Star' was being shunted into position in the sidings, supervised by Hinchcliffe. Colonel George Brown, whose firm was sponsoring the 'Flying Scotsman' locomotive, watched as engine wheels squealed and crunched over points and curved rail. He remarked, "Aren't you worried about these things coming off the rails?" Always cool, Hinchcliffe replied, "Worried? Not a bit."

That very moment a heavy bump and a grinding, tooth-gritting rasp riveted their eyes to the locomotive. Its two rear wheels had run off the rails 'on to Old England'. Everything had to stop. Willing hands hurriedly grabbed heavy timber packing. Inch by inch, aided by a diesel shunting locomotive, the wheels were levered back on the rails in about twenty minutes to sighs of relief. Colonel Brown grimaced. "Think I'd better go!"

Various firms sponsored locomotives and contributed factory time, materials and men in a complex event that was run by over thirty committees and working parties, plus paid officials. Local authorities put up handsome sums of money. Local and county councils became committed.

From the mid-1960s a few individuals had talked vaguely about a celebration – Alan Bowman, a Stockton school teacher and son of a former stationmaster at Stockton; Peter Semmens, railway historian and later deputy curator at the new railway museum at York; and Lyn Wilson, a lecturer at Durham University business school. In 1972 British Rail began to show more interest, realized that many extra trains would be needed, marketed the business under the generic term 'Rail 150' and planned an international publicity programme.

Acrimonious crossfire was exchanged between the various committees and local authorities, and the usual personality clashes were enjoyed by the more aggressive, embroiled in a one-off piece of organization that was *ad-hoc*, ad-lib, piecemeal, play-it-by-ear, never-been-done-before, not covered by in-surance, setting a dangerous precedent, etcetera, etcetera. Experienced businessmen involved really suffered.

The leading committee secured the services of Michael Satow, a keen industrial archaeologist who had retired early as managing director ICI (India) Ltd. A professional engineer, he built the full-scale reproduction working model of Stephenson's 'Locomo-tion No. 1'. He was also appointed co-ordinator (rejecting salary) for the celebrations. Lyn Wilson was seconded from Durham University to serve as commercial manager. With Satow and Wilson, Hinchcliffe completed a triumvirate of able and remark-able characters well known to the societies. In the teeth of daily mounting pressures, they virtually bulldozed a mass of complex projects into orderly and programmed events, cutting miles of red tape, that were to delight an expectant public. Among the other key people who did wonders in this great venture were Herbert Wolfe, 'Jumbo' Wilson and Norman Welch. Simply hundreds of railway societies took part.

Highlight of the celebrations was the Great Cavalcade of Steam on Sunday afternoon 31st August 1975. Viewing stands had been erected on the lineside at Shildon near the station and the Works on the Darlington to Bishop Auckland branch. During the morn-ing some 350,000 people, clad in colourful clothes and in gala mood, converged on the area by every means, a large proportion travelling on the twelve-car multi-unit diesel shuttle trains from Darlington. Later the *Daily Mail* was to report, "Thousands of people have paid £3.50 a head in the viewing stands for the privilege of sampling the soot and steam from some of the world's most famous locomotives." Masses of people stood in the enclos-ures and took any vantage-point offering a good view. (By some quirk of English linguistics, spectators in enclosures stand up, and in stands sit down.) A policeman near me grinned, "It's like Wembley on cup final day. Except that people behave them-selves!"

In the afternoon the thirty-four steam locomotives, with short distances between them, left BR Shildon Works one by one and steamed and sounded their whistles to the shouting, waving, cheering, clapping crowds. In the stands I sat with my wife and Eric Beavor, a former locomotive shed master, and his wife (Eric has published a book called *Steam was my Calling*). We four had stayed for several days, with hundreds of other spectators, at Durham University on a package tour, students being on vacation. I had also travelled in the north-east to give radio and television interviews about my new book.

But this was the event we had all been waiting for. Never before had such a collection of mighty railway history been assembled for such a large and international audience. Led by 'Locomotion No. 1' driven by Michael Satow in period clothes, all the old favourites were there: great locomotives that had been hiding their talents for too many years but now showing their paces. A 4-6-0 'Black Five' of 1947; a Caledonian tank 0-4-4 of 1907; a GWR 0-6-0 pannier tank of 1930 – a fat, squat little fellow who was overshadowed by the more glamorous GWR companions; GWR 'Hall', 'Manor', 'King', and 'Castle' classes; a Riddles 2-10-0 'Austerity' class 9F 'Gordon' No. 600 of 1943; 'Sir Nigel Gresley', a class A4 'Pacific' 4-6-2 of 1937 with a corridor in the tender for enginemen to change on a long non-stop run; that most dazzling 4-2-2 known as 'Stirling No. 1' with eight feet one-inch drivers, tall chimney, sweeping curves, in its sparkling livery of green with bold yellow, red and black lining, of 1870 vintage and claimed by many to be the prettiest engine ever built. (Unknown to most spectators, this old lady suffered from dry rot in her timber tender frame, which explained why she was running 'dead' and hauled by 'Sir Nigel Gresley'.)

Also there was the 'Flying Scotsman' of 1922, a 4-6-2 'Pacific' A3, which hauled No. 910 2-4-0, an Edward Fletcher build of 1874. (Young Fletcher had helped George and Robert Stephenson build the 'Rocket' in 1829.) No. 910 puzzled most spectators, for it was not in the official catalogue and had been 'smuggled in' at the last moment by those two grown-up boys, Michael Satow and George Hinchcliffe. 'Hardwicke' was there, a 2-4-0 Crewe-built 'Precedent' class of 1892 and a veteran of the 'Race to the North' of 1895. (F. W. Webb, her builder, said of fancy locomotive liveries, "I don't care what colour they're painted, as long as it's black.")

'Shannon' brought enormous applause. And so she should. A Wantage Tramway 0-4-0 well tank built in 1857, incredibly she had been steaming for two years before Robert Stephenson died. As this tiny little engine steamed and whistled stalwartly into view, clapping, rousing cheers and some laughter clearly spoke of admiration, tinged with amusement and sadness. For 118 years she had been kept alive and well. The footplate men bowed and waved to the television teams and a thousand amateur cameras; these men on the engine were lads when 'Shannon' was already a veteran. Now they revelled in their privileged position as she moved jauntily along the track, resplendent in green livery, neat cab, diminutive boiler, tall smoking chimney, with steam straining every rivet and spurting from every joint in careless rapture. The Didcot people who had prepared her must have enjoyed this proud moment of triumph.

In this unique Cavalcade the last steamer was 'Evening Star'; she was followed by a British Rail High Speed Train of 1973, a mass of modern technology which earned only polite applause.

My camera was already loaded. In feverish concentration I took picture after picture, fearing that each historic moment would vanish from vision for ever. My friend Beavor, a cautious and deliberate man, pointed to my camera.

"Why leave your lens cover on?"

"Damn and blast!" Angrily I whipped the thing off as nearby spectators chuckled. The presence of the two wives restricted my line in expletives.

"Not to worry," Eric assured me. "You can have copies of mine."

That day I am sure that many enthusiasts touched the threshold of ecstasy, with a loaded camera in their trigger-happy fingers and a classic locomotive steaming into the view-finder.

At four o'clock on a sunny afternoon this glorious and stirring procession came to an end. Michael Satow driving 'Locomotion No. 1' had been up the night before and could hardly remain awake, even on the footplate. Lyn Wilson, also working up to the last minute, sat in a deckchair just as the Cavalcade began, dozed off into a deep sleep and came to just as it ended and crowds were dispersing. George Hinchcliffe, who had not slept for about thirty hours also slept throughout the Cavalcade that he had worked so hard to organize – surprising, for he was having a rattling and shaky ride in the vintage carriage hauled by 'Locomotion No. 1' heading the Cavalcade. Planeloads of enthusiasts flew back to countries as far apart as America and Australia, China and Japan, to take back home their own personal memories of their beloved steam from the very place where it had all started, and perhaps acquired mementos designed specially for this great occasion.

To mark the anniversary date itself – 27th September – the new National Railway Museum was opened at York by HRH Prince Philip, the Duke of Edinburgh, and must now be rated as one of the finest of its kind in the world. On 17th July the Queen Mother had opened the Hackworth Museum at Sedgefield near Shildon. Two adjacent cottages housed many historic relics and models connected with Timothy Hackworth, a renowned railway engineer who had helped Stephenson on the S&DR. A museum was also opened at North Road station in Darlington. Among other supporting and related events, a BR exhibition train, depicting railways ancient and modern, was launched at Marylebone station in London by HRH Princess Margaret on 30th June to visit twenty-three towns and cities in Britain.

Countless sporting, social, musical, historical, leisure and school events and exhibitions were held in many parts of the country, initiated and sustained by a tremendous surge of nostalgia for the old steam railways. Commemorative postage stamps were issued. In Blackpool a quarter of the golden mile of brilliant lights was devoted to railway pictorial history. Of the many related celebrations overseas, two were staged in Australia at Sydney and Melbourne, and a major railway commemoration was launched in Japan.

By the time the Stockton & Darlington celebrations had finished, Michael Satow and Lyn Wilson were planning something similar for the Liverpool & Manchester Railway. They had been so impressed by the enormous public response to the Darlington project and the splendid work of the railway societies that a celebration in 1980 seemed irresistible. After all, the L&M was the world's very first steam locomotive railway regularly to carry both passengers and goods. Here was something to shout about. Besides, Merseyside could do with a boost. Government, local authorities and trade and industry welcomed the idea and would use the opportunity to tell the world about the facilities of the north-west region.

By 1976 Satow was already busy planning a full-scale working reproduction of Stephenson's 'Rocket' which had won the famous trials held at Rainhill in 1829 to find the best locomotive for the new railway, and the Science Museum commissioned him to build it. On my visit to his home near Middlesbrough, Satow showed me his drawings and several steel stays he had already made. In autumn 1979 the 'Rocket', hauling replica wagons, steamed along on a short track in Kensington Gardens, Hyde Park, in London, a prelude of things to come. Passers-by, minding their own business, were astonished to see and hear this piece of railway history trundling along, just inside the park and opposite the Albert Hall. For the Rainhill event, full-scale working reproductions were built also of Hackworth's 'Sans Pareil' and Braithwaite & Ericsson's 'Novelty', the originals of which had competed against the 'Rocket' at Rainhill in 1829.

At the planning stages for the 1980 celebrations, British Rail stepped in early, in co-operation with the county authorities, tourist boards, industrial bodies, railway societies and other organizations, and appointed Tony Quirke, of the Liverpool BR division, as project manager. BR named the whole programme 'Rocket 150', mounted a massive international publicity campaign, commissioned the building of viewing stands on both sides of the railway at Rainhill and closed the Liverpool and Manchester line for three days for the major events. Dates selected were Saturday, Sunday and Monday, 24th, 25th and 26th May, the spring bank holiday.

Each day, from early morning to late at night, shuttle trains of multi-unit diesel trains ran back and forth from Liverpool and Manchester to Rainhill to fetch and carry great throngs of spectators.

On the first day the Rt. Hon. Norman Fowler, the Minister for Transport, and Sir Peter Parker, chairman of the British Railways Board, arrived for the formal opening ceremony, travelling in the former L&NWR royal train, hauled by 'Jumbo'-type 2-4-0 No. 790 named 'Hardwicke', whose fame has already been mentioned.

In a vast field nearby, a large number of marquees and stalls offered a variety of food and drink and assorted relics and railwayana of interest to enthusiasts.

On each of the three days, vintage locomotives, carriages and other vehicles, plus the modern HST and the new APT (Advanced Passenger Train), ran in cavalcade along the track near

Rainhill station, then returned in reverse order. Forty separate entries were listed in the official programme. Many locomotives seen at Shildon five years earlier were here to cavort and show their steaming prowess to the cheering crowds.

'Rocket' was scheduled to lead the field, but slight technical difficulties kept her off the course on the first day: a disappointment for first-day visitors, and the cause of anguish and hours of extra work for Michael Satow, her creator. But on the following two days she did wonderfully well. Such magnificent specimens in those fleeting hours recreated something of the magic of the great days of steam railways, brought a lump to the throat and reminded us that the railways were cradled in Britain and had changed a way of life that had altered little for centuries past.

# 19

# Goodbye to Diddle-ee-dee Diddle-ee-da and All That

Ask any steam enthusiast what the attraction is, and each time you could get a different answer. Even a dirty and neglected old locomotive, breathing wheezily, taxing every rivet and groaning at every steaming joint in an effort to pull its load, exudes a captivating impression of majesty and might that always remains part of the mystery.

Most of us who get caught up in the grip of steam railways accumulate bits and pieces that are precious to us because of their special associations. Apart from books and photographs, maps and models, one of my treasured possessions is a June 1946 Bradshaw timetable, a fat volume with tiny print on more than thirteen hundred pages. Among the 140 pages of advertisements – presumably necessary to finance a monthly publication – are announcements that themselves reflect the period. Blotting-paper, advertised by Fords, was quickly rendered redundant after World War II by the sudden popularity of the ballpoint pen, invented by an American John J. Loud as far back as 1888. The National Provincial Bank has since vanished, along with the magazine *Everybody's Weekly*; seventeen NAAFI clubs around Britain were serving the armed forces; Ashley Courtenay was personally recommending hotels; booksellers were offering Denise Robins romances, Dennis Wheatley murders and Nancy Spain mysteries at 10s 6d a time.

But the most interesting feature of the 1946 Bradshaw is that it lists train services in a network of nearly twenty thousand route miles, a mere few hundred below the peak mileage for Britain's railways of 20,445 in 1930. As in British Rail's own timetables, station mileages are given route by route. In this Bradshaw you can trace detailed train services for practically the entire network that existed in those vintage years of railway steam in the 1920s and 1930s, even to such timetable idiosyncrasies as "Sats. only, runs 13th July to 14th Sept. incl.". The table below from British

Rail shows the punishment the post-war years have inflicted on the route miles:

| 1940 | 19,931 | 1965 | 14,920 (post Beeching) |
|------|--------|------|------------------------|
| 1950 | 19,471 | 1970 | 11,800 |
| 1960 | 18,369 | 1983 | 10,700 (est.) |

An entrancing characteristic of travel by the old steam trains was the rhythmic diddle-ee-dee diddle-ee-da diddle-ee-dee diddle-ee-da as the wheels struck hammer blows on the joints in the rails. Whenever my thoughts roam down memory lane to childhood railway journeys, this rhythm springs to the fore.

On a long journey, its lulling beat could drift you into a restful snooze. And if, like me, you had fun in estimating the speeds of the train, you could count the number of joints in forty-one seconds, and that would give you the miles per hour. For those with itchy fingers and a pocket calculator, a check can be made: one mile is still 1,760 yards, one rail is still 20 yards long (usually known as 60 feet) and the variable gaps at the rail joints are anybody's guess! Today, on almost all British Rail's principal routes, tracks have been relaid with continuous rails welded at the joints. But if you really concentrate, a sensitive ear can still pick up faintly the rhythm even of welded joints, enough to do that speed check. That same old rhythm can still be heard on private railways, adding to their nostalgic charm.

Roger Woodis in a short poem 'The Sentimental Things' published in an issue of the *Radio Times*, caught a perceptive philosophy in the lines:

> Regardless of the future, or how our fate is cast,
> The ugly facts of life are such, we'd rather hug the past.

Sentiment is certainly an ingredient in the pleasures that blandish the railway enthusiast. There is something fresh and individual about steam railways as offered by the preservation societies. Individuality in this prepacked, standardized, egalitarian, plasticated life-style is a welcome and precious relief. We notice this when visiting some of Britain's less spoilt villages and small towns; it is a joy to see a charming old place without the standardized and unsurprising shop facias of Boots and W. H. Smith, Woolworths and Marks & Spencer, Tesco and Sainsbury, splendid services though we acknowledge these great houses provide. The more technological and automated and computer-ized and complicated our society becomes, the more it seems that people look back into the past and begin lovingly to restore the simple mechanical gadgetry and machinery, take up the handi-crafts, grow food in the garden and recreate the ambience of a traditional way of life, trends particularly noticed among young people.

When you are very young, you think that everything around you is permanent and will never change. For instance, I remem-ber being shocked to learn that the terrace house we lived in on the edge of Hanley had been built the year before I was born. I thought it had been there for ever. One of the subtle elements in the railways is the feeling of permanence; even the track is called the permanent way.

Many people, I find, love to recall memories of steam-railway journeys. My friend Kenneth Wheaton, a life-long railway steam enthusiast, tells me of his unusual commuting journeys of happy days, he says, on the dear old Great Western. From his lodgings in Teignmouth he travelled three miles by steam train to Dawlish, where he worked in a bank. Within that distance, the train steamed along the sea coast, past the Devon-red cliff known as 'the Parson and Clerk', through a tunnel, along a stretch of line overlooking the sea, through the second, third and fourth tun-nels, another coastal stretch, through the fifth tunnel, then finally along the sea wall into Dawlish station. Commuting for six miles through tunnels ten times daily must be a record.

Those local trains generally ran between Newton Abbot and Exeter, sporting the famous chocolate-and-cream carriages and hauled by a fine old tank engine with plenty of polished brass. Sometimes high seas whooshed through an open carriage win-dow, soaking the occupants. The coast did not just meet the sea, it collided head-on. This particular stretch of line, built by Brunel in the 1840s, was probably the most costly on the Great Western Railway: first to construct, then to maintain. Many times the relentless sea washed away the track, started landslides, caused train accidents. Costs in maintenance never abated. Unquestionably the railway along the Devon coast is glorious – rather like a beautiful and impetuous woman: breathtaking, but deucedly expensive to maintain.

Moving north now: bred and reared in the steam age of Yorkshire, Philip Wilson, a colleague and friend who often lectured to railway staff about steam operations, retired early. Commuting for years to London from Sittingbourne in Kent, he travelled forty-five miles each way each day.

I told him, "Now you're retired, you can get a nice little job locally and go home for lunch."

"What, me? Never! I'd miss the journey. I've always travelled to work by train. I just love travelling by train. There's always been a travel ticket in my pocket. I'd miss it."

A few weeks later he telephoned me in my office. "I've just landed a part-time job."

"Great! In Sittingbourne?"

"No. In London. The office is on King's Cross station, main line. So I have a travel ticket again. Isn't that just marvellous!"

My sentiments too.

Working at headquarters, I commuted between St Albans and London for twenty-six years, notching up over a quarter of a million miles. At close quarters I saw on this line the revolution from steam to diesel power. It was electrified between London (St Pancras and Moorgate) and Bedford in 1983. When I said I enjoyed commuting, people found it hard to believe. Some friends said, "That's because you don't pay!" Partly, perhaps. Commuting I found therapeutic. If you had had a bad night because one of the children had been screaming with earache or you had had words with your wife, by the time you had travelled with friends and read in your newspaper that the world was coming to an end in many places, your own corner seemed quite cosy, and you were ready to meet the day's problems. Conversely, if you leave the office seething with frustration, by the time you step off the train at your home station, your mind has been purged and the office tucked into a corner of your mind and filed under 'pending' until tomorrow. For most of us, work and home are two entirely different life-styles, and we are two different people, and commuting by steam train I found an excellent way of bridging them. In commuting, people of like interests seem to congregate by instinct in their own sections of the train, and often lasting friendships are made. Besides, by commuting one can bring up a family in the country and work in the world's greatest city.

For me, commuting holds happy memories. From my early commuting days between Bucknall, Stoke-on-Trent and Derby (over twenty thousand miles a year), I recall long panels of sepia photographs in the carriage compartments. These illustrated places of interest on the LMS such as Ludlow Castle, the walled city of Chester and the beautiful sandy bay of Llandudno with Great Orme's Head standing sentry at one end and Little Orme's Head at the other.

A reminder of these youthful days came out of the blue in a recent letter from a lady named Mrs Mabel Ratcliffe (née Pedley) from her adopted home in North Wales. On a visit to Stoke-on-Trent she had seen one of my railway books. It seems she remembered me from our teens when she and her friend, both factory girls, flirted with me and mine, since when I have never seen her again. She enclosed a short unpublished typescript entitled 'Memories of Steam'. Here are extracts:

Each time I return to my hometown in the Potteries, I sadly miss the dear little steam railways I used to know so well. Did Beeching's axe have to be so drastic? A way of life wrenched and clawed and cast into oblivion. I think of those little wayside stations with nostalgia; they capture the days of my long lost romantic youth.

My friend and I enjoyed our twenty minutes' walk each morning to the station at Bucknall, to travel nine miles to Leek. From the brow of the hill we could see it nestling down below, with its brown timber structure and tesselated awnings.

Then through a wicket gate, down a slope and onto the station platform. In the winter the iron stovepot in the booking hall glowed hot, its warmth as warm as the greetings from our friends who worked with us in the silk mills factory at Leek. We joked as we waited for the iron horse that would soon come snorting along from Stoke. Hardly does the train come to a halt when heads pop out of carriage windows. Our friends from the mills are calling for us to hurry and join them.

Small compartments, no corridors. Once inside, you couldn't get out. So we liked compatible companions. Such a hive of industry. Knitting needles clicking busily, embroidery and crotcheting quietly weaving. Hair curlers taken out. Toast and marmalade eaten from white paper bags. Some read novelettes.

For ever will I remember those mornings waiting for the train at Bucknall station to take us to work; those carefree teen-age girls I travelled with have long since been scattered on the winds of time, like tiny dandelion seeds on their fluffy white parachutes on a blissful summer's day. Those dear little stations and the dear little trains. All now faded and gone forever, like a haunting dream that never was.

Mabel Ratcliffe's sentiments surely must be echoed by countless women who, in the 1920s and 1930s, travelled by steam train to work, in the mills and factories, shops and offices, of every part of Britain and created their own ephemeral little world of those bygone times.

Not everybody loves the railways. Some, inexplicably, hate them; many seem to love to hate them. This has been the way since railways began. In Queen Victoria's days John Bright MP (1811–89) wrote: "Railways have rendered more service, and have received less gratitude than any other institution in the land." Things don't change much.

Looking back on forty years of working with steam railways, I have noticed in later years that in the railway service family ties are fewer. And though I had no relatives on the line and it took me some years to feel I 'belonged', pride stole up on me uninvited; and with pride in one's work comes loyalty.

With such a wide range of leisure and study activities, many people found that the railway and their railway colleagues and mates became their entire life. Shift work had an influence. Youngsters with older brothers, fathers or uncles in the service were much less likely to do something stupid; and something stupid on a railway line could mean disaster. These youngsters were also well briefed at home on how to conduct themselves at work and the best ways of promotion.

Loyalty to employers seems today less fashionable than it once was; yet in the railway service (and no doubt elsewhere) loyalty to the employer means to serve and satisfy the customer who ultimately pays our wages.

Steam on British Rail has been gone since 1968 (and I retired from BR eight years later). But the steam locomotive that roared across Britain from the days of the Industrial Revolution to the dawn of the electronic age has left its indelible marks. The great traditions of steam railways are now in the capable and dedicated hands of amateur enthusiasts in the railway preservation societies, in railway museums and on privately-owned lines, and we can rely upon them to keep the spirit alive.

For me, a working life on steam railways has been a fascinating and rewarding experience, and I would not have changed it for anything else in all the world.

# Index